# STRATEGIC MANAGEMENT IN THE MARITIME SECTOR

He stood in front of the Tegel Prison gate and was free. Yesterday in convict's garb he had been raking potatoes with the others in the fields behind the building, now he was out in a tan summer topcoat; they were still raking back there, he was free. He let one tram-car after another go by, pressed his back against the red wall, and did not move. The warder at the gate walked past him several times, showed him his tram-line; he did not move. The terrible moment had come.....the four years were over. The black iron gates, which he had been watching with growing disgust..... for a year were shut behind him. They had let him out again. Inside, the others sat at their carpentry, varnishing, sorting, glueing, had still two years, five years to do. He was standing at the tram-way stop.

His punishment was only just beginning.

Alfred Doblin (1929) *Berlin Alexanderplatz*, Martin Secker and Warburg.

# Strategic Management in the Maritime Sector

A case study of Poland and Germany

*Edited by*
**MICHAEL ROE**
*Institute of Marine Studies*
*University of Plymouth*

Routledge
Taylor & Francis Group

LONDON AND NEW YORK

# Contents

# Acknowledgements

The usual crowd have all done their bit on this one and these acknowledgements are an attempt to thank them for their efforts.

In particular, Marie Bendell at the Institute of Marine Studies, University of Plymouth has dug me out of the usual number of word processing holes; Kate Trew, Lindsey O'Brien and Anne Keirby have been as amenable as always at Ashgate - no mean feat when dealing with academics; and a variety of people across Eastern Europe have provided stimulation to keep persevering through the many distractions that exist not the least being the English play-off finals and the World Cup. These include Helena Vráblová in Žilina, Valentina Pomazan in Constantza, Hajni Semro in Budapest, Professor Janusz Zurek in Sopot, Professor Karl-Heinz Breitzmann in Rostock and Professor August Ingerma in Tallinn. However, the greatest debt has to go to Aleksandra Wrona at the University of Gdańsk who had the horrendous task of preparing the contributions from Poland into English before they were sent to me in Plymouth. Her ability to manipulate a Polish email system with a mind of its own and a shortage of reliability at the same time as meeting her university commitments and caring for her family, and all with a sense of humour, has been remarkable. Having done her job so well, she can now take a welcome and deserved rest on her posh porch in Żabianka.

Finally, as always, I have been given the greatest support of all from Liz, Joe and Siân who seem to still think that Charlton Athletic can survive in the Premiership this season - we shall see.

Plymouth, January 30th, 1999.

# Preface

It was with shock and dismay that I learned of the death of Hanna Figwer in a house fire in Poland on 28 January, 1999 shortly before this book including her contribution, was to be published. She was a close colleague and friend to Aleksandra Wrona and acted as my administrative contact in Sopot. A talented academic and delightful young woman, she will be missed by those who knew her.

Michael Roe, February 6th, 1999.

# 1. Introduction

*Michael Roe*
*Institute of Marine Studies*
*University of Plymouth*

This is the third in the series of books produced from the combined research interests of the leading research groups with a specialist interest in shipping and ports in the Baltic Sea region. For the first time this volume includes two papers from the Institut für Verkehr und Logistik at the University of Rostock in Germany, representing the premier centre for teaching and research in the new Germany and the only survivor in this sector from the former German Democratic Republic times. The two collaborators on the previous three volumes from the Institute of Marine Studies, at the University of Plymouth in the United Kingdom and the Institute of Maritime Studies and Seaborne Trade at the University of Gdańsk in Poland have long established links with the University in Rostock dating back to the 1980s and beyond and well into the era before transformation and reunification. Thus in this volume we have papers from the leading East European research centre (in Gdansk), the leading German Baltic Sea research centre (in Rostock) and the leading research centre in Western Europe for East and Central European maritime studies (in Plymouth).

Current collaborative interests include research projects spanning work between all three establishments funded from a variety of sources including the British Council, the European Union (Phare) programme, the Polish and

UK shipping industry, the Polish government and the universities themselves. This set of papers represents a selection of the work carried out in the last year up to April 1998, with a particular orientation towards the issues that stem from strategic management in the maritime sector - an issue that did not even exist up to the time of transformation in Poland and reunification in Germany.

The papers are divided into three sections. The first set represent the work of the University of Gdańsk under the leadership of Professor Janusz Zurek who has long directed the work of the Institute in Sopot and has been prominent in developing the University's international collaboration and reputation. It begins with the paper by Aleksandra Wrona who has also played a vital administrative role in bringing this text to a conclusion. Her paper looks at the application of computer simulation tools to port management including a series of case studies from around the world and then applying the techniques to a practical example. The SLAM II application model is applied and its advantages (and difficulties) are outlined and discussed.

Wrona's paper is followed by a paper by Hanna Figwer which begins the process of looking at the application of marketing tools to Polish seaports where before 1989, the issue of marketing was entirely ignored. This paper begins by examining the role and importance of marketing generally in the seaports sector and then discusses in some detail the characteristics of a general approach to the process. It concludes with an application of a strategy to the Polish situation and discussion of some lessons for the immediate future.

The paper by Miotke-Dziégiel provides an original analysis of the activities of two significant ancillary companies in the maritime sector - that of Polfracht and the Gdynia Maritime Agency - and the attempts being made by each to increase their marketing activity particularly focusing upon their strategic marketing initiatives and the organisational impacts. Meanwhile the paper by Zurek takes developments in the ship operating companies in Poland, and in the state owned companies of PŻM, PŻB and Polish Ocean Lines in particular and examines the changes taking place in organisational structure and the effects of a strategic management approach upon their activities.

Misztal presents a detailed analysis of the development of marketing practices in Polish seaports in the context of the specific nature of service marketing and goes on to examine the effect of these developments in the ports of Gdynia, Gdańsk and Szczecin. He concludes with a discussion of strategy.

Adam Salomon presents a full review of the present state and planned development of the Port of Gdynia which includes a general background to the port's activities and ownership and then a discussion of the planned investments over the coming years. The final Polish paper comes from the joint authorship of Krzysztof Dobrowolski and Stanisław Szwankowski who take a look at the legal and institutional developments in Polish seaports. In particular they examine the effects of the new Ports Act upon the ownership structures of both the major and minor ports within Poland.

The paper by Michael Roe represents the major contribution to the text from Plymouth and provides an extensive discussion of the relationships between international transport investment and the development of the economy using transformation and the Polish maritime sector as an example. The wider issues of how the old system worked and the changes that have taken place in recent years are used as the framework for discussion in addition to an analysis of the impact of European Union issues on the maritime sector.

The third and final section of the book is provided by the University of Rostock with two papers. The first is by Karl-Heinz Breitzmann and analyses in some detail the privatisation of ports on the Baltic Coast in the Former German Democratic Republic with particular reference to the ownership issues that have emerged and the need to transform their markets. The ports of Rostock, Wismar, Stralsund, Sassnitz and Mukran provide the case study material. Meanwhile the final paper is an extended discussion by Falk von Seck, also of the University of Rostock and looks at the substantial impacts of the developments in the Baltic Region upon the shipping sectors with particular emphasis upon the industries in the Former East Germany, Poland, Russia and parts of the Baltic States. This extensive article provides an in depth analysis of recent events in the region and unrivalled coverage of the significant issues that abound.

# 2. The application of computer simulation tools to port management

*Aleksandra Wrona*
*Institute of Maritime Transport and Seaborne Trade*
*University of Gdańsk*

**Definition of efficient port management**

A series of Polish maritime transport transformation developments are having the effect of changing existing management concepts which have proved to be inefficient and have failed to meet the requirements of a rapidly evolving market economy. Professional knowledge of modern management techniques is probably the primary element that provides for economic success within an enterprise and as a result its social and economic environment. However both the professional experience and managerial skills have to be supported and extended by modern tools which have been designed to support decision processes. These issues particularly concern developments in maritime ports where a large number of operations of a various nature are carried out, many partners from different business backgrounds are involved, and the interests of the region and whole country are in question.

In the current competitive environment, carriers, shippers, inland and seaport terminal operators and other participants within intermodal transport, need to understand each other's operations far more than they did in the past. This requires the use of tools capable of accommodating the entire intricacies of port operations in sufficient detail.[1] It is for this reason that the computer simulation of economic and technological processes needs to be considered in full.

---

[1] Kondratowicz L.J. (1990) Simulation methodology for intermodal freight transportation terminals. *Simulation*, July 1990, p. 49.

## A seaport as a system represented by a model

There are many definitions of systems as a concept. Generally speaking it is accepted that a system is an organised group of entities - including for example people, equipment, methods, principles and/or parts - which come together to work as a unit. A simulation model characterises a system by mathematically describing the responses that can result from the interactions of the system's entities. The system state is the collection of variables, either stochastic (which can change randomly) or deterministic (not influenced by probability), which contain all the information necessary to describe a system at any point in time.[2]

The port system is an organised unit within which elements such as loading equipment or infrastructure, are subjected to a main goal - in this case normally servicing transportation means and cargoes. The port system can be the port as a whole, a specialised loading and storage terminal, a berth, a loading site, etc.

A maritime port provides us with a typical example of a queuing analytical model. It is a complex system because it is characterised by many variable processes with complex relationships and its external environment changes and evolves very quickly, subjected to world trade trends and many other external forces. The main features of the port system can be identified as follows:

- – dynamic,
- – non-linear,
- – changeable,
- – stochastic,
- – discrete,
- – very complex.[3]

The port system is *dynamic* because its operations are affected by frequent qualitative and quantitative changes in characteristics of equipment, their organisation and the technologies employed. Operations depend upon the current and anticipated demand for services created by the port's economic environment.

---

[2] Smith Sh. A., (1989) Maximising the return from the simulation of material handling systems. Paper presented at AGVS 89 conference.

[3] Kondratowicz L. (1984) *Symulacja komputerowa systemów portowych (Computer simulation of port systems).* Wydawnictwo Instytutu Morskiego, Gdańsk, Słupsk, Szczecin.

The maritime port is also a *non-linear* system. This means that functions describing its operations, e.g. time in storage, are not a linear function of a limited number of variables but tend to be highly complex and non-linear, and as a consequence, very difficult to formulate.

The port system also can be described as *changeable*, i.e. the efficiency it displays over a longer time scale tends to be variable. For example a gradual increase in loading capabilities will result in changes in services output. Seasonal fluctuations, in particular in the demand for the servicing of particular goods, can influence the system's stability resulting in congestion at some time during the functioning of the port.

Another feature of the port system is its *stochastic* property. A port operates in risky conditions. Most of its operations are of random character and they follow common theoretical or empirical distribution patterns.

Any changes in the functioning of the port system tend to occur gradually - they are of *discrete* character.


## Application of modelling and computer simulation in port management - some practical examples

Here we present some examples of the use of modelling and computer simulation in the process of port management.

Firstly we can take an example from *Israel* - which includes the preparation and implementation of a simulation project for a cost prognosis of the Ashdod port operations

A process of preparation and building a port simulator constitutes a very interesting question in itself. One could ask why look for new solutions when there is an abundance of existing port simulators of many different profiles, which vary both in complexity and flexibility? In practice, finding and adjusting an instrument and completing a very comprehensive analysis turns out to be difficult. Simulation software designed to solve one particular maritime problem might not meet the requirements set by another experiment goal. On the other hand employing a tool which provides flexibility normally means using procedures that have to be standardised to some extent. Adopting a general-purpose simulator suggests accepting a compromise for a number of levels of detail.

There are three main ports in Israel: two on the Mediterranean leading to Southern Europe and the Atlantic Ocean, and one on the Red Sea leading to the Indian Ocean. They are managed individually whilst port policy is directed by a national Ports Authority, which is overseen by the Ministry of

Transportation. The need to estimate the timing and amount of investment necessary to provide for the national port system and to ensure it works efficiently as a whole encouraged the government to turn to the Wydra Institute of Shipping and Aviation Research. The aim of this project was to combine the experience from various scientific disciplines (i.e. marine sciences, economics, labour productivity and mathematical modelling), and to recommend an optimal investment volume and schedule.

The researchers first considered using extrapolation methods and conventional port design methodologies. However the complexity of modern marine terminals, the dynamics of port and shipping technologies and the enormous costs involved required more sophisticated and flexible planning tools - involving computer modelling and simulation. Having reviewed a variety of existing port simulators (i.e. CASM, DYNATRACK, G2, PORTLOG/YARDLOG, PORTSIM, and those designed by Gogol, Hansen, Hoong et al., Lawrence and Ward), the team decided to design a new and unique suite of software. The comprehensive approach of the study required the construction of a unique simulation model that would relate to multiple functions and components of a single port and would even consider co-ordination between two neighbouring ports. It was soon realised that the available products could not meet these specific requirements. For example issues relating to the impact of labour were commonly neglected. Also some of the above simulators were old and did not reflect recent technological changes.

The next step the Wydra Institute team faced concerned the choice of hardware and software. A resource matrix was constructed. It combined three crucial resources: the human component, available equipment and computer languages. Finally it was decided to develop the product on PC, run it on a SUN computer and to use the C language because it was compatible with both computers.

When the hardware and software was decided upon, the input and output designs were discussed. The goal was to provide for simplicity, ease of use and the quick maintenance of data input. Data were implemented in the form of text files and keywords which were specifically meaningful to the researchers involved. It was not necessary to bother with a more user-friendly format since the persons working on the project were also its main operators. The output had to serve different purposes: debugging and validation, and also efficiency analysis. The debug and validation functions facilitates not only finding omissions in the execution of the programs but also first of all checking the integrity of all the input data, e.g. if a ship was waiting for a berth even when there was one available, or any data misprints.

The objective of the project was to show the impact of a given decision under a certain scenario upon the overall performance of all the ports over the course of 17 years. Therefore the output had to provide easy access to data in many different formats including for example, monthly reports, detailed reports of given (commonly 'suspicious') selections of output data in order to pinpoint problems, or a variety of charts.

The simulator was event-driven, the main entity being the ship and an auxiliary entity serving as work scheduler. Arrival times of ships were calculated based upon statistical distributions. One of the unique characteristics of the simulator was its approach to manpower sources - the availability of labour was not presumed as constant, as is usually the practise in other simulators, but a number of variations, including work priorities or overtime rules, were also taken into consideration.

Finally the program was constructed so that it could be run on any computer, powerful but portable, requiring only the minimum size of memory space (depending upon the input data quantity). It was fully operational in less that three man months, which is remarkably short for a project of this kind.

The Wydra simulation project played a pivotal role in decisions regarding investments in Israeli harbours. In order to analyse the impact of different assumptions regarding economic developments, four scenarios were prepared, ranging from the pessimistic to the optimistic. For each scenario the simulation was run five times starting with present conditions. The process was stopped after 17 years or when the monthly costs hit a high threshold. After reaching the threshold, pre-set minimal changes were introduced, involving variables such as the timing or rate of works.

The Port Authority policy now closely follows the suggestions included in the final report. It proves the value of the simulator approach for port investment planing purposes.

An *Indian* interactive simulation model provides a suitable example for logistical planning of container operations in seaports.

At present more than 80 per cent of world seaborne cargo is carried in containers. It has thus become an imperative for major seaports to manage their container operations both effectively and efficiently. The basic tasks in the management of a port container terminal consist of berth allocation, yard and stowage planning and logistical planning of container operations. The complex character of a modern container terminal suggests that using a computer simulation method is the best way to support the wide range of crucial operational decisions that exist. Other solutions, for example constructing analytical queuing models, were discounted as being inadequate or unsuitable in particular because the condition that ships' arrivals and service times should belong to the Erlang family of distribution functions cannot be met.

As in the previous Israeli case, other popular port simulators were reviewed, including the UNCTAD port model (for analysing conventional loose cargo operations), PORTSIM (a project appraisal tool useful for evaluating the costs and benefits in changing general conditions) and the MIT port simulator (permitting the analysis of a multipurpose seaport). However none of these models were found to be suitable for the analysis of operations within modern container ports. Technological advances and the growth in volume of serviced cargo have been too rapid and these substantial and fundamental changes had to be reflected in the model to be used.

As a result a new model was developed in co-operation with port officers who provided the necessary empirical data on ship turnaround time, berth occupancy and ship outputs following various operating strategies. Port practitioners' participation in the project contributed not only to improving its integrity but also enhanced the project with interactive features making it as a result, that much more useful.

Since the simulation model was to be implemented as a modelling tool to be used by a wide range of people with differing experience and skills, its designers decided to prepare it in menu driven form - including a data input menu, a run simulation menu, an output statistical menu and an exit menu.

*The data input menu* prompts the user to input data for ship and port characteristics and an operating strategy for the assignment of port equipment to the ships. The required port characteristics include a number of features e.g. the number of shift operations per day, the number of working hours in each shift, the number of berths, quay cranes and their productivity, yard cranes and their productivity, the number of prime movers and all the respective probability distributions. Ship characteristics include assigning the number of quay cranes, primary movers, yard cranes, etc.

*The run simulation menu* demands from the user specific initial and final conditions of the system state and the number of runs.

*The output statistical menu* facilitates interaction between the port managers and the simulation model in order to select the required output statistics upon port performance at the desired level of aggregation in the form of a table or chart. For example berth occupancy, i.e. the level of demand for port services, is defined as the percentage of the total time a berth is occupied. Ship waiting time is the sum of waiting times in the harbour for a berth, at berth for servicing, and at berth after completing all operations. Ship output measures the rate at which containers are handled between a ship and quay side, consisting of containers per ship working hour, containers per ship at berth, and containers per ship in port. Ship turnaround time equates to the total time a ship spends in the port from its arrival at the harbour to its departure.

The project's implementation turned out to be highly successful. Its efficiency and effectiveness to support decisions for the logistical planning of container operations were clearly established. Port executives were provided with a powerful tool enabling prompt evaluation of port performance in different conditions and thus in choosing optimal operational strategies. Many actual examples of the project's usefulness could be given. For instance analysis based on the simulation model resulted in saving almost two hours in the average ship turnaround time (Table 1.1).

**A theoretical model of a crude oil loading terminal in changing services' contract conditions using the SLAM II simulation package**

The main goal of this example was to study the effectiveness of a crude oil loading terminal under given conditions and the opportunities to use the existing potential of equipment even more efficiently. Using the SLAM II simulation package we could observe how the waiting time for services by servers and the use of given resources, for example berths and tugs, changed. The issue of utilisation of resources was regarded as of key importance to seaport operation profitability because of the existence and significance of penalties for delays caused by a port. It is also very important to define the system's sensitivity to particular changes, i.e. to what extent waiting times and equipment utilisation can be increased.

**Table 1.1**
**Comparison of operating strategies**

| Estimation port performance indicators | Strategy A (proposed) | Strategy B (existing) |
|---|---|---|
| a) average berth occupancy (%) | 58.11 | 58.78 |
| b) average waiting time for berthing (hrs) | 01:11 | 01.56 |
| c) average time for container operations (hrs) | 19:42 | 20.52 |
| d) average number of container/ship hours | 40.42 | 38.27 |
| e) ship turnaround time (hrs) | 22:46 | 24:35 |
| f) average waiting time/average time for container operations (%) | 6.01 | 9.27 |

Source: Ramani K.V. (1996) An interactive simulation model for the logistic planning of container operations in seaports. *Simulation*, May, p. 299

The port in question provides services to tankers. Each of the ships can be serviced at the same time. Three main types of tankers visit the port with uniform probability distribution - from 4 to 8 hours. The first type of ship requires from 16 to 20 hours, the second from 21 to 27 hours, and the third from 32 to 40 hours. After completing unloading operations all ships (if it is possible) leave the port at once. The probability of arrival of a certain type of tanker is respectively for the first one 25%, for the second one 55% and for the third one - 20%.

There is one tug necessary for the berthing of every tanker. The approach and departure from each berth takes exactly one hour; however all departing port activity has priority.

Storms occur regularly, (with an exponential probability distribution), disturbing smooth terminal operations. Each storm lasts from 23 to 26 hours and it paralyses the activities of the tug which is necessary for berthing and leaving the port.

In order to study terminal operational efficiency we ran a simulation for a one year period, defined in this case as a total of 8,640 hours.

The first stage of the simulation consists of building a model using SLAM II symbols. The process is initiated by implementing a set of control instructions.

**Table 1.2**
**The SLAM II model of a crude oil terminal operations**

Source: prepared by the author

After checking the integrity of input data against SLAM II standards with the ECHO function and correcting any mistakes, the report is ready to be generated. For the data from the above model the report is as follows:

**S L A M   I I   S U M M A R Y   R E P O R T**

SIMULATION PROJECT TANKER        BY WRONA
DATE 1/ 1/2001        RUN NUMBER  1 OF  1
CURRENT TIME  .8640E+04
STATISTICAL ARRAYS CLEARED AT TIME  .0000E+00

# Table 1.2 (continued)

## **STATISTICS FOR VARIABLES BASED ON OBSERVATION**

| | MEAN VALUE | STANDARD DEVIATION | COEFF. OF VARIATION | MINIMUM VALUE | MAXIMUM VALUE | NO. OF OBS |
|---|---|---|---|---|---|---|
| T1 TIME IN PORT | .239E+02 | .601E+01 | .251E+00 | .181E+02 | .574E+02 | 186 |
| T2 TIME IN PORT | .288E+02 | .535E+01 | .186E+00 | .230E+02 | .656E+02 | 460 |
| T3 TIME IN PORT | .407E+02 | .554E+01 | .136E+00 | .344E+02 | .669E+02 | 144 |

## **FILE STATISTICS**

| FILE NO. | LABEL/TYPE | AVERAGE LENGTH | STANDARD DEVIATION | MAXIMUM LENGTH | CURRENT LENGTH | AVERAGE WAIT TIME |
|---|---|---|---|---|---|---|
| 1 | AWAIT | .238 | .554 | 4 | 2 | 2.587 |
| 2 | AWAIT | .020 | .139 | 2 | 0 | .213 |
| 3 | AWAIT | .020 | .147 | 2 | 0 | .220 |
| 4 | CALENDAR | 4.456 | .630 | 6 | 5 | 2.714 |

## **RESOURCE STATISTICS**

| RESOURCE NO. | RESOURCE LABEL | CURRENT CAPACITY | AVERAGE UTIL | STAND DEV | MAXIMUM UTIL | CURRENT UTIL |
|---|---|---|---|---|---|---|
| 1 | BERTH | 3 | 2.50 | .617 | 3 | 3 |
| 2 | TUG | 1 | .18 | .387 | 1 | 0 |

| RESOURCE NO. | RESOURCE LABEL | CURRENT AVAIL | AVERAGE AVAIL | MIN AVAIL | MAXIMUM AVAIL |
|---|---|---|---|---|---|
| 1 | BERTH | 0 | .5043 | 0 | 3 |
| 2 | TUG | 1 | .7344 | -1 | 1 |

During the simulated period (8,640 hours), 186 type one entities, 460 type two and 144 type three entities were processed by the system, corresponding to particular types of tankers. Average times in the system of given ship types are displayed in Table 1.3.

## Table 1.3
## Average times within the system of different ship types (mins)

| Tanker type | Average time in system | Standard deviation | Minimum value | Maximum value |
|---|---|---|---|---|
| Type I | 23.9 | 6.01 | 18.0 | 57.4 |
| Type II | 28.8 | 5.35 | 23.0 | 65.6 |
| Type III | 40.7 | 5.54 | 34.0 | 66.9 |

Source: Author

12

Output data was allocated to files which gathered information upon waiting for 'berth' resource activity (i.e. an available berth), waiting for 'tug' resource activity after allocating a unit of the 'berth' resource (i.e. waiting for the tug after freeing space at the berth), and waiting for the 'tug' resource unit after activity has been completed (i.e. waiting for the tug in order to leave the berth). The average length of queue for the first activity in given conditions amounted to 0.23 of an unit, and for the second and third - 0.02. A maximum of four ships waited for a free berth, reducing to a minimum of two. The longest queues that occurred whilst ships waited for units of the 'tug' resource to berth and depart the port consisted of two tankers, whilst the shortest was none.

The most interesting conclusions can be drawn when studying the level of resource utilisation, i.e. berths and tugs. Respective values were 83% and 18%. It suggests that berths were used almost all the time the simulation was run.

Let us consider that the port authority contemplates signing a contract for servicing an additional five tankers requiring 21 hours with three hours of deviation. Their round trip travel time would last 10 days with a one day deviation. The type IV tankers would call at the port every two days. The goal of the experiment is to check whether without any investment, the port authority could operate the service required efficiently. To do it one has to expand the model including elements connected with the type IV tankers.

The report generated by the simulator after introducing these changes, showed that the number of type II and II tankers decreased insignificantly while the number of the new, type IV, ships was at the same time 154. However the waiting time for the 'berth' resources increased eight times and for the 'tug' resource by about one third. The resources utilisation also rose to 22% in the case of the 'tug' resource and to almost 100% in the case of the 'berth' resource.

The results of the SLAM II simulation experiment seem to suggest that efforts to increase the oil terminal's utilisation should be aborted because of the congestion threat to the port that would be caused.


**Conclusions**


Running a port efficiently means gathering, transforming into decisions and generating a considerable amount of information. The flow of cargo is also likely to be faster - logistical solutions applied by modern big companies allow stocks to be limited to minimal volumes, thus facilitating savings in storage costs. However their partners, including transportation links, need to be extremely reliable. To be competitive a port has to be run smoothly - no margin for experimentation or failure is allowed.

Modelling and computer simulation provide new possibilities for a port manager. For example it enables results to be checked which emerge from a given decision before its execution in real life, and it can supply information of a system's integrity e.g. revealing bottlenecks and the waste of resources. It is also very important that most of the simulation software is user-friendly, enabling easy application by persons not acquainted with computer programming.

There are many examples of the successful implementation of modelling and computer simulation. The methods are widely used in maritime ports throughout the world because of their easy application compared with, for example, more mathematical models. Despite the complexity of the port system, the construction of a simulation model with readily available software is not difficult, as the practical example of a crude oil loading terminal model has proven. However although there exist a large number of simulators, very often it is necessary to construct new ones specific to the situation in question. For example, the SLAM II simulation package with Fortran inserts is a powerful tool. However, as was shown in both the Israeli and Indian case studies outlined earlier, large and very detailed models very often require a unique approach to be successful.

## References

G. S. Fishman (1981) *Symulacja komputerowa. Pojécia i metody*, Państwowe Wydawnictwa Ekonomiczne, Warszawa.

L.J. Kondratowicz (1978) *Modelowanie symulacyjne systemów*, Wydawnictwa Naukowo-Techniczne, Warszawa.

L.J. Kondratowicz (1990) Simulation methodology for intermodal freight transportation terminals. *Simulation*, July, p. 49.

M. Pidd (1989) *Computer modelling for discrete simulation*, The Management School, University of Lancaster.

M. Pidd (1992) *Computer simulation in management science*, The Management School, University of Lancaster.

A.B. Pritsker (1989) *Introduction to simulation and SLAM II*, A Halsted Press Book, John Wiley & Sons, New York and Systems Publishing Corporation, West Lafayette, Indiana.

*SLAM II Quick reference manual*, Pritsker Corporation, Indianapolis, 1992.

S.A. Smith (1989) *Maximising the return from the simulation of material handling systems*. Paper presented at AGVS 89 conference.

Z. Szuwarzyński (1995) *Materiały do laboratorium metod symulacyjnych*, Wydział Zarządzania i Ekonomii, Politechnika Gdańska, Gdańsk.

# 3. Marketing orientation in Polish seaports

*Hanna Figwer*
*Institute of Maritime Transport and Seaborne Trade*
*University of Gdańsk*

## Changes in seaport situation during the transformation period of the Polish economy

For almost half a century, the functional system of Polish seaports was based upon a centrally planned economy which resulted in, amongst other things, monopolies within the port services market and port management organised by the state. This structure of Polish seaports depended upon relationships mainly with the state-owned sector with large monopolistic firms having an exclusive right to provide certain port services. Such a system totally eliminated competition in port services or the port related manufacturing sphere which consequently led to a slow down in technical and organisational development, and as a consequence, it adversely affected efficiency and effectiveness of the operation of Polish ports.

For a number of years now, Polish seaports have operated within a new internal and external environment. The internal conditions are a result of both political and economic changes in Poland, resulting from the implementation of a shift from a centrally planned economy to that of a market economy. Changing external conditions that have to be met by Polish ports come from a new political and economic configuration in Central and Eastern Europe and the increasing integration processes within the European Union. Together these factors have had an impact upon spatial changes within the Polish ports' hinterlands which are now defined mainly by economic criteria rather than strictly geographic controls as were imposed throughout the old CMEA system period. Both the domestic and transit hinterland of each of the Polish seaports have become a prospective hinterland for a sizeable number of foreign ports.

The domestic hinterland of Polish ports has developed into an international one as a result of the opening of the Polish marketplace to the free exchange of goods and services. This has brought about the loss of monopolistic character of the hinterlands along with the need to compete for Polish international trade loads with foreign ports and in particular, German and rather less so, Adriatic ports.

Changes in the transit hinterland of Polish ports have also occurred - and the share of traditional transit cargo flows to and from the Czech Republic, Slovakia and Hungary through the Polish ports has diminished. This is a direct consequence of the removal of the transferable rouble payments system between the member countries of the CMEA. The use of this artificial currency meant that the final payment for port services was much lower than when using West European ports. Since transformation, the countries of Eastern Europe have intensified their trade exchange with the European Union countries and this new direction of trade is characterised primarily by transport through inland routes with clear impacts for the ports industry. At the same time cargo from the transit partner countries for Poland has been taken over by more competitively located ports. However, at the same time, the opportunity has arisen to obtain transit cargoes for Polish ports (Gdańsk and Gdynia in particular) from Belarus, north-western Ukraine, the Baltic States and from the Kaliningrad enclave of Russia. Meanwhile, the Szczecin-Świnoujście port complex is still largely supplied by cargo coming from the eastern region of Germany.

The limited trade turnover by sea resulting from the newly established benefits of inland transportation, particularly that by road, is the next factor that has influenced the volume of cargo throughput in Polish seaports in a negative way. Inland transportation has become increasingly more competitive as compared with transport by sea resulting from an increase in trade exchange in an East-West direction, and exacerbated by the inhibitions of inadequate road links between the Polish ports and their hinterland. Further to this, the continuing process of the integration of the international transport sector of Poland and the EU countries, and the increasing transportation of containers and general cargo from domestic hinterlands to the North Sea

17

countries by road has made the moves away from the sea, and thus ports sector more noticeable.[1]

The discussion above brings us to the conclusion that growing competition is the main determinant of the current functions and development of Polish seaports. Besides the competition from foreign seaports, which not long ago was concerned only with transit cargoes but now includes also Polish foreign trade goods, there is now intense competition between Polish ports for cargoes from both domestic and transit economic hinterlands, which was non-existent until recently, and also competition within each port between the enterprises that provide port services. Inland transportation has become competitive with Polish ports as well. In the new political situation Polish seaports were forced to accept both liberal and competitive rules within the domestic and international market. As a result, they found themselves in a very competitive environment, and to win access to any new (or even existing) cargo they have had to take up marketing operations within their organisations as a serious activity.

## The necessity for adaptation to the new economic conditions by Polish seaports

Based upon the observations of Kohli and Jaworski,[2] it is clear that in the situation when there is a lack of competition, a firm can still be very effective whilst not being marketing-oriented because buyers are conditioned to its products and services (there is no competitive offer) and they operate within a monopoly. In contrast, the opposite to this situation is very different when the competition is fierce and a buyer has a choice amongst offers from various firms, who can meet to the same extent, his needs. In this context, a firm that is not market-oriented would probably lose its clients to the benefit of competitors. Marketing orientation is therefore a factor which helps to determine positive economic results within a company operating within a highly competitive environment.

---

[1] K. Misztal (1997) *Wewnętrzne i zewnętrzne uwarunkowania restrukturyzacji polskich portów morskich, (Internal and external implications of Polish seaports transformation)* in: *Restrukturyzacja transportu morskiego Polski, (Transformation of maritime transportation in Poland)*. Gdańsk, p.13, (in Polish).

[2] A.K. Kohli and B.J. Jaworski (1990) Market orientation: the construct, research propositions, and managerial implications. *Journal of Marketing*, no. 2, p. 57.

The new economic conditions within which Polish seaports have been operating for the last few years, have meant that maintaining the pre-transformation level of competitiveness within the international market for port services has become very difficult if not impossible and an urgent need to implement extensive and proactive marketing operations has arisen. Taking up these operations has proved necessary for a number of reasons:[3]
the stronger the marketing orientation of a firm, the better the economic outcome;

1. the stronger the marketing orientation of a company, the closer the involvement of employees and identification with the market;
2. the more radical the changes in the market, the stronger the interactions between marketing orientation and the firm's financial outcomes;
3. the more rigorous the competition, the stronger the interactions between marketing orientation and the firm's financial outcomes;
4. the weaker the standing of the economy, the stronger the interactions between marketing orientation and the firm's financial outcomes.

In the new economic situation, reliable and professional marketing activities in Polish ports become necessary because without efficient marketing structures they will not manage to cope with the demands of the competitive market.

**Characteristic features of marketing orientation**

Defining marketing orientation principles for seaports is closely tied up with entering what is identified by fully developed countries as 'the prosperity society'. The market in this period becomes a consumer market and more and more markets grow into trans-national and even further into global ones. Besides this, but at the same time, this period is characterised by rapid development in science and technology, a shortening of product life-cycles within the market, an increase in the capital requirements of research and development work and investment connected with product launches and the introduction of new products into the market. These factors then require taking up policies that will diminish the investment risks. The suitable adjustment of products, according to needs and requirements of a prospective buyer, serves this purpose. A positive analysis of the chances of a new product launch is a major presumption before making decisions to begin investment financing. It is necessary to undertake fundamental reorientation of a firm's

---

[3] A.K. Kohli and B.J. Jaworski, Market orientation. *op. cit.*, p. 53-68.

management based upon conclusions drawn from the acceptance that the firm's future will be determined by the market. In addition to a choice of goals and resources to implement change, all activities should be subordinated to the existing and prospective needs of clients and other actors in the marketplace. Consequently this results in:

1. the rapid growth in demand for market research studies as a basic source of information upon which to make decisions;
2. the harmonisation of all means of influencing the market by a company, including concepts such as the 'marketing mix', comprising not only rationalised forms of distribution and sales promotion but also an adequate pricing policy for the product itself, expressed commonly through the use of utility categories.[4]

Desk research has proven that despite the wide scope of marketing orientation studies there remains a lack of an homogenous and commonly accepted criteria defining marketing orientation for a company. Putting together all the elements from the work of a large variety of authors one can distinguish the following characteristic features that attempt to define marketing orientation:

1. concentration upon buyers' needs - tastes and preferences - and needs and desires of current and prospective clients are the base for the operation of a firm;
2. conducting market research (studies of buyers, competition and other elements of the environment) as an indispensable element of recognising buyers' needs;
3. concentration upon the longer-term perspective of the firm's operations;
4. directing a firm's offer to a chosen segment (or segments) of the market, i.e. carrying out segmentation analysis and choosing an appropriate target market;
5. impacting the market using a series of co-ordinated marketing operations;
6. the offer of a company should be an answer to target group expectations;
7. including all divisions of a firm in the process of gathering information upon buyers' preferences;
8. efficient communication inside a company - vertical and horizontal information flows among different divisions regarding client needs and their expectations of products;
9. making every employee aware of his place and role in providing value to a buyer.

---

[4] J. Altkorn (1995) *Podstawy marketingu (Marketing basics)*. Instytut Marketingu, Kraków, p. 15 (in Polish).

## Introducing marketing into Polish seaports

Introducing marketing concepts to Polish firms, including seaports as well, meets a variety of substantial barriers. The main sources of these difficulties can be identified as follows:

1. marketing requires long-term, strategic thinking and the current transformation period in Poland is not conducive to shifting from a short-term to a strategic approach.
2. the needs of marketing orientation depends not only upon developing a marketing function for a company but also devising its strategic and leading role. In particular it necessitates co-ordinating marketing functions with other operations of the company. Interactions between the company's functions will become stronger and it contributes towards a process of flattening the organisational structure (otherwise known as decision decentralisation). In addition, employees of every division of a company have to identify themselves with the corporate marketing goals. Implementation of these requirements is not easy in practice.
3. commonly there is a problem of the slow acquisition of marketing skills and also a tendency for rapid degeneration.
4. there is an understandable aversion to bear the substantial and constantly growing marketing costs, particularly the ones that only show any impact after a long period of time.[5]

Despite these difficulties which are faced when adopting a marketing orientation, it remains necessary to accept fully and implement a strategy of this type in conditions of fierce and growing competition - the situation in which Polish seaports find themselves at present.

Within the organisational structures of Polish seaports, marketing units have been created and they have started to play a growing role. They are responsible for research into transportation markets including competition analysis; they have attempted to attract investors in the utilisation of port areas within a set development strategy; they have attempted to create a positive image of the port both domestically and abroad; they have gathered and analysed information on price levels and quality of services provided by competitive ports; and they carry out advertising operations for the ports

---

[5] J. Dietl (1997) *Orientacja marketingowa, (Marketing orientation)*. Nowe Zycie Gospodarcze, no. 43.

(promotional materials preparation, organisation of fairs and exhibitions, etc.).[6]

The activities surrounding marketing services in Polish seaports needs to cover a large scope of function, comprising for example:

1. planning marketing projects and estimating the costs of their implementation;
2. lobbying for the development of domestic transport infrastructure, supporting maritime transport development and for an increase in seaports' importance;
3. finding partners for co-operation in the development of complementary services contributing to improvement in a seaport's attractiveness;
4. looking for new contacts by active participation in port orientated events organised by various institutions;
5. co-ordinating packaged contracts for loading and warehousing services for a specified partner;
6. maintaining close relations with servicing bodies operating in a port;
7. preparing international and national policies for port promotion and services.

It is worthwhile underlining here that considering the specific nature of other services provided by seaports, the elements of promotion, canvassing, advertising and public relations should be regarded as of particular importance. During the last few years for example, the canvassing policy in ports gained a particular meaning. It covered identifying and acquiring buyers, gathering orders and signing contracts for port service provision. As a consequence of this canvassing policy, a gradual increase in the number of clients using given port services can occur thus providing for production continuity and consequently having a positive impact upon the economic efficiency of port companies.

In seaports where marketing has a major role to play, all production, trade and investment decisions should be made based upon a knowledge of current and prospective clients (which together create a target market), and the competition that threatens or is capable of threatening the company's future well-being. That is why gathering information about the market and its development trends and the threats from competition is a necessity rather than a luxury. This information gathering should create an information system upon the range and prices of port services offered by other domestic and foreign ports, upon prospective clients, upon export and import development

---

[6] H. Klimek and K. Sulima-Chlaszcza (1997) Inwestycje w polskich portach morskich (Investments in Polish seaports). *Ingynieria Morska i Geotechnika*, no. 6.

trends, etc. and should be considered as a primary task of any marketing services sector. To accomplish this process effectively, the full range of techniques of marketing research need to be utilised.

Marketing research methods appropriate to seaports do not differ from methods applied in other companies. One of the better known is the SWOT analysis and it is a starting point for much broader and rational decision-making. The port's geographical location, the location of heavy industrial centres, the relations of a port with other economic bodies, can be the strengths of a port. Problematic workforce issues, and a location far from important industrial centres may well constitute weaknesses. Opportunities for a port can be represented by the chances of development and an open attitude towards the implementation of new technology. However the most significant threat will always come from the activities of competitive ports and the competition from other modes of transportation.

Another, also very popular method for conducting market research, is portfolio analysis exemplified by the work of the Boston Consulting Group. It refers to the classification of products with respect to their market share compared with competitors and their sales growth. It facilitates adequate allocation of financial resources between different product lines in a way that provides for long-term profitability.[7]

A port which has a strong market-led management focus has to possess a good knowledge of its operational marketplace and of those markets it intends to enter. A market analysis conducted systematically enables the:[8]

1. identification of acceptable markets in order to impact upon them in a beneficial way;
2. assistance to ports in gaining profits in the market; a final goal of port service sales should be to make profits for shareholders although this is not always possible, particularly within a short period of time;
3. constant observation of market developments and the environment in which they take place (domestic and international); information on this subject can be extracted from local agents, media contacts etc.;
4. setting direction for a long-term market development which helps to prepare and implement a port services sales strategy;
5. preparation of market reports containing information on the depth of the market, its profile and development directions, and upon the market situation;

---

[7] F. Suykens (1988) The marketing of a seaport. *Hinterland*, vol 137, no. 1.
[8] K. Misztal (1994) *Porty morskie w Unii Europejskiej, (Seaports in the European Union)*. Gdańsk, p. 70.

6. support for development of more competitive operations in the marketplace, e.g. by adequate structuring of tariffs;
7. creation of a more efficient information system for a port and its operations that can be offered to a prospective port user;
8. port to follow technological and organisational progress as far as port services are concerned.

The scope of marketing information, necessary for effective functioning within the port services market, is very important from a port company's point of view. Marketing units should provide:[9]

1. information upon current and prospective port clients and their activities within the maritime transport sector;
2. information upon technological and economic changes in a port, within maritime transport, within inland water transport, land and air transportation and combined systems;
3. information upon economic, trade and industrial changes which have an impact upon the volume of cargo turnover and the direction of its flow;
4. information upon the situation and development of other ports, particularly competitive ones (e.g. equipment, capacity, pricing, technical development);
5. information upon the situation in the port itself and its servicing companies;
6. information upon competitive threats and the level of an undertaking's risk.

In marketing research, market segmentation (including issues relating to the requirements of various port users, their specialisation and the regionalisation of the market) should be taken into account because it is not advisable for port companies to provide services just generally as a more targeted approach is likely to be more fruitful. It is necessary to identify areas within the hinterland and the foreland that have the greatest potential and which thus form a very important element of the strategic management process in seaports.[10]

Marketing research needs to be the primary stage within the marketing management process in seaports because it is important that the boundaries of the market for port services should be identified, and internal and external conditions of port functions within the market analysed before further progress can be made. Following this, the next stages of a properly conducted marketing management framework are as follows:

---

[9] *Port marketing and the challenge of the third generation of port.* UNCTAD 1991, TD/B/C.4/AC.7/14, p. 33.
[10] S. Szwankowski and A. Tubielewicz (1992) *Planowanie strategiczne w portach morskich, (Strategic planning in seaports).* Wydawnictwo Instytutu Morskiego, Gdańsk-Szczecin, p. 83.

1. setting goals and defining a strategy for the port in the marketplace;
2. deciding upon a strategy and the techniques appropriate for a port functioning in that market;
3. taking steps to operate within the market efficiently;
4. controlling and assessing the effects of operations and activities and drawing conclusions for the future.[11]


**The effects of marketing operations within Polish seaports**

The results of adopting a marketing orientated strategy within the Polish ports sector can be identified on a number of levels and in a number of ways.

*Firstly,* a new style of management within Polish seaports, taking into account the competition that exists, has started to have effect in the form of a broadened range of services and in the quality provided by ports. Amongst other things it is possible to see this through the numerous investments implemented in Polish seaports and those that are currently planned. These investments have improved the loading capacity of these ports and enriched the range of services offered there.

For example in Gdańsk:
1. storage for heavy general cargo developed on the Oliwski wharf;
2. a container terminal has been built on the Szczeciński wharf;
3. the Free Trade Zone in the old part of the port has been created (and within its boundary both loading and storage terminals for bananas and citrus fruits will be soon opened);
4. on the Westerplatte wharf a ro-ro ramp has been constructed (meeting the requirements of a series of partners as far as, amongst other things, the loading of heavy road trucks is concerned);
5. a terminal for liquid gas loading is under construction;
6. a new unit for liquid fuels loading is being built.

Meanwhile in Gdynia:
1. a grain terminal is being modernised (including both an elevator and a fairway);
2. dredging works on the approach way to the port are in progress;
3. the second stage of building a container terminal, building a ferry terminal and opening a paper servicing terminal are planned;
4. a coal sorter is under construction.[12]

---

[11] K. Misztal (1996) Zarzádzanie marketingowe w portach morskich, (Marketing management in seaports). *Spedycja i Transport*, no. 10, p. 9.

[12] H. Klimek and K. Sulima-Chlaszczak *Inwestycje...*, op. cit.

In addition, the Szczecin-Świnoujście port complex, in order to improve its market standing, undertook the development of a set of enterprises connected with the modernisation of both wharves and storage. The largest investments were undertaken through the modernisation and enlargement of the general cargo facilities, including conventional and containerised systems, and particularly concentrating upon the loading potential of the port.

*Secondly,* marketing policy has a significant impact upon both the economic and exploitation results of the ports. The economic and financial situation of the commercial seaports of Poland has been improving gradually for the last few years. The improved results which were realised in both 1996 and 1997 in Polish international seaports, had not been approached in any year prior to then since the transformation period began at the end of the 1980s.

In particular, 1997 was a very good year for the port of Gdańsk not only in terms of loads but also in terms of the profit gained which was higher by 32% in comparison with the previous year. In terms of infrastucture renovation and port investment, some 16 million złotys were spent in 1997. In the same year in the Gdynia port about US$30 million was spent for renovation, investment and dredging works. The gross profit of the port, compared to 1996, increased by more than 50%. The total income of the capital group - Port Gdynia Holding S.A. - exceeded 470 million złotys and the gross profit was almost 67 million złotys. This included setting a new record in terms of general cargo loads - almost 4.4 million tonnes - which was clearly a substantial success. In addition to this, companies within the holding generally achieved a positive financial result reflecting their new market orientation.[13]

Meanwhile, during 1997, 4.5% less cargo was loaded through the wharves of the Szczecin-Świnoujście complex compared with 1996. This was largely a result of the severe summer floods which occurred in southern Poland. However despite a lower cargo turnover, the financial outcome for the eleven months of 1997 was approximately 50% higher than that achieved during the whole of 1996, and investments in 1997 were over 30 million złotys.[14]

Since the economic crisis of the beginning of the 1980s, a slow increase in cargo turnover in Polish seaports has been observed until recently. This includes not only Polish foreign trade but also cargo in transit. Its characteristics are presented in Table 3.1.

---

[13] P. Kuciewicz (1998) Rok 1997 w gospodarce morskiej: coraz lepsze obroty i zyski, 1997 in the maritime economy: gradually growing turnovers and profits. *Budownictwo Okrętowe i Gospodarka Morska*, no. 1, p. 2, (in Polish).

[14] *Morski bilans, (The maritime balance sheet)*. Kurier Morski, Feb. 1998, p. 4-5, (in Polish).

**Table 3.1**

**Loads within Polish seaports ( '000 tonnes)**

|  | 1990 | 1991 | 1992 | 1993 | 1994 | 1995 | 1996 |
|---|---|---|---|---|---|---|---|
| Gdańsk | 18613 | 17001 | 20447 | 23261 | 22413 | 18618 | 16875 |
| Gdynia | 9987 | 7274 | 6286 | 7759 | 8055 | 7739 | 8661 |
| Szczecin-Świnoujście | 18123 | 17229 | 17458 | 19307 | 21727 | 22659 | 22659 |

Source: Rocznik Statystyczny 1995 i 1997 (Statistical Annual 1995 and 1997), GUS, Warszawa.

The location of Poland in relation to Scandinavia and in close proximity to 'Middle' Europe suggests that Polish seaports could achieve a larger share of cargo turnover including cargo in transit in the North-South direction, and not only that moving in an East-West direction. According to a prognosis prepared by Prof. Andrzej Tubielewicz,[15] cargo turnover of Polish ports in the year 2010 will increase to as much as 74.9 to 110.4 million tonnes. It would appear to be a realistic forecast if Polish seaports broadened the scope of their marketing operations, improved their image within the international transport services market and then could meet the expectations both of current and prospective clients. In that context, the development of a new marketing orientation presents a great opportunity for all Polish seaports.

**References**

J. Altkorn (1995) *Podstawy marketingu, (Marketing basics)* Instytut Marketingu, Kraków, (in Polish).

J. Dietl (1997) Orientacja marketingowa, (Marketing orientation) *Nowe Zycie Gospodarcze*, no. 43, (in Polish).

H. Klimek and K. Sulima-Chlaszczak (1997) Inwestycje w polskich portach morskich (Investments in Polish seaports), *Ingynieria Morska i Geotechnika*, no. 6, (in Polish).

A.K. Kohli and B.J. Jaworski (1990) Market orientation: the construct, research propositions, and managerial implications, *Journal of Marketing*, no. 2.

---

[15] A. Tubielewicz *Prognozy obrotów, kierunki inwestowania oraz Ÿródła i sposoby finansowania priorytetowych inwestycji infrastrukturalnych w portach polskich do 2010 r. (ekspertyza), (A prognosis on turnovers, directions of investment and sources and ways of financing priority infrastructural investments in Polish ports till 2010 (an expertise), p. 8.*

P. Kuciewicz (1998) Rok 1997 w gospodarce morskiej: coraz lepsze obroty i zyski, (1997 in the maritime economy: gradually growing turnovers and profits). *Budownictwo Okrętowe i Gospodarka Morska*, no. 1, (in Polish).

K. Misztal (1994) *Porty morskie w Unii Europejskiej, (Seaports in the European Union)*. Gdańsk (in Polish).

K. Misztal (1997) *Wewnętrzne i zewnętrzne uwarunkowania restrukturyzacji polskich portów morskich, (Internal and external implications of Polish seaports transformation)* in: *Restrukturyzacja transportu morskiego Polski (Transformation of maritime transportation in Poland)* Gdańsk (in Polish).

K. Misztal (1996) Zarządzanie marketingowe w portach morskich, (Marketing management in seaports) *Spedycja i Transport*, no. 10 (in Polish).

*Morski bilans, (The maritime balance sheet)*. Kurier Morski, Feb. 1998, (in Polish).

*Port marketing and the challenge of the third generation of port* UNCTAD 1991, TD/B/C.4/AC.7/14.

*Rocznik Statystyczny 1995 i 1997 (Statistical Annual 1995 and 1997)* GUS, Warszawa, (in Polish).

F. Suykens (1988) The marketing of a seaport, *Hinterland*, vol. 137, no. 1.

S. Szwankowski and A. Tubielewicz (1992) *Planowanie strategiczne w portach morskich, (Strategic planning in seaports)*, Wydawnictwo Instytutu Morskiego, Gdańsk-Szczecin, (in Polish).

A. Tubielewicz *Prognozy obrotów, kierunki inwestowania oraz Ÿródła i sposoby finansowania priorytetowych inwestycji infrastrukturalnych w portach polskich do 2010 r. (ekspertyza), (A prognosis on turnovers, directions of investment and sources and ways of financing priority infrastructural investments in Polish ports until 2010 (an expertise)* (in Polish).

# 4. Servicing maritime transportation firms - a marketing management perspective

*Joanna Miotke-Dziégiel*
*Institute of Maritime Transport and Seaborne Trade*
*University of Gdańsk*

## Structural changes in the maritime transport service sector

The systemic economic, political and social transformation occurring in Poland in the 1990s has especially influenced the functioning of the broadly defined maritime transportation community and a particularly substantial reorganisation has taken place within the maritime shipping sector. A number of state-owned enterprises, and primarily the maritime agencies which until 1989 had a monopoly in this sector, have started the process of privatisation. These agencies, commonly transformed into workers' shareholder companies with limited liability, have thus effectively become the employees' property. For example, in the Gdynia Maritime Agency between 40 and 50% of the shares belong to the management of the company, whilst the rest are owned by employees. However, the number of employees engaged in ownership is a small proportion of the total representing only about 10%.

Polfracht, the previously sizeable state-owned company, initiated a privatisation process based upon workers' company principles as recently as 1996. Earlier, within the framework of the so-called Polfracht Group, small private companies had been created, each concentrating upon (for example) vessel clearance or containerised cargo forwarding. Reorganisation and ownership changes in state-owned companies, including the Gdynia and Szczecin Maritime Agencies and also Polfracht in Gdynia, were necessary for survival in the rapidly evolving auxiliary services market. However the position of these companies in the marketplace still became weaker despite the changes made.

Despite the worsening situation in the maritime marketplace as the 1990s proceeded, the Gdynia Maritime Agency managed to limit reductions in its employment to only a small extent: thus in 1992 the number of employees was 207 and in 1998 - 190 persons worked there. As a result it is still a very large firm considering the nature of the market in which it operates. In Polfracht, where re-organisational processes have been rather more delayed, a considerably greater reduction in employment has taken place, i.e. from 82 persons in 1992 to as few as 34 in 1998.

## The position of the Gdynia Maritime Agency and Polfracht within the maritime services market

As a result of the transformation processes in the auxiliary services sector which are proceeding at present within the free market economy, firms characterised by a variety of organisational, legal and ownership forms are operating; some are state-owned firms (e.g. Polfracht), there are numerous limited liability companies; and there are also private ones - including family businesses.[1] The rapid development of ship-brokerage firms (in 1990-1997 from realistically only one monopoly supplier to more than 70)[2] radically changed the structure of the maritime service sector. Despite the fact that newly established firms are usually very small, employing a few persons and sometimes only one (in very rare cases they reach up to twenty employees but this is undoubtedly the exception), their presence within the market has induced extended competition and deprived the large, state-owned companies (mainly the Gdynia Maritime Agency and Polfracht) of their comfortable monopolistic position.[3] The main competitive activity takes place in the fields of ship clearance and servicing within ports, and also in the conduct of seamen employment agency services. This network of ship-brokerage and

[1] J. Miotke-Dziégiel (1997) *Service sector in maritime transport*. Paper presented at the International Conference on Maritime Transport and Economic Reconstruction, Gdańsk. Oct. 17-18.
[2] Around 10% of the firms created went bankrupt. Based on data from 'Maritime Economy. Statistical Review' from 1991 and 1997 and 'Maritime Economy Bulletin' 1997.
[3] The increase in number of ship-brokerage firms in Poland differed from trends in other countries. For instance in Hamburg from 200 firms in 1980 only five were left by 1997 - based on 'Namiary na morze i handel' ('Direction of sea and trade') no. 7/1997, p. 17.

private firms is accompanied by agencies established by key Polish and foreign shipowners. It is worth underlining here that the trend of launching agency organisations independently by shipping lines, has been done to promote the name and profile of the firms involved and to make them more visible in the marketplace. This process has also facilitated the utilisation of information by the service sector from within the shipping company itself, and thus creates a serious threat for the independent agencies, unrelated in any way to a shipowner. The trend towards offering ship-brokerage services by international forwarding firms has made this situation even worse. Each of these factors has the effect upon both the Gdynia Maritime Agency and Polfracht of requiring new methods of operation, including adapting modern forms of management, if they are to survive in the highly charged competitive environment that has now developed.

## The role of marketing in a firm's management structure - organisational conditions

An analysis of organisational structures of a number of maritime service companies reveals that there is rarely a focus or even an orientation towards marketing within any of the functions or tasks of the firms concerned.[4] This is typified particularly by the Gdynia Maritime Agency where it is difficult to distinguish any concentration of activities employing marketing tools. There are three units in the organisational structure of the Gdynia Maritime Agency which can be identified as carrying out some form of marketing operations:
1. within an organisational team - marketing of the firm's general image (creating image, advertising, etc.);
2. within a specific marketing and/or freight team providing a general marketing service;
3. within a line operations team - providing direct and specific marketing.

To provide a summary of what occurs within the Gdynia Maritime Agency, there are three units and seven persons dealing with the co-ordination of marketing operations. However the people in question do not strictly belong to the management of the firm. Although the managerial staff is aware of the need to create an adequate marketing organisation this, as yet, has not resulted in any significant changes in the company structure. The result is that marketing functions have not been placed within a higher managerial level and remain disaggregated at the operational level.

---

[4] Based on analysis of the organisational structures of firms and a worker survey.

However, the necessity to distinguish these functions has been recognised by the second of the firms researched, i.e. Polfracht. In this firm since 1997 internal structures have been created which have the objective of facilitating its functioning as a private firm and its adaptation to new market conditions.

It is for these reasons that an organisation was created consisting of five divisions, instead of ten teams working on particular cargo groups. It is worth underlining that besides three cargo divisions and another for administration, a completely separate and dedicated marketing division was also established. The number of companies and representatives operating abroad was reduced to a minimum as well because they were too expensive and in some ways could be viewed as superfluous nowadays in an era of increasingly efficient communications and rapid information flows. Besides ships' agency service operations (for which a new and separate company with a majority of Polfracht shares was established) all other shipping operations were given up.

Generally speaking it is probably fair to conclude that both firms are characterised by a 'flattening' of their organisational structures which has facilitated decentralisation of decision-making and, to a variable extent, the role of the organisational structure as an active marketing management instrument as well.


## Conditions for the implementation of marketing management in maritime service companies

In connection with changes that are internal (i.e. mainly ownership issues) and external (i.e. those activities within their direct environment, including other agency and shipbroking firms) and also changes with respect to those purchasing their services (i.e. transportation firms) it is worth taking a closer look at the management methods adopted by recent state monopolies. It is even more interesting considering the fact that in the conditions of economic liberalism and competition in the market that now prevail, and which continue to grow even further because of the rise in demand for transhipment services, the management organisation of service companies will have to adopt a series of new operational strategies.

These state monopoly firms, having recently lost a substantial number of service buyers which were previously guaranteed by law, can no longer afford to concentrate exclusively upon producing their standard mainstream product. Instead, implementing a market oriented strategy towards the marketplace is now a requirement, and the companies should consider first of all the needs of their clients and the operations of the numerous competitors that now exist. In other words research into the conditions which exist in the external environment is needed, including an examination of the existing laws and processes that control and characterise shipping transhipment servicing, and this ought to be accompanied by the development of activities orientated towards service clients whilst recognising the activities of competitive firms.

## Strategic marketing - the scope of implementation

First it is worth considering to what extent key features of marketing strategy are used, i.e. market segmentation and at least some instruments of the marketing mix (7 Ps). With respect to this, it is important to underline that the Gdynia Maritime Agency conducts service activities on a very large scale as far as operations within the contexts of maritime transport and foreign trade are concerned. The main activities in which they are active can be structured as follows:

1. ships, cargo and agency services, i.e. they provide all the activities that are involved in shipowner representations;
2. facilities for providing foreign ships with crews of Polish seamen;
3. representation of shipowners' Protection and Indemnity Clubs (in this case the North of England P and I Club) covering cargo, ship, damage claims etc.;
4. servicing multimodal container transhipments (including global services);
5. finding optimal solutions to problems stemming from the services provided above;
6. servicing ocean voyage vessels.

Besides these activities, the Gdynia Maritime Agency also offers a variety of specialised services which include:

1. chartering and organising transhipments of heavy and over-sized cargo, vehicles, and steel products; and
2. servicing all kinds of floating units built and repaired in Polish shipyards.

These specialised services require considerable efforts in finding clients in the respective market niches. These operations are commonly treated as a priority because here lie the best opportunities to increase market share and consequently profits. Gaining superiority of the firm in this type of field will normally result from either its size, experience and/or image.

Polfracht however, has also used segmentation in its market strategy applied to the provision of ship-brokering services:

33

1. first of all to bulk cargo, both dry and liquid categories. These operations are a key source of income for the company. In the near future the plan is to concentrate upon the chemicals market as a priority:
2. semi-bulk cargo, in particular cooled, frozen, and a limited concentration upon over-weight items;
3. over-sized general and containerised cargo (which will form a new segment of the market for the company).

Despite the fact that the services mentioned above are provided primarily to Polish shippers, more and more often offers have been directed towards foreign partners.

Polfracht also provides specialised services including:
1. purchasing and selling second-hand ships and other floating units;
2. signing contracts for sea towing.

It is worth adding that the newly created Polfracht-Agencja company also provides complete agency services to ships in all Polish ports. It competes in this area with the Gdynia Maritime Agency.

One can draw a number of conclusions from the above discussion that indicate that operations of both the companies outlined here are characterised by the following features:
1. firstly, an increase in market share (based upon the development of traditional operations using the firm's own resources and skills);
2. secondly, vertical diversification (offering a more complete range of services better meeting the varying needs of buyers, and thus sharing a risk among a larger scope of services);
3. thirdly, finding partners in a number of identifiable market niches.

The companies clearly apply at least to some extent, a number of the elements of the marketing mix. While applying these elements the main stress is placed upon:
1. the quality of services offered, including amongst other things choosing the best option, a guarantee of completed work, another related to punctuality (and much of it based around the principle of 'my word, my bond');
2. a competitive price: discounts and preferential payment conditions are offered to clients, particularly regular and large ones (this is mainly a policy of the Gdynia Maritime Agency);
3. offering for example, 24 hours a day access to services and also the application of skilful negotiation techniques.

In addition, comprehensive market information can be supplied, along with a variety of payment conditions and a series of consultancy services offered. The importance of each contact with a service client is now clearly and explicitly valued and seen to contribute to the firm's image. Market information gathered by shipbrokers and agents, including data on the firms' organisational methods (including for example a SWOT analysis when applied), is used comprehensively, with the objective of, amongst other things, meeting clients' expectations.

The companies that have been included in this research use service promotions as part of their marketing strategy to rather a lesser degree. Written, printed information and advertising materials, booklets, bulletins and small gifts with the company logo are the main methods of promotional operations.

In addition, the increasing levels of staff professionalism should be underlined. As a result of the high level of qualifications of the employees, particularly the ones working closely with clients (most of them have successfully completed university studies), this facilitates the creation of a positive image of the firm's operations in the marketplace. In addition, shares in the company are offered to the most competent and successful staff members, and the future tasks, goals and vision for the company can be disclosed to them for their consideration and discussion. Working in the friendly environment that this implies, with enhanced promotion chances that this suggests, means that employees identify themselves more with the company with all the obvious advantages that this sort of environment brings.

Generally speaking one can confidently state that in spite of the existence of the formalised planning approach that dominated during the last 40 years, planning at the micro scale of the firm has not been abandoned and it remains an element of effective company management. Both of the enterprises examined here conduct market research and analysis which utilise in the main:

1. internal documentation providing data on amongst other things, sales and costs of services, payments and debts;
2. comprehensive marketing research conducted by the staff. Whilst carrying out macro-economic analysis they search for market opportunities (primarily an activity of the Gdynia Maritime Agency) and emphasise possible threats that are felt to exist. In estimating marketing opportunities, the management of both firms follow trends that characterise the environment, studying the state of the national economy reflected in trade turnover, the specific shipping situation, etc.

Within the planning process, the focus was shifted from that of formal plan preparation to the creation and formulation of development strategies (e.g. increasing the firm's market share in a chosen segment). In addition, the process of marketing operations is also contained within the strategic planning framework of both companies (but particularly within Polfracht). Strategic presumptions are detailed within prepared operational plans, e.g. marketing goals are defined for given cargo markets (Polfracht) or service groups (the Gdynia Maritime Agency).

## Closing remarks and conclusions

The characteristics of market operations within the Gdynia Maritime Agency and Polfracht presented above, bring us to the conclusion that they are relatively efficient in their organisation and operations: both firms have been operating for over eight years in a new environment, maintaining (particularly the Gdynia Maritime Agency) a relatively strong position in the marketplace. It is without doubt that this has resulted from the maintenance of a traditionally good brand image, in addition to the adoption of a series of modern management models. Thus, through the introduction of a formalised buyer strategy, both firms are intent upon formulating marketing developments, improving the service quality that they offer, continuing to introduce service delivery differentiation, maintaining and developing frequent and strong ties with both existing and new clients (Polfracht, for example maintains contacts on a daily basis with over 200 partners) and in so doing, not neglecting even the smallest or least prospective ones. There remains the significant ambition of retaining a leading position within the marketplace (in other words a leader strategy has been adopted) and this is being implemented as we have seen, with some evident success.

It is also worthwhile underlining that the constant monitoring of competitors' actions is now carried our by both of the firms on a regular and frequent basis. This is undertaken on two levels:

1. By conducting market studies, an increase or decline in competitors' positions can be analysed. It particularly concerns those companies that enjoy a strong market position, whilst amongst the others, the goal is to consider the potential for co-operation with them.
2. At a level of direct contact with customers whereby nearly every shipbroker and agent of the Gdynia Maritime Agency and Polfracht, cautiously studies the methods adopted by partners' actions (and of course they borrow ideas from the best ones).

On the other hand, the strategy of both firms in question, does not suggest that they wish to become price leaders in their approach towards competitors. Special preferences and incentives are granted occasionally, particularly to regular customers. However, because of constantly growing competition in the marketplace for both firms, ways to lower costs (including human resources) are constantly being sought.

Within the third area of marketing operations of the two companies, which concentrates upon market share, the companies (particularly the Gdynia Maritime Agency) have the objective of retaining or regaining the leading position they had in the past in the Polish market, but also to achieve the position of market specialist (Polfracht). In the Gdynia Maritime Agency to a larger extent, it is possible to identify trends towards broadening the range of services offered, whilst in Polfracht there is an identifiable attempt to concentrate strategy towards a limited number of services.

Generally speaking it is possible to conclude that in both of the researched companies, although they do not apply fully developed, model structures of marketing management and they do not reveal a strong market orientation within their organisational structures, they are clearly beginning to follow at least some of its principles.

The companies, currently concentrating upon directing the main elements of their efforts upon the market environment (i.e. their clients and competitors), are beginning to shift from a process characterised by marketing orientation towards one that is essentially a strategic marketing phase. Within this process they are beginning to move closer to the market strategies that are commonly implemented in modern firms and thus they increasingly carry out their own market plans. Not having the opportunity to return to recent monopolist positions they have begun to design and implement a range of realistic strategic goals.

## References

*Gospodarka Morska. Przegled Statystyczny 1991, 1997 (Maritime Economy. Statistical Review 1991 and 1997)* (in Polish).

*Informator Gospodarki Morskiej (1997) (The Maritime Economy Bulletin)* (in Polish).

Kotler P. (1994) *Marketing - analiza, planowanie, wdrazanie, kontrola (Marketing - an analysis, planning, implementing and control)*, Warszawa (in Polish).

Miotke-Dziégiel J. (1998) *Service sector in maritime transport.* Paper presented at the International Conference on Maritime Transport and Economic Reconstruction, Gdańsk, Oct. 17-18th.

*Namiary na morze i handel (Direction of the sea and trade)*, No. 7/1997 (in Polish).

Payne A. (1996) *Marketing usług (Marketing of services)*, Warszawa (in Polish).

# 5. Refining management systems in Polish maritime development

*Janusz Zurek*
*Institute of Maritime Transport and Seaborne Trade*
*University of Gdańsk*

## Maritime shipping companies under market economy conditions

The economic transformation, introduced in Poland from 1989, changed the economic management system by creating a totally different legal, economic, organisational and social basis supporting the launch of market mechanisms which might help to induce innovation and an improved level of economic effectiveness. Within the transformation process, the principle of economic freedom was adopted as a fundamental market economic principle whilst still recognising that the economy cannot be entirely released from state involvement. State involvement should first of all be limited to legal and economic spheres however, only so far as defining and governing the basic economic parameters, i.e. the rate of currency exchange, the level of interest rates and the selection of tax rates, in such a way that they promote self-regulation and the instruments needed to achieve redefinition of the marketplace.

The market economy forces companies to adjust to market conditions and ideally, requires them to be as completely self-sufficient and self-financing economic bodies as possible. It also encourages companies to take up activities that contribute to an improvement in their property structure, management system, their organisation and financial management. The operations should be directed at one primary goal - the improvement of company market competitiveness.

The market, which provides excellent evidence of a company's value and effectiveness, should provide the prompt for adequate reactions from a company. Market economic structures require from a firm, a high level of flexibility of operation and speed in response to conditions both from the domestic and international environments. Besides and in addition, companies which want to be competitive should also be able to foresee changes expected in the nearest future and try to implement them within their operational development programmes. The absence of a well defined concept for the development of a firm and of the current operations to be undertaken, which allow at least for adjustment to needs and market trends, may consequently lead to the bankruptcy and liquidation of the company.

These operations should first of all concern companies which function in direct contact with the international market. This means that it has special relevance to maritime transport companies and particularly maritime ship operating companies. Competition within the shipping market continues to grow stronger in Poland as the new market economy develops. Maritime shipping companies, in order to survive and maintain their market position, must be able to foresee and accurately assess their situation, i.e. have the ability to operate and develop effectively to adapt to the changing environment. Besides this, they have to make decisions upon the direction, rate and scope for transformation changes. These operations are beneficial not only as far as a firm's survival and restoring its balance with the environment are concerned but also they influence the company's further development and its ability to function efficiently.

**The transformation and diversification process and its impact upon changes in the managerial system of maritime shipping companies**

The transformation process for companies began in earnest following the implementation of the Act on the Financial Transformation of Firms and Banks ('ustawa o restrukturyzacji finansowej przedsiębiorstw i banków'), dated 1993. The goal of the Act first of all was to:
1. secure suitable economic and legal conditions for the operation and development of companies in such a way that they would be able to meet the growing competition requirements;
2. eliminate those companies that had poor prospects for efficient operation when they were exposed to the new free market;
3. create conditions for an effective banking sector which would then be able to enter into the process of structural change with companies.

Transformation, which is a very important element preceding the privatisation of a company, is an extremely difficult and complex process and it requires substantial financial resources. It is for this reason that it has proceeded in Polish shipping companies relatively slowly. It is a result of not only external conditions, i.e. those pertaining to the international context, but also to a large extent, of domestic and internal factors, which are located within a firm. A severe lack of financial resources and the high level of debts from foreign and domestic creditors that continue to exist, are a source of particular complaints by these companies. The rate of transformation was also affected by the excessively large organisational structure of the companies and an inefficient managerial system which was closely connected with it.

The gradual introduction of the transformational processes has led to the creation in Polish maritime shipping firms of so-called state-owned 'quasi-holdings' of a capital group character. A capital group is here understood as a set of self-sufficient economic bodies joined with each other by capital ties and accompanied by a dominant unit as a leading body within the organisation.

This adopted 'quasi-holding' structure has improved the process of managing organisations with some clear and significant results. Management has became more effective, efficient and, first of all, it has provided conditions for adequate leadership within an organisation including setting the development directions that are its priority. The existence of mutual capital ties and the possibility of making operational decisions self-sufficiently and at a dependent company level, has supported the concept. Improving management efficiency has also facilitated, to a large extent, the gradual preparation of state-owned shipping firms for the full privatisation process. The holding structure that has been developed allows the possibility of buying shares and/or bonds and in this way, shifting money from sites where its productivity is low or it is presumed that it will not bring any positive effects, to ones where its utilisation has the potential of providing a much better output. The principles of these relations and ties are based upon the signed contracts and regulations contained within the legal body of regulations known as the Polish Commercial Code.

The adoption of a transformation strategy and the development of a capital group operating within maritime ship operating companies is commonly closely accompanied by a process of management decentralisation, reflected in a functional and operational division between what is not incorrectly called a 'domineering parent body' and a series of infant 'dependent companies'. Within the management system that has been commonly adopted, the sphere of strategic and administrative decisions has been visibly separated from the

40

location of exploitation decisions which are made totally independently on an infant company level, including decisions relating to shipping issues along with those from other sectors of activities.

Meanwhile, in the 'quasi-holding', the dominant body tends to be a specific managerial centre connected both by capital and organisational ties with other self-sufficient economic bodies, dealing with the activities of shipping and other equipment, including both containers and land transportation means amongst other sectors. Whilst some ships are already owned by the dependent companies, some of them remain leased from the parent.

Within this new structure of a carefully designed managerial system, the tasks of the dominant body tend to be normally concentrated upon at least some of the following:

1. setting directions for a basic strategy for the capital group as a whole in co-ordination with its dependent companies;
2. controlling cash flows;
3. co-ordinating and supervising the implementation policy of the holding, and influencing strategic and exploitation decisions within dependent companies (this is commonly ensured by placing the control of shares of the dominant body in the hands of dependent companies).

This last task is normally executed in Polish maritime ship operating companies by the participation of representatives from the parent body on the boards of directors of the dependent companies. A goal of this is to provide an adequate policy for the development of the organisational structure of the whole capital group, and advice upon introducing other managerial structures or inviting the participation of external shareholders. On the other hand, as far as dependent companies are concerned, the managerial system designates to them tasks connected with shipping or other operations, directed solely at profit generation.

According to the principles of the management system outlined here, dependent companies are obliged to pay dividends and to bear payments for leasing ships, containers and container equipment, office space and equipment, telecommunication and energy charges, costs of maintaining the holding, goodwill payments, and payments connected with leasing land transportation means.

The transformation process and the managerial system closely connected with it will be more efficient if the co-operating bodies pursue an open policy towards one another, making genuine attempts to consider seriously, economic arguments presented by each other and at the same time more probably achieving satisfactory solutions for everyone engaged in the ship operating process.

41

The managerial system adopted in managing a capital group of this type allows for and even promotes the process of diversification, i.e. by broadening the scope of operations of the parent body and in addition those of the dependent, infant companies. Diversification, when the shipping market is still difficult and where there is still severe competition in primary operations, becomes an important element of the process of ensuring a profitable operation and, in addition, it improves the company's image and its market value at the same time. Polish maritime ship operation companies have expanded the range of their operations, and in so doing have entered areas close to the company's primary operations and in some cases, taking into consideration market trends, they have gone well beyond this. These actions have become a necessity stemming from the market economy conditions and changes occurring in the international background that have occurred. Their impact means that the traditional distribution of ship operating tasks, originally set by strictly administrative decisions of central government under the old regime, which was characterised by the presence of three Polish shipping firms (PŻM - bulk shipping; PŻB - ferry operations; and Polish Ocean Lines - liner shipping services), should be changed. The present market conditions make concentrating upon only one form of tonnage exploitation, a highly risky strategy. The Polish liner shipowner - Polish Ocean Lines (PLO) - is a good example of this in that liner shipping is very difficult as far as exploitation and profit-taking is concerned whilst at the same time, it is extremely capital-absorbing. In addition to this, the lack of modern potential in this company makes the process of diversification indispensable if the company is to survive.

The managerial system used in a capital group structure, as has been applied to Polish Ocean Lines (PLO), contributes to various forms of diversification and helps to broaden the scope of group operations. It results in the establishment of dependent companies within the group that operate in branches other than the shipping but which support primary operations of the group. The diversification process was particularly visible in the period when the shipping company was preparing for privatisation. Diversification became an element enabling a more comprehensive entry into the market by these firms with an offer to would-be purchasers, not only comprising their primary operations but also a variety of related but supplementary operations.

Observing the changes which have occurred in the domestic market as far as company diversification is concerned, a general trend can be distinguished - the way and the scope of diversification depends upon whether the sector in which a firm operates is regarded as one that is attractive to the market and shows promise for the future. If the prospects of the sector for the future are optimistically estimated, then vertical diversification usually prevails. Only to an insignificant degree is there any evidence of horizontal diversification, similar in character to the firm's primary operations. However within commercial sectors where the market is estimated to be risky, the trend of diversifying horizontally, concentrating upon entering totally new spheres of operation, different in characteristics from the primary ones, is more common.

## Changes of organisational structure within shipping companies with the objective of improving managerial effectiveness

One of the main goals of changes in an organisational structure should be to make the management system more efficient which means providing for not only the efficient functioning of the company but also the development of a communications system within the group as a whole. Management solutions that are directed at exploitation activities which concentrate upon shipowning companies and which attribute strategic and management functions to the dominant parent body, would support this goal. In addition, organisational changes have resulted in the establishment of companies with service characteristics that conduct activities other than those associated with shipping. These actions have prepared Polish shipping companies for the gradual building of state-owned 'quasi-holdings' which consist of the dominant parent body company and a variety of dependent companies. This structure also reflects the fact that 13 shipping and other related companies operate within the Polish Ocean Lines group structure. Polish Ocean Lines, as the dominant body, is linked with the dependent companies by contracts and capital/financial agreements reflected in the prevailing shares of Polish Ocean Lines in dependent companies. In some of these dependent companies, Polish Ocean Lines owns as much as 100% of the company shares. Meanwhile, a reasonable number of the dependent companies have shares in a series of other companies. Thus there are close relations not only between the dominant parent body and the dependent infant companies but also amongst a variety of far wider ranging organisations.

There is also a new direction creating efficient and competitive structures that induces changes in the management system - alliances. These are very often, by necessity, of an international character. Among them strategic alliances and joint ventures can be distinguished.

Alliances are more than agreements between two or more partners brought together by a particular common strategic goal; they are relationships directed towards providing improved development possibilities and, besides a large number of advantages that can be realised in a short time period, they also offer a range of new operational opportunities to the partners concerned. They require very close interpersonal ties to work and also contacts on various levels of partnership.[1]

In order to manage a strategic alliance or a joint venture in a modern and efficient way one has to follow closely the guidelines below:-[2]

1. maintain an open system within the framework of existing structures;
2. exchange extensive and detailed information with partners;
3. have an objective of open co-operation;
4. use the alliance as an organisational framework to facilitate the acquisition of resources in order to sustain a competitive edge;
5. conduct joint training sessions in order to integrate personnel and provide an opportunity to exchange experiences;
6. create conditions for adequate communication building towards achieving the principles of the collective agreement.

Following the guidelines given above is especially important for the companies operating in a dynamic environment typified by the fast changing conditions of the shipping market. It particularly concerns shipping companies that have to be aware of operational effects within a long-term development perspective, the emergence of a wide range of communication patterns with partners and the incorporation of speed and elasticity within company operational practises.

One also has to remember that creating such a strategic alliance or joint venture can turn out to be very difficult. For example partners use different approaches to management, there can be a lack of a flexible approach, a substantial variety of goals, problems in accepting the mutual relationships of partners, a lack of trust or even harmful intent as far as fulfilling contract obligations are concerned.[3]

In the very near future, Polish shipping companies will face the necessity of establishing such relations considering first of all, the opportunities emerging from scale economy effects and the much easier access that now exists to new markets. Entering alliances between Polish shipping companies with foreign operators is important for the Polish partners because it can contribute to

[1] R. Moss Kanter (1994) Collaborative advantage, The art of alliances. *Harvard Business Review*, July-August.
[2] N.M. Vyas, W.L. Schelburn and D.C. Rogers (1995) An analysis of strategic alliances; forms, functions and framework. *Journal of Business and Industrial Marketing*, Vol. 10, no. 3.
[3] C.L. Hung (1992) Strategic business alliance between Canada and the Newly Industrialised Countries of Pacific Asia. *Management International Review*, vol. 32, no. 4.

strengthening their position within the international shipping market, it can improve their efficiency and at the same time it can help to speed up the privatisation process. An alliance's participants can improve their competitive standing, improve their management system and more effectively compete with other firms, or co-operate with them instead, with relatively less effort owing to their strengthened capital position and the possibilities for mutual exchange of experience.

A company strengthened in this way can find a strategic investor much easier which can provide financial resources thus increasing its market value and making it more attractive for prospective business partners.

In Polish shipping companies whose market standing is rather weak, there is the problem that they face at the moment in formulating the privatisation process and in particular, finding a strategic investor whose role in the process is both significant and beneficial. A strategic investor can be a person or a firm owning adequate financial resources and who possesses operational abilities and knowledge which enables active involvement in the management of the company.

Polish shipping companies, which at present are following the principle of improving their competitive position within the market and thus, aim to make their management system more efficient, also commonly consider establishing a consortium, a form of co-operation varying between an alliance, strategic alliance or joint venture. This form of business organisation consists of operations directed at linking financial resources, skills or other assets of the firm in order to fulfil given economic tasks too large to be handled by one member of the partnership alone. In addition, the potential risks of the commercial venture are divided amongst the members and not faced by a single organisation. This form of co-operation would appear to be very beneficial for many Polish shipping companies. It facilitates combining the capital of the firms involved and at the same time it makes their market position stronger stemming from the joint presence in the marketplace. In addition, creating a consortium eliminates a certain amount of sectoral competition which would otherwise exist amongst companies.

According to Polish law, a consortium can be established by banks and various other firms, regardless of who is their owner. Thus state-owned firms or the ones operating with capital participation of the state can be consortium founders. In addition it is quite permissible for there to be foreign capital as a part share in a state-owned company. State Treasury companies and joint ventures can also be placed within this group. Profits and losses can be split according to volume (calculated by quantity or by percentage) of involvement in a joint undertaking and this is a common approach within many consortia.

This form of co-operation can visibly speed up the privatisation process in many maritime shipping companies.

**Strategic management in maritime shipping companies as a condition of creating true competition in the marketplace**

Strategic management can be defined as an approach that facilitates the combination of strategy and operations in an efficient way thus creating the conditions for the efficient functioning of a firm and its harmonious development in close co-operation in order to diminish both risk and uncertainty.

Thus the core theme of strategic management is to prepare a company to function under unfavourable conditions in a constantly changing environment and to take such actions that would comply with the qualitative and quantitative needs of the market.

In conditions of growing competition within the marketplace, each company, when considering its future development has to implement some sort of process of strategic management. The strategy chosen, defines the direction of company development and specifies a way to accomplish the goals set by the firm. The process as a whole must be efficiently managed and strictly controlled if it is to be effective. It is a basic condition of succeeding with the implementation of a chosen strategy that this is the case, and in addition it will strengthen the competitive position of the firm within the market.

Strategic management is particularly important for maritime ship operating companies which function in direct contact with the world market and thus within an international framework. To function in this market, companies have to take into account the conditions and trends, and they have to adjust to a continuously changing environment.

Polish maritime ship operating companies find themselves at present, in a difficult economic situation. There is a shortage of financial resources which prevents them from making new tonnage investment and, at the same time - updating their transit potential. The transformation process gradually introduced in these companies is undoubtedly an element contributing to the improvement of their competitive position within the market. However the scope of management transformation and rate of its implementation cannot be defined as sufficient at present. A formulated development strategy, and a management system adjusted to match it, should first concentrate upon necessary organisational changes, and then move on to changes in property structure (in the case of the shipping sector, selling old tonnage and other redundant equipment), changes in the structure and volume of employment, and finally focusing upon the gradual repayment of debts that have been accumulated both under the old regime and the new authorities post transition.

As far as new tonnage investments are concerned, the Polish Steamship Co. (PŻM - Polska Żegluga Morska) is by far the leading firm. In 1997, the PŻM group continued the process of gradual tonnage restoration - focusing in particular upon their core interests in bulk shipping - which had begun in 1996. This included a big investment contract with the Mitsui and Co. corporation of Japan for building five ships of a laker-max (34,600 DWT) type. In addition, contracts were agreed with the Warna shipyard for building four ships of a handy-max (41,200 DWT) type. The first ship from the series was completed in the summer of 1997. In 1998 a contract signed two years ago with the Szczecin Shipyard will be implemented. It is also anticipated that in the years up to 2000, five ships (two sulphur carriers of 15,500 DWT and three bulk cargo carriers of 16,900 DWT) will be built.

However there are no plans for new tonnage investments by the Polish Ocean Lines group. There are plans to buy only a few second-hand ships for servicing Far East and North American lines plus the possibility of buying used ships or chartering them by the POL-Levant subsidiary company and employing them on their Mediterranean lines.

The Polish Baltic Steamship Co.(PŻB) faces a pressing need to modernise its transit potential as well. The company deals first of all with servicing ferry lines in the Baltic Sea where there is strong competition from both Swedish and Finnish shipowners. Modernisation of the 'Pomerania' ferry, completed in 1997, and the 'Boomerang' catamaran purchase has only to a limited extent, improved the quality of services provided by the Polish shipowner.

The changes taking place in the managerial system of Polish maritime companies in general terms can be described as positive. This managerial reorganisation is necessary before even considering privatisation involving a strategic investor and before an improvement in the firms' competitive standing within the market can be anticipated.

With regards to financial issues, the need to ensure the maintenance of a positive cash-flow has primary importance and is thus another very important element in the process of managing a company efficiently. The lack of readily available financial resources inhibits taking on board any new development possibilities.

Maritime ship operating companies are aware that maintaining positive cash-flow cannot be considered as the solely sufficient condition to ensure a positive financial balance in the long-term. Further actions directed at repaying firms' debts, particularly the ones owed to foreign creditors, and then adjusting the structure of capital covering the current development operations of a company is also highly necessary. The subsequent financing requirements of maritime shipping companies with a debt should be allowed only following detailed consideration and extreme caution as is normally the case when taking up investment decisions based upon company capital. Solving these rather thorny financial questions is unquestionably a primary strategic problem for Polish maritime ship operating companies and one that needs to be addressed in conjunction with the wider structural management issues.

## References

N.M. Hung (1992) Strategic business alliance between Canada and the newly Industrialised countries of Pacific Asia, *Management International Review,* vol. 32, no.4.

Konsorcjum jako struktura kooperacyjna (1998) *Gazeta Prawna,* no. 3 (in Polish).

A. Kreja (1997) Holding - Nowa forma organizacyjna w polskiej gospodarce, *Organizacja i Kierowanie,* no. 4 (in Polish).

H. Minzberg and J.B. Quinn (1996) *The strategy process. Concepts, contexts, cases.* Prentice Hall International.

R. Moss Kanter (1994) Collaborative advantage, The art of alliances, *Harvard Business Review,* July-August.

J. Penc (1998) Programowanie rozwoju firmy, *Zycie Gospodarcze,* no. 4 (in Polish).

B. Pomykalska (1998) Strategia finansowania rozwoju przedsiébiorstwa. *Ekonomika i Organizacja Przedsiébiorstw,* no.2 (in Polish).

Ph. Very (1993) Success in diversification: Building on core competencies. *Long Range Planning,* no. 5.

N.M. Vyas, W.L. Schelburn and D.C. Rogers (1995) An analysis of strategic alliances, forms, functions and framework, *Journal of Business and Industrial Marketing,* vol. 10, no. 3.

# 6. Marketing management in seaports

*Konrad Misztal*
*Institute of Maritime Transport and Seaborne Trade*
*University of Gdańsk*

## Some specific characteristics of port services marketing

The marketing of services is derived from the cognitive and methodical basis of general marketing knowledge. A marketing style of thinking and the ways of conducting business that come from it are basically the same for goods as they are for services. However the specific instruments that are applied and the nature of the organisation of practical operations within enterprises that are based upon a marketing concept are clearly different with particular respect to the scope of the actions they take.

In contrast to the marketing of goods, the core of services marketing is not linked to the variety of needs and buyers' behaviour but to the characteristics of the service itself which normally consists of:[1]

### Immateriality

Services are of an operational character, i.e. they are invisible, and accordingly they do not possess any physical features. This makes estimating the quality of a level of service particularly difficult. To limit the uncertainty that stems

---

[1] M.Pluta-Olearnik (1993) *Marketing usług*. Warszawa (in Polish).

from this, buyers may look for documentary evidence of the service quality. Opinion will be moulded by the place of service origin, its provider, the technical and exploitation equipment utilised, any information material that is available, the existence of 'quality' symbols and, of course, the price charged. The task of the service provider (in essence its 'manufacturer') is to give reality to the features of a service, i.e. to something that is effectively immaterial. However, the opportunities to do this are further limited to a large extent because services are not secured by patent law, they cannot be presented in a direct way during sales promotions, they cannot be stored, any other basis for pricing differently from the prices of competitive services are commonly difficult to establish, and also it is hard to check and preliminary estimate a service project.

*Inseparability of a service and its provider*

There is no physical way to separate a service and its provider. Material goods are produced, sold and consumed and services are sold, provided and consumed. It means that in the service providing process the presence of the provider is required, the scope of operations is limited, direct marketing processes have to dominate, and the   evaluation of a service purchased depends upon the skills and qualifications of the provider.

*Simultaneous nature of service production and its consumption*

The place and a time of the rendering of a service are convergent with the place and time of its consumption. A service is consumed for the same length of time as the process of rendering lasts.

*Versatility*

Services tend to be highly diversified and thus characteristics are very difficult to compare. Services differ between one another depending upon who provides them, when and where. The inherent versatility of services limits to a large extent, the possibilities of standardisation and in addition, the ability to control the level of their quality.

*Impermanence of services*

Servuces are impermanent and therefore cannot be stored. One cannot produce and store a stock of services; and neither is it possible to store the potential to provide them as well. It means that the provision of a continuity of sales demands presents completely different conditions from those found with material goods.

*Impossibility of buying ownership rights to a service*

A buyer has access only to a given service or the facilities connected with it. This lack of possibility of owning a service constitutes a substantial difference between service and material goods; the latter can be used by a buyer in the way that meets his preferences in terms of timing, duration location etc.

*The complementary and substitutive character of material goods and services*

These characteristics indicate the relationships that exist between selling goods and services. They can be of a complementary or substitutive nature depending upon the services and material goods involved and the markets to which they are directed.

This range of features presented above has differing impacts upon different kinds of services in the context of marketing and this results in the need to diversify the marketing mix according to the purpose to which the service is being directed and both the specific and general characteristics of the buyers.

**The marketing of seaport services**

The primary objectives of seaport marketing are as follows:
1. designing particular seaport services within the port marketplace by adjusting them to the requirements and preferences of buyers, in other words the port users;
2. attempting to impact upon the seaport services market, i.e. by shaping the consumption (purchasing) of services through selecting an appropriate means of influencing buyers;
3. carrying out an 'outlet' policy, i.e. managing the seaport services sales process within the market.

These operations should be based upon the presumption that sales of particular port services within seaport markets grow faster than the demand for them (despite the fact that it can be to the contrary) which may result in there being difficulties in selling them. In terms of both producers and buyers of port services this should stimulate a situation that requires both the manufacturing and selling of those services that are most expected and preferred by buyers in the marketplace.

The following information is necessary for a port operating effectively within the seaport services market:

1. details of both present and prospective port clients and their activities in international trade exchanged by sea;
2. an appreciation of technological, organisational and economic changes in maritime and inland transportation and ports;
3. details of economic, trade and industrial changes in the hinterland that have an impact upon the level of port turnover and their relationships with transit;
4. information about competitive ports including for example, their technical and exploitation equipment, loading capacity, applied technologies, level of fees and prices, etc.;
5. the technical and economic situation inside the port and the service companies that are functioning there;
6. threats and the level of risk from operations undertaken in the seaport market.

There are many factors of various character that influence the volume and structure of the demand for seaport services. For the seaport, the most important feature of a potential or existing port services buyer is his attitude towards services purchased. Buyers make their choices based mainly upon economic premises. They buy services closely meeting their needs and which will provide for profitability. The task of a port services producer is to facilitate making these choices by adopting an adequate and appropriate set of measures that will influence the buyer. It is for this reason that such great importance is attached to the process of seaport market research.

## The organisation of seaport marketing management

The process of marketing management is of a complex character. It consists of specified steps arranged in a particular order and requisite to each other. There are six distinguishable stages within a correctly conducted marketing management process in seaports:[2]

1. identification of what constitutes the seaport services market;

[2] A. Podobiński (1994) Zarządzanie marketingowe w handlu zagranicznym. *Handel Zagraniczny*, no. 7-8, (in Polish).

2. an analysis of external and internal conditions of the port as it functions within the market;
3. defining the goals and strategy of the port within the market;
4. deciding upon the tactics and the appropriate techniques for a port operating within the market;
5. conducting effective operations within the market;
6. control and assessment of the results and drawing conclusions for the future.

Firstly one has to identify a market and then carry out a process of market identification and undertake an analysis of the port's situation within the given market. The assessment should result in the assembly of data upon the kinds of port services that customers expect, whether the services offered by the port meet these expectations, how the level of services offered by the port can be estimated compared to similar services provided by competitive ports, and what actions should be undertaken to make the seaport services offered by the port more competitive. To compete successfully with other ports within the market one has to study them thoroughly. It is necessary to gather as much as possible, genuine and comprehensive information upon competitive ports.

Based upon conclusions drawn from the above analysis, the external and internal conditions of the functioning of a port within the market and changes in the marketplace should be assessed within a defined time range. The assessment is necessary to specify the port marketing strategy and it should normally contain the following:
1. trends in changes in the shape of the market situation as far as the sales and demand for seaport services which are on offer are concerned;
2. trends in changes of the level of seaport service prices and conditions, and a measure of the level of access to a given port;
3. directions of changes in the main competitors to the port within the market analysed;
4. the primary directions of the economics and politics within countries of competitor ports.

This information outlined above is indispensable for the process of defining marketing strategy, and designed to accomplish the operational goals set by the port, (e.g. broadening the scope of diversification) for services offered, improving their quality level, attracting new port customers, or undertaking appropriate and efficient organisational, technological and investment actions. In this phase of the marketing management process, the main long-term strategic goals of the port are formulated; however, it should also include those concrete tasks that need to be implemented within a particular period of time.

53

Definition of the substantive tactics and techniques of operations within a given port services market, and also the process of effective market operation aimed at achieving the set goals, usually forms the next stage. In this phase an estimate is also made of the conditions needed to support the plans of the port and the decisions which would be required to achieve anticipated efficiency during their implementation.

The port's chances of success within a given market depend upon the implementation of adopted goals and the conduct of effective market operations. A major goal of these operations is to create or enlarge a group of loyal port services buyers and strengthen their relationship with the port, induce an increase in the demands of buyers by means of offering new services and an increase in their diversification, and also propagating new forms and methods of selling port services.

The goals of a marketing management strategy are completed by conducting a control and operational effects analysis upon the market that has been researched. This means first of all, an assessment of the changes that have occurred within the market as a result of port marketing activities and an estimation of the changes in port customers' opinion of the specific services provided and the overall port image. The information upon changes in volume and structure of the services sold and the broader economic outcome is also necessary. The results of the analysis facilitate not only the assessment of a port's position within the marketplace compared with its competitors but also helps to draw conclusions upon the effects of up-to-date marketing operations and suggest directions for the future. They constitute a basis for making decisions upon future policies within marketing management.

Within marketing management, the fundamental role of the process is established by research into port services in the market within which the port functions or intends to function. Correctly conducted research of a market should provide fundamental data upon its characteristic features, volume and structure of demand for port services, and the competitive conditions that exist.

Marketing management is a core element within the activities of seaports and their development and thus it should be treated as an equal to other managerial functions. Such understanding of the role of marketing management constitutes a basic condition of the economic development of the port and all port operations should be subordinated to its requirements.

# The conditions of marketing operations within Polish seaports

Marketing in seaports in countries which were until very recently, Socialist dominated, was regarded as unimportant and as a consequence was completely neglected. This negative attitude to marketing stemmed from the basic rules of the social and political system which were centred upon the centralised planned economy, in which the ownership by the state of all production means was a fundamental principle. As a result, this led to the strong monopolisation of economic operations in decision-making and executive spheres as well, and to restricting the self-sufficiency potential of enterprises. As a consequence, they were separated from the marketplace.

In ports the structure of the system existed based mainly upon a state-owned sector with large monopolistic companies having an exclusive right to particular port services. It led as a consequence, to high monopolisation of the port services market and an elimination of any competitive aspect within the port services operational sphere. The ports also functioned in a monopolistic economic and transport environment and according to the rules of this market, they did not have to compete as far as domestic foreign trade cargoes were concerned because the rule of planned division of domestic cargo was applied - i.e. cargo was allocated to them in guaranteed fashion. Meanwhile, transit cargo flow from the (then) Socialist countries, i.e. those of the CMEA, was determined through non-economic criteria as well.

This system brought about a lowering of managerial staff skills and standards through taking away any initiative in deciding the key issues of company development, creating a strict hierarchy of decision-making that could not be avoided regardless of the operational effects, applying further strict political criteria in assessment of activities accompanied by the virtual elimination of economic criteria and an absence of self-sufficiency in decision-making the latter because all decisions had to be confirmed at a higher level within the company.

The transformation of the Polish economy and its economic environment, particularly in the context of the development of other Central and East European countries, has brought about far reaching consequences for the world economy and for Polish foreign trade and its ties with the international market. This process, directed at creating a market economy environment, is strongly reflected by developments within the Polish port economy. The Polish seaports faced a need to solve numerous strategic problems stemming from the new conditions of operation and development, including:
1. spatial changes in the economic hinterland of ports and growing international competition from foreign ports and alternative inland

transportation, in particular trucks, resulting in substantially limiting the immediate and exclusive hinterland of Polish ports;

2. a change in customer and shipper attitude whereby they now regard a seaport as an element of the complete land-sea transportation chain from sender to recipient;
3. changes in the volume, characteristics and direction structure of the cargo turnover of Polish foreign trade;
4. introducing market economy mechanisms producing a cost and quality orientation in the operations of ports and improving their competitive potential.

The factors that are influencing changes within both the external and internal environment of Polish seaports have many aspects and characteristics. Amongst internal elements the liberalisation and decentralisation of national economic management is the core one. With regards to Polish ports it tends to have the effect of facilitating:

1. freedom for finding an optimal transportation route for cargo;
2. an increase in domestic and international competition;
3. modification of the national transportation network.

However the external environment of Polish seaports is influenced by a variety of elements which include:[3]

1. the removal of the 'the iron curtain' between East and West Europe, resulting in an impact upon the increase in goods exchange in an East-West direction and, as a result, a growth in the importance of land transportation in the process of this exchange;
2. the integration within the European Union and its implications for the freedom of goods, services, capital and persons flow, whilst demanding at the same time an adjustment to the structure and standards which a united Europe needs and support for an increase in land transportation's importance in trade relations between and with all the European Union countries;
3. the process of economic liberalisation in Central and Eastern Europe enabling the choice of optimal route for cargo transportation and thus growing competition for cargo;
4. the reunification of Germany resulting in increased goods turnover and again, growth in competition.

As a result of the changes noted above, what was the domestic hinterland of Polish seaports has become 'internationalised' which consequently means

---

[3] *The Study of the National Transport Plan in the Republic of Poland. Final Report.* JICA, Tokyo, 1992.

competition for Polish foreign trade cargo (particularly containerised) with foreign ports and the acquisition of Polish cargoes by foreign carriers. On the other hand the use of foreign ports by Polish importers and exporters (i.e. those ports competing with the Polish ports) may well grow because of the abolition of the state monopoly in the foreign trade.

At the same time one can observe fundamental changes in the direction of Polish foreign trade. At present (late 1996) about 60% of Polish foreign trade turnover occurs in relations with European Union countries. Germany is the main trading partner of Poland and its share is 52.3% of total turnover with foreign lands. Germany also dominates in Poland's foreign trade with the European Union countries (47.8% of imports and 56.9% of exports in 1996).

Meanwhile, inland transportation routes, as an alternative to Polish seaports, are emerging more and more often. As a result of the limited efficiency of transportation links between the Polish ports and their hinterland, and also the advancing process of transport integration of Poland with the European Union, inland transportation gradually has become a stronger competitor for Polish seaports.

The shifting cargo flows of Polish foreign trade from eastern to western directions limits the share that the sea route can take in their servicing. This particularly concerns high-advanced industrial goods which tend to gravitate to a land route anyway. This phenomenon is accompanied by strong development and liberalisation of the road transit industry which now directly links Poland with nearly every European country.

Polish maritime transport still maintains its importance in exports and imports of many cargo groups, particularly bulk cargo but also general cargo in transport with overseas countries (see Table 6.1). Meanwhile, compared with inland transportation the share of shipping routes in servicing Polish foreign trade is shown in Table 6.2.

**Table 6.1**
**The share of shipping routes in servicing Polish foreign trade during 1985 and 1995 (per cent)**

| Specification | 1985 | 1995 |
|---|---|---|
| Total | 38.5 | 32.5 |
| Import | 24.6 | 26.9 |
| Export | 51.5 | 36.6 |

Source: 1985 prepared based upon *Rocznik Statystyczny GUS (Statistical Annual of the Main Statistical Office)*, Warszawa 1986; 1995 - *Rocznik Statystyczny Gospodarki Morskiej 1996 (Statistical Annual of the Maritime Economy 1996)*, GUS Warszawa 1997

The internal and external conditions for the functioning and development of Polish seaports indicate the necessity to carry out large-scale and intensive marketing operations.


## The organisation of marketing operations in Polish seaports

Polish seaport marketing divisions have been located within an organisational structure of the port managing body (i.e. the Port Authority). Their structure can be presented as in Figure 6.1.

The organisational structure presented in Figure 6.1 will inevitably change following the implementation of the new Act on Seaports and Harbours and the appointment of a separate port management body for the public utility and the separation of the operational activities undertaken by private firms from this body.

According to the Act, senior Port Management will carry out marketing operations for the port as a whole, representing it for both internal and external contacts, and the port service companies will organise marketing of their own needs at local (in-port) market level.

Defining a marketing strategy and implementing strategic planning in the port as a whole is the main task for the highest port management level, whereas marketing operations within port companies consists of planning, implementing and controlling tasks based upon an analysis of the present and anticipated state of the environment, i.e. the constant and reciprocal adjustment of the firm's goals and resources to meet market opportunities which have to be picked up relatively early and adequately exploited. The co-ordination of decisions and operations as far as all port's functions are concerned at every management level, are also the tasks of the Port Authority.

Up until the present day, marketing research for the port services market for Polish seaports was completely ignored within any marketing operations undertaken. Port promotion, widely appreciated as important in communication with the market and regarded as an indispensable development factor, tended to be the main, if not sole focus.

The Promotion Division deals first of all with advertising, publishing and exhibitions, and also the organisation of promotional events in addition to receiving visitors.

**Table 6.2**

**Polish foreign trade turnover by main transportation branches in 1995 (per cent)**

| Transportation branch | Total | Share according to total turnover | |
|---|---|---|---|
| | | *Import* | *Export* |
| Maritime transport | 32.5 | 26.9 | 36.6 |
| including: | | | |
| conventional and containerised cargo | 31.6 | 25.7 | 35.8 |
| Railway transport | 37.3 | 33.0 | 40.5 |
| Road transport | 15.3 | 14.9 | 15.7 |

Source: *Rocznik Statystyczny Gospodarki Morskiej 1996 (Statistical Annua of the Maritime Economy 1996)*, GUS Warszawa 1997

**Figure 6.1**

**Organisational structure of marketing in Polish seaports**

Director of the Port Authority

Deputy Director -  Finance
Ownership supervision
Staff and administration
Property management
Marketing and development

Marketing and development is then divided into:-
Port dispatching
Marketing
Promotion
Port development

Source: Author

## The marketing strategy of Polish seaports

As a consequence of the transformation of the Polish economy the maritime sector has borne a high economic cost deepened by substantial differences in the development level that exists, and the economic, financial and legal base from which it has had to begin its reformation. Indifference in state policy towards the sector has meant that development opportunities for Polish maritime transport firms, unlike the case of many of their foreign competitors, have not been provided. That is why the adoption by the state of both a protective and promotional function towards domestic ports in competition with foreign stronger ports, is indispensable.

The Ministry of Transportation and Maritime Economy has prepared a policy document '*Presumptions of a program to increase the international competitiveness of Polish maritime transport*', but in this it does not propose any form of support for maritime transport from the state. It merely concentrates upon adjusting Polish economic and commercial conditions in the sector to OECD and EU standards necessary for the eventual accession of Poland to the EU sometime in the near future.

According to the document, the program's goal is 'defining opportunities and ways to take up operations directed at reducing an unfavourable gap between conditions of Polish seaports and shipping companies' activities compared with the operational conditions of their direct competitors within the international transport market, with respect to the liberalisation rules of the maritime policy of the OECD and EU members, applying the chosen tools and procedures of maritime polity implementation used by these countries'.[4]

The program aims at facilitating integration between the Polish maritime economy and the policy of the EU countries and making structural changes in adjusting Polish maritime transport so that organisational and technological co-operative solutions with the European transportation system are possible. The next task is to adapt Polish maritime transport to shipping safety, natural environment protection and employment conditions' standards. In addition it aims to stimulate the regional integration of the maritime economy contributing to the development of port agglomerations and export-import companies.

The development of land-sea transportation systems requires that ports should become fast and efficient links in cargo transit between sender and recipient. Improving the competitiveness of ports cannot be achieved without

---

[4] *Presumptions of a program to increase the international competitiveness of Polish maritime transport*. Ministry of Transportation and Maritime Economy, Warszawa 1995 (in Polish).

improving their links with maritime, railway, land, inland water and pipeline transportation. Creating the many facilities needed with regard to an efficient transportation chain as a whole is thus an important element in the process of improving competitiveness. The factors that this process relates to are listed below.[5]

Improvements within an organisational sphere include:

1. creating multi-subject and close branch relations within the land-sea transportation chain.
2. creating and activating marketing operations within transport representatives (i.e. ports and shipping, railway and ports, etc.) in transit countries;
3. creating duty free zones in port territories which would provide particular duty, transport and trade facilities to firms from transit countries.
4. organising joint shipping ventures, lines and services in Polish ports.
5. introducing uniform competitive tariffs for transit partners, with the possible application of an internal cost calculation system amongst transportation system participants;
6. applying exceptional and special tariffs following the examples of the EU countries.

In the technical sphere:

1. modernisation of the transportation infrastructure and trans-shipment potential. The rate of motorway construction needs to be increased (initially the A1 and A2), enabling the implementation in Poland of an independent strategy for international trans-shipments (including transit) and the modernisation of railway links in main transportation corridors;
2. stimulating the development of multi-modal transhipments.

The program also indicates the need to enlarge and modernise Polish seaport potential accompanied by creating logistic and distribution centres for cargo at their territories or in the near vicinity. It was also noted that implementation of the Act on ports, creating a basis for adequate functioning of port managing bodies, is of great importance for adjusting organisational structures and operational conditions within seaports.

However a very capital-absorbent port, road and railway infrastructure, despite its significance for port competitiveness, was excluded from the sphere of state influence. Two projects are being prepared: *'The project on access to ports and port managing'* and *'The port modernisation project'*. For their implementation, US$ 300 million was assigned from the World Bank loan project. Ports should conduct their own investments, not only those

---

[5] *Presumptions of a program...*, op. cit.

relating to transformation, but also the ones concerning development, and look for sources of foreign capital as well.

In the meantime governmental projects set the following tasks for ports to undertake:

1. raising the level of economic efficiency and service quality;
2. diversification of operations, broadening them with trade, industrial, distribution and logistic functions;
3. integrating ports with the land transportation system within the framework of multimodal transportation;
4. raising the competitiveness level following liberalisation rules;
5. employment rationalisation and the introduction of modern work principles of organisation into ports;
6. developing co-operation amongst Polish seaports;
7. strengthening the position of Polish seaports within the European transportation network;
8. facilitating port development that is friendly towards the natural environment.

The responsibility for Polish port strategy implementation falls almost entirely upon the seaports themselves. No direct or indirect support from the state is expected. However, it is highly improbable that the ports can manage by themselves - the tasks required are numerous and very costly.

**References**

K. Misztal (1994) *Porty morskie w Unii Europejskiej (Seaports in the European Union).*Gdańsk (in Polish).

K. Misztal (1996) Zarządzanie marketingowe w portach morskich (Marketing management in seaports), *Spedycja i Transport* no. 10, (in Polish).

M. Pluta-Olearnik (1993) *Marketing usług (Marketing of services)*, Warszawa (in Polish).

A. Podobiński (1994) Zarządzanie marketingowe w handlu zagranicznym (Marketing management in foreign trade), *Handel Zagraniczny* no. 7-8 (in Polish).

*Rocznik Statystyczny GUS (Statistical Annual of the Main Statistical Office)* (1986), Warszawa (in Polish).

*Rocznik Statystyczny Gospodarki Morskiej 1996 (Statistical Annual of the Maritime Economy 1996)* (1997), Warszawa (in Polish).

*The study of the National Transport Plan in the Republic of Poland. Final Report* (1992), YICA, Tokyo.

*Ustawa z dnia 10.10.1996 o portach i przystaniach morskich (the Act on ports and harbours dated October 10th 1996)*, Ministerstwo Transportu i Gospodarki Morskiej, Warszawa (in Polish).

*Załowenia programu zwiêkszenia miêdzynarodowej konkurencyjnoœci polskiego transportu morskiego (Presumptions of a program to increase the international competitiveness of Polish maritime transport)* (1995) Ministerstwo Transportu i Gospodarki Morskiej (Ministry of Transportation and Maritime Economy), Warszawa (in Polish).

# 7. The present state and development opportunities in Gdynia Port

*Adam Salomon*
*Institute of Maritime Transport and Seaborne Trade*
*University of Gdańsk*

## General remarks

The Port of Gdynia (Lat. 54°32'N; Long. 18°33'E) is an artificial pier-quay port, protected from the Baltic Sea by cement breakwaters of 2.5 km length in total. There are 11.1 km of wharves, including 10.3 km for loading, located within its territory. The volume of loading in the Port of Gdynia in 1995-97, broken into cargo groups is presented in Table 7.1.

**Table 7.1**
**Loadings at the Port of Gdynia in 1995-1997 (thousand tons)**

| CARGO GROUP | 1995 | 1996 | 1997 | Dynamics (%) 1996=100 | Dynamics (%) 1995=100 |
|---|---|---|---|---|---|
| Coal and coke | 2,154 | 1,717 | 1,867 | +9 | -14 |
| Ores | 77 | 110 | 93 | -16 | +20 |
| Other bulk | 858 | 838 | 801 | -4 | -7 |
| Grains | 529 | 1,619 | 826 | -49 | +56 |
| Timber | 0 | 2 | 1 | -50 | 0 |
| General cargo | 3,659 | 3,632 | 4,521 | +24 | +23 |
| Liquid cargo | 356 | 648 | 736 | +14 | +6 |
| TOTAL | 7,634 | 8,565 | 8,845 | +3 | +15 |

Source: Namiary na Morze i Handel (The direction of sea and trade), no. 1/1998, p.48

Commencing on November 19th 1991, the fundamental process of ownership transformation in the Port of Gdynia commenced. The separation of the management function of infrastructure and port territory from its operation (consisting mainly of loading and storage), trading and servicing, has already been achieved, resulting in the implementation of a holding structure, which is regarded as the best for the port.[1] A holding structure, providing the specific framework for the port, was considered to be the most flexible body, ideal for implementation within a variety of structures of organisation and economic systems, providing the necessary facilities for an effective utilisation of resources both for current and prospective needs.[2] According to the work schedule prepared by the Supervisory Board in 1994, two territories were separated from the Maritime Commercial Port of Gdynia structure and two limited liability companies, fully owned by the MPH Gdynia S.A. were established: the Baltic Grain Terminal Ltd., launched July 1st, and the Baltic Container Terminal Ltd., launched December 1st. In 1995 the next five economic bodies belonging to the Maritime Commercial Port of Gdynia S.A. were created. They were as follows: the Port Technical Company Ltd. (April 1st), the Maritime Bulk Cargo Terminal Gdynia Ltd. (June 1st), the 'Trans-Port' - Port Transport Company Ltd. (June 1st), the Port Supply Company Ltd. (July 1st), and the Baltic General Cargo Terminal Gdynia Ltd. (August 1st). Since May 1st, 1996, the WUŻ-Shipping and Port Services Gdynia Co. Ltd. and the 'SIEÆ' - Hydraulic and Power Net Company Ltd. have been operating as independent companies. In all the companies where there is 100% ownership by the MPH Gdynia S.A., the suprastructure necessary to provide basic services was provided as a contribution in-kind, together with a financial contribution, depending upon the organisation, varying from złoty 0.35 to 3.0 million. On September 25th 1996, the Board of the MPH Gdynia S.A. was transformed into Port Gdynia Holding S.A. (PGH S.A.) with an operational mission based upon the 'non-profit' principle, i.e. it was presumed that any incomes have to be assigned for the development and maintenance of the port infrastructure. The current organisational chart of the Capital Group Port Gdynia Holding S.A. is presented in Figure 1. Dependent companies are here divided between the ones belonging to PGH S.A., external

---

[1] Z. Gralak (1995) Na nowej drodze. Rozmowa z Ryszardem Wocialem, dyr. ds. nadzoru właścicielskiego MPH Gdynia S.A., (In the new direction. An interview with Ryszard Wocial, the director for the ownership supervision of MPH Gdynia S.A.). *Gazeta Portowa*, no. 26.
[2] B. Nogalski, P. Dwojacki, T. Białas and J. Waśniewski (1996) *Budowa i funkcjonowanie holdingów, The construction and functioning of holdings.* Bałtyckie Zespoły Doradcze 'Port 2000', Gdynia, p. 8.

companies operating in the port and maritime sector, and remaining external companies.

## Figure 7.1
## The capital structure of Port Gdynia Holding S.A.

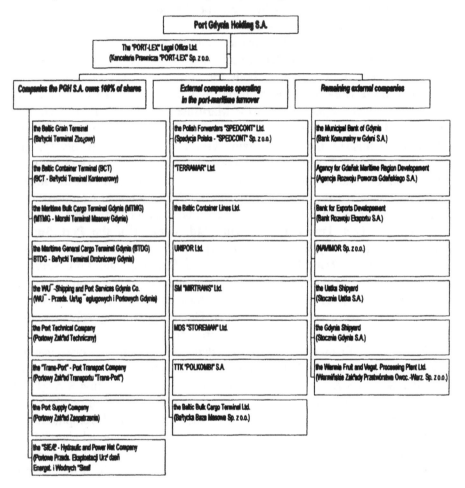

Source: The official home page of the Port Gdynia Holding S.A., April 29th, 1998, *http://www.port.gdynia.pl/pl/struktura_kapitalowa/struktura_kapitalowa.htm*

## Main investments of the Port Gdynia Holding S.A.

New economic trends coming from the political and economic transformation in the Central-Eastern European countries in addition to progress in transportation technologies, has brought about the need for changes in all links of the international transport chain and at the same time within seaports. The Port of Gdynia has made efforts to meet these requirements and its investment programme is directed towards achieving this task.

The Port Gdynia Holding S.A. is amongst other things, engaged in two major enterprises which extend in their scope far beyond the port territory. The successful implementation of them would contribute to a large extent to the efficient operation of the terminals and the port system as a whole.

The Trans-European Motorway/Trans-European Railway (TEM/TER) Scandinavia project is the first of these projects. Cities located along the route of the planned road-railway corridor, connecting Oslo with Athens, have conducted together a series of lobbying actions in order to make a joint and therefore stronger, impact upon governments and institutions responsible for the preparation and implementation of the project. The newly constructed Ferry Terminal/Ro-Ro ramp facility, part of the Baltic Bridge project, together with Karlskrona port developments, will be the Port Gdynia Holding S.A. contribution. The TEM/TER Scandinavia will run from Oslo, through Göteborg, Karlskrona, Gdynia, Toruń, Łódź, Częstochowa, Katowice, Bratislava, Budapest, Belgrade to Athens. The second project, is essentially a continuation of the first one and assumes the construction of the Polish section of the A-1 (TAPP) motorway. When the Kwiatkowski highway is completed and connected to the Tricity ringroad through the forest section, the Baltic Container Terminal will be the starting point of the motorway to the continent. The decision to join the 'BALT TAPP' stock company by the Port Gdynia Holding S.A. at its launch was made early on. It is a goal of the port company to establish participation in the bid, and finally to engage in the project, including the construction and exploitation phases of the toll A-1 motorway from Gdynia to Tuszyn near Łódź.[3] Cities located within the motorway corridor including Częstochowa, Toruń, Płock, Włocławek, Grudzidz, Gdańsk, Sopot, Gdynia, Tczew; significant Polish companies involved in the investment include BIG Bank Gdański, Bank Gospodarki Śywnościowej,

---

[3] *Grupa Kapitałowa Portu Gdynia - dzień dzisiejszy i perspektywy rozwojowe, (The Gdynia Port Capital Group - today and development perspectives).* Dział Rozwoju Portu Gdynia, Gdynia 1996, p. 25.

Elektromontaż, Gdańskie Przedsiébiorstwo Robót Drogowych and a number of overseas firms.

On October 8th 1997 the cement loading terminal was incorporated into a major development within the Baltic General Cargo Terminal in Gdynia. The investment was carried out by the Scancem International A/S firm. Annual cargo turnover was estimated at 100-150,000 tonnes, destined mainly for planned Polish motorway construction, and the cost at approximately US$5 million. The newly opened facility is a distribution terminal and offers Portland cement of a high quality (manufactured by a concern belonging to Kunda Nordic Cement Corporation of Estonia) with a loading rate equivalent to 200 tonnes per hour. The cement terminal, whose storage capacity is as much as 10,000 tonnes, is equipped with electronically controlled systems, protecting the natural environment from dust.[4] The first ship arrived at the new terminal wharf on July 11th, 1997.

The Baltic Grain Terminal, following modernisation carried out in 1994 at a cost of złoty 300 billion, at present has a yearly loading capacity equal to 1.2 million tonnes.[5] Transhipments are conducted using Bühler Portalink Combi 300 equipment, and the technological process as a whole is controlled by computer. The natural environment is fully protected from pollution by special filtercycles. There are also the possibilities of unloading ships carrying grain using four floating elevators owned by the port. Further modernisation of the Baltic Grain Terminal will consist of erecting a second Bühler equipment unit which will double the daily transhipment capacity. A further stage consisting of enlarging the terminal with six tank silos, each of 2,250 tonnes capacity, and two further ones of 300 tonnes capacity, has been completed already resulting in an increase in capacity of the elevator and the accompanying equipment by around 14,000 tonnes and as a consequence reaching now a total of about 40,000 tonnes. Their final capacity is planned to increase to around 75,000 tonnes. The next investment project provides for doubling the transhipment capacity of the Baltic Container Terminal in the next few years to about 300-350,000 TEU per year. In addition, there are plans for a free trade zone and a car terminal of a PDI type, as well as the development of a number of minor terminals located adjacent to the Baltic Grain Terminal.

---

[4] K. Sudziarska (1997) SCANCEM inwestuje w Polsce, (SCANCEM invests in Poland.) *Namiary na Morze i Handel*, no. 10, p. 16.
[5] M. Grzybowski (1996) *Strategia konwersji do gospodarki rynkowej, (A conversion strategy to the market economy)*. 'BOiGM' no. 3, p. 23.

The port development plan covers the eastern part of the port territory as well, i.e. the territory around basins and wharves located on the city side and areas in the vicinity of Gdynia Shipyard S.A., the 'Nauta' Repair Shipyard S.A. and the 'Dalmor' Fishing, Processing and Trade Company. Bulk cargo (loose, liquid and grains) and general cargo are currently stored there. To make this part of the port more attractive, the storage area is going to be enlarged. It will facilitate broadening the scope of services supplementary to those providing for basic distribution.

Other development undertakings also include, in addition to those already noted, constructing a distribution terminal in the Gdynia-Port railway station area constituting one of the new 'distri-parks' of about 15 ha. and creating a new general or bulk cargo terminal of 7.1 ha. with a depth of 12.4-14.5 meters.

## Ferry terminal construction

Gdynia is located at a central point along the future transit corridor of the North-South Trans-European Motorway. This creates good prospective conditions for the development of communications with the port's prospective hinterland. The direct hinterland of Gdynia has significant meaning for the future expansion of ferry shipping in the port especially given that the Tricity agglomeration of Gdańsk, Gdynia and Sopot, inhabited by over a million people, has a well developed economic potential, and a clear tourist, cultural and entertainment infrastructure.

Considering its geographical location, production potential and transit advantages, there are sizeable opportunities to intensify cargo and passenger services in Gdynia by ferry. The existing port potential is also promising in terms of providing the experience and back-up for these facilities - the complete logistical background of the port is directed towards servicing general cargo and is specialised in the use of modern transhipment technologies particularly in the Baltic Container Terminal. There are also favourable communication conditions within the area chosen for the construction of the new ferry terminal. It is not a coincidence that the leading international ferry shipping company - Swedish based Stena Line - located its headquarters for the south-eastern Baltic in Gdynia.

The predicted significance of the growth in ferry related traffic is behind the plans for ferry terminals forming one of the major elements of the Gdynia Port development strategy and is the reason why the port is making efforts to build a new, large and modern ferry terminal during the next few years. It will be the biggest investment in the port for many years and the very first stages of its implementation have been already started.

The terminal is a part of the Trans-European Motorway/Trans-European Railway Scandinavia. It is one part of an investment enterprise called the *Baltic Ferry Bridge*. Gdynia is planned to be a continental bridge-head with the port of Karlskrona-Vekko in Sweden forming the other port across the Baltic Sea. All issues connected with the implementation of this sizeable undertaking are included in the special works programme designed on behalf of the World Bank. It is also a product of the research of a joint Polish-Swedish team created by the Baltic Institute in Karlskrona, the Swedish Institute of Transport and Communication Analyses, Swedish Railways, the Institute of Railways Future, Karlskrona City Authorities, the Blekinge Region Management, Gdynia City Authorities, the Polish National Railways and the Port of Gdynia S.A.[6] In 1996-2005, new cargo and passenger ferry terminals will be constructed in both ports. In the Gdynia port territory, the investment will comprise an area of about 25-28 ha. in the western part of the port in the neighbourhood of the Container Terminal, near the existing temporary ferry terminal where approximately 25% of passenger ferry turnover and 10% of cargo turnover coming through Polish seaports is already concentrated.

According to the investment project under the working name 'Baltic Ferry Bridge', prepared within the framework of the TEM/TER Scandinavia project,[7] four ferry service ramps will be built in Gdynia: two for car-passenger units and two for railway-cars, together with the necessary technical infrastructure. These new facilities will enable five ferries to be serviced at the same time. The estimated amount of investment from the Polish side is equal to approximately US$ 40-50 million.

## The prime strategic investment for companies established by Port Gdynia Holding S.A.

In order to increase container shipments and the attractiveness of the port, a regular container feeder system was organised from the Polish interior to the Baltic Container Terminal in Gdynia. Transportation services are provided based upon container terminals located up-country in Łódź, Poznań,

---

[6] Z. Gralak (1997) Bałtycki Most Promowy Gdynia-Karlskrona, (The Baltic Ferry Bridge Gdynia-Karlskrona). *Namiary na Morze i Handel*, no.3/1997, p. 18.
[7] Grupa Kapitałowa Portu Gdynia, op. cit., p. 13.

Warszawa, Sosnowiec and Kraków. To improve the quality of services the Port Gdynia Holding S.A. decided to develop a container road and railway connection with the established shipping routes, encouraging efficient links between the point of loading and the destination port.

On September 19th 1995, the first regular shipping link with Hamburg and Bremerhaven serviced by Baltic Container Lines (BCL) was established in the Baltic Container Terminal. BCL is a joint venture of the Port Gdynia Holding S.A. (who hold 40% of shares), the shipping company of the PLO Group - POL-America S.A. (40% of shares) and a forwarder - C. Hartwig Gdynia S.A. (20% of shares). Its goal is to develop commercial feeder services to and from Gdynia port and to enter the short-range transportation market in the Baltic and North Sea region. So far it has achieved substantial profits and as a result, since March 1998, further lines to Antwerp, Kłajpeda, Riga and Kaliningrad have been opened. The connections between Gdynia and these ports is provided by 25 units.[8] All these projects require a considerable financial investment. At present the Baltic Container Terminal is preparing a series of organisational changes which, including those projects outlined above, will facilitate servicing as many as 300-350,000 TEU and about 1 million tonnes of general cargo per year.

Adopting an organisational and developmental model for Gdynia port, of the type that has been applied previously in many highly-developed countries, is the goal of the current development strategy of the port. In addition to an expansion of the loading capacity of the port, it should establish a series of distribution centres for imported goods, specialising mainly upon agricultural and food products. The distribution centres, which will service exported, re-exported and imported goods, are designed to deal with storage, processing, packaging, refining, accumulating and distribution functions. In Gdynia Port, the development of distribution activities based upon goods such as citrus fruit imports (storage, refining, distributing, dispatching), fruit and vegetable exports (refining, storage, repackaging, dispatching), steel (storage, palettage), sacked goods (storage, palettage), spices and beverages (storage, preparing for sales and dispatching), cars (storage, preparing for sales and dispatching) and heavy lift goods (storage) are planned. In the Free Trade Zone located in

---

[8] More information on Baltic Container Lines can be found in J. Kujawa (1997) *Baltic Container Lines - nowe polskie przedsiębiorstwo żeglugowe, (Baltic Container Lines - a new Polish shipping company)*. Studia i Materiały Instytutu Transportu i Handlu Morskiego (The transformation of maritime transportation in Poland. Studies and materials of the Institute of Maritime Transport and Seaborne Trade), Wydawnictwo Uniwersytetu Gdańskiego, Gdańsk, p. 75-82.

Gdynia Port, the following kinds of economic activity are planned to be carried out:

1. loading goods to all destinations;
2. providing passive and active services to ships;
3. renting and leasing property to carry out production and trade activities to foreign and domestic bodies;
4. cargo handling and processing.

The preferred enterprise partners involved in these activities are those derived from the existing port supra- and infrastructure, and primarily the ones who have invested in the port. The impacts and profits Port Gdynia Holding S.A. expects from this Free Trade Zone activity are as follows:

1. service diversification, including, primarily, an increase in added value;
2. an increase in transit turnover;
3. an increase in loading area capacity enabling a better utilisation of the transhipment potential of terminals;
4. strengthening the position and improvement of competitiveness level of the Port of Gdynia;
5. the creation of new jobs;
6. gaining access to foreign capital, prepared to invest in the Free Trade Zone and Gdynia Port as a whole;
7. creating incentives to stimulate the port's industrialisation;
8. implementing and encouraging new technologies by foreign investors;
9. creating mechanisms to enable the lowering of imported goods prices;
10. international trade facilitation, because:- goods shipped by foreign firms are not burdened with customs duties; goods located in the Free Trade Zone area can be further sold, re-exported, refined and processed; there is the possibility to store, manipulate and process cargo without any time-limit.[9]

For many years the limited storage capacity of the grain elevator has been the biggest problem in the Baltic Grain Terminal. At present, increasing the storage facilities has become an indispensable factor in meeting market requirements, servicing larger ships, facilitating high daily processing rates and making the most of the chance to create a modern fodder terminal in the southern part of the Baltic Sea. In order to succeed in implementing an elevator enlargement project of this sort, which requires substantial financial resources, the investment has been divided up into a series of segments. In the first stage, six steel elevators of 2,250 tonnes capacity each and two 300 tonne

---

[9] *Ekonomika portów morskich i polityka portowa, (Economics of seaports and port policy)*, edited by L. Kuŷma (1993) Wydawnictwo Gdańskie, Gdańsk, p. 271-273.

silos with a joint technological system were built, increasing storage capacity by more than 14,000 tonnes.

To improve the turnover volume of grains and fodder and to finance the part of the investment connected with the second stage of elevator enlargement, it was necessary to attract an external collaborator who would participate in the investment and at the same time would be a cargo provider for the grain terminal. Talks with the 'Agros' and 'Rolimpex' companies have been held which reveal great interest in the idea to create in Gdynia a grain turnover centre. Simultaneously the purchase of a second stationary piece of Bühler loading equipment is planned which will increase daily loading capacity of the terminal to 12-16,000 tonnes. As an auxiliary investment, dredging works around the elevator were carried out, providing access for ships with a draught up to 11.5 metres and eventually up to 12.5 metres.

In order to intensify the turnover of grain, there exists in addition a plan to build in the vicinity of the elevator an industrial and port complex, dealing with grain processing, plant oil manufacturing, etc.

All these proposals and undertakings are a result of decisions adopted by Port Gdynia Holding S.A. to specialise in the port upon containers, grain and fodder transhipments, and in addition, ferry servicing, whilst attempting to retain the universal character of the port at the same time.

Within the territory of the Maritime Bulk Cargo Terminal Gdynia, in addition to a number of other developments, a specialised storage-loading terminal for artificial fertilisers (mainly imports) has been constructed[10] based upon a roofed tank of 9,000 sq. meters area and a storage capacity of 35,000 tonnes. Its segmented construction enables the storage of various kinds of fertiliser when servicing large vessels. The investment is a joint venture of Port Gdynia Holding S.A. and the 'Puławy' Nitric Plant, and named the Baltic Bulk Terminal Ltd. The contract value is estimated at złoty 40 million (about US$13 million), and the first use of the terminal is anticipated for the end of 1998.

The construction of a highly controversial liquid gas (LPG) loading terminal, in competition with the Gaspol terminal in Gdańsk port (Port Północny Northern Port) is another investment taking place. It is anticipated that the yearly turnover at this fuel terminal will reach as much as 60-100,000 thousand tonnes, and the storage capacity of liquid gas will be 400 tonnes at

[10] G. Golis, J. Dubicki, W. Budkowicz and M. Bendkowski (1996) *Wizja zagospodarowania i rozwoju Morskiego Portu Handlowego Gdynia S.A. do roku 2000, (A vision of utilisation and development of the Commercial Seaport Gdynia S.A. until 2000)*. Dział Rozwoju Portu Gdynia (Gdynia Port Development Division), Gdynia, p. 12.

any one time. Remaining investment consists of the building by the OK Petroleum Swedish company of a terminal for processed liquid fuels with an annual loading capacity of about 500,000 tonnes and modernising the liquid chemicals loading terminal. All these investments are aimed to meet a constantly growing demand for infrastructure, loading equipment and mechanical devices for servicing bulk cargo.

Besides the above mentioned project to establish the Free Trade Zone in the Baltic General Cargo Terminal in Gdynia, preliminary works are also underway upon a number of other projects:

1. construction of an aluminium oxide loading terminal in collaboration with the Konin steelworks, one of the biggest consumers of this raw material. It should be noted that the Maritime Bulk Terminal Gdynia has provided the terminal location and this is particularly suitable as there are no conflicts of interest with regards to the environment and in particular agricultural production in the vicinity. The emission of aluminium oxide dust - $Al_2O_3$ - is a possibility that might occur despite protection facilities included within the loading technology design;

2. a highly controversial project is to drain part of the port basin in order to enlarge storage capacity and possibly to relocate the ro-ro terminal;

3. constructing a specialised wharf for citrus fruit;

4. constructing a ceramics loading and storage terminal in the neighbourhood of the cement terminal.

Development plans of the biggest terminal within the Port Gdynia Holding S.A. include intentions to diversify services considerably. The Port of Gdynia is, and undoubtedly will remain, a major general and containerised cargo port not only for Poland but also in the southern part of the Baltic Sea as well. This means that it will be subjected to the strongest international pressure amongst the Polish seaports, including competition from powerful ports such as Hamburg, Rotterdam and Rostock.[11] To meet these new pressures it has to strengthen its position within the port services market systematically. This situation also demands a considerable number of highly capital-absorbent investments. The necessity of implementing proposed changes in the Baltic General Cargo Terminal and in addition, the other operating companies in the eastern port was also stressed by the authors of the Rotterdam Maritime Group

---

[11] K. Sudziarska (1996) Efektywnie i z determinacjł na europejskim rynku usług portowych. Rozmowa z prof. A. Grzelakowskim - przewodniczłcym Rady Nadzorczej MPH Gdynia S.A., (Effective and with determination in the European port services market. An interview with Prof. A. Grzelakowski - president of the Supervisory Board of the MPH Gdynia S.A.). *Gazeta Portowa*, no. 6, p. 8.

Report. There would appear to be reasonably good chances that financial support from World Bank funds will be obtained.

## Conclusions

Overcoming political and economic barriers in Central and Eastern Europe has resulted in changes in the functioning of all Polish seaports. They have found themselves suddenly placed within a highly aggressive market for port services and as a result, improvements in competitive position in order to participate actively in servicing cargo transhipped through Polish seaports became a basic goal of each port. The hinterland of Polish ports located adjacent to the Gdańsk maritime border has turned from one largely guaranteed, instead to one in considerable dispute with strong and experienced competitors. Now even the closest regional hinterland of the Polish ports is being successfully cultivated and penetrated by a series of foreign ports, dominated by Hamburg, Bremen/Bremerhaven and Rotterdam.

At the same time in the next few years, one can expect a significant increase in the competition between ports in the Baltic. To meet these growing competition requirements, the Port of Gdynia has to be linked by efficient railway and road connections with its hinterland and offer a high frequency of shipping services of all types: conventional, container, ro-ro and ferry. It is for that reason that Gdynia, whilst working on improvements to its competitive position must realise improvements mainly by modernisation and enlargement of the existing loading and storage potential, together with broadening the scope of manufacturing and refining services offered. Many of these developments are now planned and beginning to be implemented, thus meeting the requirements of increasing cargo flows whilst achieving significant profits at the same time.

The gradual growth of Poland's economy and an increasing volume of foreign trade turnover are reflected in the growing transhipments that are now occurring in the port of Gdynia. The most important investments in Gdynia Port over the next few years are presented in Table 7.2.

**Table 7.2 Planned development investments for the Port of Gdynia**

| SUBJECT | COST | INFRASTRUCTURE ELEMENTS | NOTICE |
|---|---|---|---|
| Ro-ro terminal | $ 24 million | construction of two ramps and quay wall, filling in the basin, purchase of ro-ro and lo-lo equipment | feasibility study, own investment, period: 1998-2001 |
| PREEM | $ 21 million | construction of fuel terminal for transhipment and storage of liquid fuel, reconstruction of North Jetty | completion of technical project, foreign investment, period: 1998-1999 |
| Aluminium oxide | $ 6 million | storage/loading facility for aluminium oxide and equipment for unloading from ship and loading to wagons | feasibility study, own investment, period: 1998-1999 |
| BBM | $ 5.7 million  $11.4 million | storage/loading facility for liquid fertiliser with steel tanks, storage/reloading facility for dry bulk fertiliser with 'DOME' type semi-spherical storage | completion of design project, PGH S.A. and Z.A. PUŁAWY investment, period: 1998-1999 |
| Fruits | $ 4.6 million | modernisation of existing storage, purchase of equipment for loading goods on pallet | feasibility study, period: 1998 |
| Distri Park | $ 10 million | construction of back-up facilities and infrastructure | feasibility study, own investment, period: 1999-2002 |
| Indyjskie Quay | $ 7 million | construction of new quay line | technical project, own investment, period: beyond 2000 |

Source: The official home page of the Port Gdynia Holding S.A., April 17<sup>th</sup>, 1998, http://www.port.gdynia.pl/pl/struktura_kapitalowa/struktura_kapitalowa.htm

# References

J. Drzemczewski (1996) Powtórka z historii (A repetition from history). *Namiary na Morze i Handel*, no. 3-4, (in Polish).

G. Golis, J. Dubicki, W. Budkiewicz and M. Bendkowski (1996) *Wizja zagospodarowania i rozwoju Morskiego Portu Handlowego Gdynia S.A. do roku 2000, (A vision of utilisation and development of the Commercial Seaport Gdynia S.A. until 2000).* Dział Rozwoju Portu Gdynia (The Gdynia Port Development Division), Gdynia, (in Polish).

Z. Gralak (1995) Na nowej drodze. Rozmowa z Ryszardem Wocialem, dyr. ds. nadzoru właścicielskiego MPH Gdynia S.A. (In the new direction. An interview with Ryszard Wocial, the director for ownership supervision of MPH Gdynia S.A.), *Gazeta Portowa*, no. 26, (in Polish).

*Grupa Kapitałowa Portu Gdynia - dzień dzisiejszy i perspektywy rozwojowe,. (The Gdynia Port Capital Group - today and development perspectives),* Dział Rozwoju Portu Gdynia (The Gdynia Port Development Division), Gdynia 1996, (in Polish).

M. Grzybowski (1996) *Strategia konwersji do gospodarki rynkowej (A conversion strategy to the market economy).* BOiGM, no. 3, (in Polish).

Inwestycje w polskich portach na tle prognoz (Investment in the Polish ports compared to forecasts), *Gazeta Portowa*, 1995, no. 10, (in Polish).

J. Kujawa (1997) *Baltic Container Lines - nowe polskie przedsiębiorstwo żeglugowe (Baltic Container Lines - a new Polish shipping company),* Studia i Materiały Instytutu Transportu i Handlu Morskiego, Wydawnictwo Uniwersytetu Gdańskiego (The transformation of maritime transportation in Poland. Studies and materials of the Institute of Maritime Transport and Seaborne Trade), Gdańsk, (in Polish).

*Oficjalna internetowa strona domowa Port Gdynia Holding S.A. (The official home page of the Port Gdynia Holding S.A.),* http://www.port.gdynia.pl, (in Polish).

Perspektywy rozwojowe portu Gdynia (Development perspectives of the Gdynia Port). *Gazeta Portowa*, 1995, no. 6, (in Polish).

*Port Sector Study Poland, Phase 3A Report for The World Bank,* Rotterdam Maritime Group, September 1993.

A. Tubielewicza (ed.) (1994) *Koncepcja programowa zagospodarowania obszaru międzytorza w porcie Gdynia (A programmatic concept of utilisation an area between rails in the Gdynia Port),* Gdańsk (in Polish).

# 8. New legal regulations for seaport management in Poland. Institutional aspects of Polish seaport management compared with ports of the European Union

*Krzysztof Dobrowolski and Stanisław Szwankowski*
*Institute of Maritime Transport and Seaborne Trade*
*University of Gdańsk*

## Introduction

For a number of years, Polish seaports have been carrying out a complex process directed at adjusting their structures and rules of functioning to meet the new market requirements that have emerged and also to meet the rigorous conditions of international competition. In particular, the second aspect - improving competitiveness - should be regarded as the strategic goal of Polish port operations. Its implementation ties in with Polish ports' adjustment to the verified standards which characterise the ports of the European Union.

The basis of effective seaport functioning is first of all achieved by the existence of one separate and identifiable body managing the whole territory of the port and its fundamental technical infrastructure.

In Poland during the period after the Second World War period until the mid 1990s, a seaport management system, which was centred around the existence of one separate managing body, did not exist. During this time, the economic management function - i.e. managing port territory and organising port infrastructure maintenance - was carried out by many and various port companies together with servicing and production operations, and providing transfer services to ships and a variety of other transportation facilities as well. Only the functions of a public and legal character, i.e. implementation of the

78

control and supervisory tasks across port territories, were separated and concentrated into a central maritime administration body.

In the new social and economic climate, which has functioned since the beginning of the 1990s, Polish seaports have faced the necessity to implement changes in their management system, adjusting to European and world standards. Improvement of operational efficiency within Polish ports and raising the level of their competitiveness in order to enable them to cope with the fierce and constantly growing competition from foreign ports are now the primary goals of this process.

The management sphere of Polish seaports was regulated by the Act on Ports and Maritime Harbours (Ustawa o portach i przystaniach morskich), enforced by the Polish Parliament on December 20th 1996.

The Act on Ports and Maritime Harbours, which came into force on August 6th 1997, is a legal act fundamental to port management in Poland. It regulates the ownership relationships within the port territories, provides rules for the utilisation of these territories, and also establishes bodies responsible for port and maritime harbour management.

Regarding the major Polish ports in Gdańsk, Gdynia and Szczecin, the Act invoked a rule to create one new management body for each port. New management bodies operate in the form of a limited liability, public utility company which means that their goal is not in making profits but investing in port infrastructure development in order to create the most advantageous conditions for the numerous commercial enterprises that are functioning in ports and which use the infrastructure against payment to the authority.

The Act created the legal basis for the operation of Polish ports under market economy conditions. It separates the sphere of management in particular ports from the broader economic activity sphere of central government. It introduces an advanced management model, commonly known as 'port-landlord', where economic activity is not separated from the port authority. Instead, the management body will be responsible solely for the management sphere of activities, and will be represented as a public organisation. Meanwhile, the operational activity sphere as a whole will be the domain of separate operating organisations which, as a consequence, will be able to compete freely between one another.

The Act attempts to solve many of the problems faced by the management body, its financial autonomy, the issues relating to port infrastructure maintenance and the development of the port to meet European Union standards. It introduces principles for the financing of infrastructure and providing access to a port by the State Treasury with the possibility of covering expenses connected with the development of internal infrastructure in a port from the state budget. In the case of the smaller seaports and maritime harbours, regulations were introduced stating that the local community can decide about the port's local status and whether municipalisation should be introduced or not.

## Introducing the Ports Act into Polish seaports

The procedures adopted in the Act are no doubt, to a certain extent, of a compromising nature. In the period before its implementation, the various concepts relating to the form of port management adopted (e.g. autonomous, municipal, state-owned etc.) were vying with one with one another for supremacy. Problems arose over ownership relations existing in port areas and local interests groups became active in lobbying for the introduction of the most beneficial regulations for their particular interests. The authors of the Act faced a difficult task to meet all these, very often contradictory, expectations and these conflicts of interest undoubtedly damaged the homogeneity of the solutions adopted in the Act and its internal logic. However despite some unfavourable assessment of certain regulations, the fact that it was actually enacted can be regarded as a significant element in shaping the maritime policy of the state. The Act facilitates the continued structural and ownership transformation process in commercial seaports which had commenced in 1991. The process of introducing rigorous models of port management and subordinating the ownership structure of land within the port borders to meet the conditions required in a market economy, should contribute to making the most of any development chances for Polish ports that might arise and the gradual growth of their competitiveness.

Those responsible for the preparation of the Act selected a group of ports of prime significance for the state economy. The three biggest Polish commercial ports: the port of Gdańsk, the port of Gdynia and the Szczecin-Świnoujście port complex, were each subjected to its requirements. The second group consisting of smaller seaports and maritime harbours including for example, Hel, Jastarnia, Ustka, Władysławowo, Kołobrzeg, Police, Stepnica and Darłowo were subject to a second selection of new requirements differing from those applied to the international ports.

When defining the rules of port management the authors of the Act treated the group of primary ports for the economy differently than the remaining seaports and maritime harbours. Ports in Gdańsk, Gdynia and Szczecin-Świnoujście will be managed by specially established, share limited companies, owned by the State Treasury and local communities with respect to the location of a particular port. This means that in large commercial ports a mixed, state and municipal management system will now emerge. The port of Gdańsk will be managed by the Seaport Authority of Gdańsk Co., established by the State Treasury which owns at least 51% of the shares and the Gdańsk local city community owning at least 34% of the shares. Meanwhile, the port of Gdynia will by managed by the Gdynia Port Authority Co. created by the State Treasury owning at least 51% of the shares and the Gdynia local community owning at least 34% of the shares.

The structure of the body managing the Szczecin-Świnoujście port complex will be different because it is located across the territory of two local city communities, those of Szczecin and Świnoujście. Thus this port will be managed by the Szczecin-Świnoujście Port Authority Co. (Zarzád Morskiego Portu Szczecin-Świnoujście S.A.), in which 51% of shares will be owned by the State Treasury, whilst both Szczecin and Świnoujście city communities will own 24.5% of shares each.

The legislator stipulated that the State Treasury's share in each company managing a port cannot be less that 51% of votes in relation to the whole value of its capital. This means that the State Treasury has the right stemming from the Act to maintain a dominant position within each of the port companies.

The primary tasks of these companies managing the ports include the following:
1. management of the port territory and infrastructure;
2. creating a planned programme for overall port development;
3. constructing, enlarging and maintaining the process of modernisation of the port infrastructure;
4. obtaining additional land to meet the development needs of each of the ports;
5. providing services connected with port infrastructure utilisation.

A company managing a port cannot conduct any economic operations other than the ones contained in this scope of operations. The following indicate the permissible sources of income for a port managing body:
1. payments from using, renting, leasing or other contracts, when a management body provides land, equipment and/or other port facilities;
2. income from services provided;
3. income from other sources.

Each of the three international seaport management bodies is a non-profit company which means that all of their income is appropriated for statutory tasks including financing any excess operational costs. The State Treasury can finance particular undertakings, including port infrastructure construction, modernisation and maintenance. It is however, obliged to cover in full the part of the port infrastructure costs that directly provides access to each port's maritime facilities.

The rules that regulate the process of managing particular ports arouses some questions. One has to remember that the bodies the legislator speaks about do not function in an economic vacuum but have to be seen as included within the complex structure of organisations already operating in the territory of each port. There already existed one body of a very specific character among the numerous economic organisations located in the port territories of each of the international ports. In each case it operated as a company limited by shares although before 1991 it was a state-owned firm and depending upon the period, it was variously named Maritime Commercial Port (Morski Port Handlowy) or Port Authority (Zarzád Portu). Before 1991 each of the bodies dealt with two basic functions: they managed the port infrastructure and the part of the port territory where they were located, and they also provided loading and other services to ships and cargo. It should be emphasised that as far as loading services and many other services were concerned, these bodies were acting as monopoly providers within their own port areas.

After 1991 each of the bodies underwent a transformation process which led to the separation of the port infrastructure management function from direct port operations. These operations are now conducted by specially created companies although in each of three main commercial ports the situation is slightly different.

In Szczecin-Świnoujście there is the Szczecin-Świnoujście Port Authority Co. (Zarzád Portu Szczecin-Świnoujście), which manages the port infrastructure and a part of the port territory and owns 45% of the shares in each of operational companies (the remaining shares belong to employees of the companies created based upon the structure of the Szczecin-Świnoujście Port Authority Co. and the financial contributions of the staff). The Port Gdynia Holding Co. operates in Gdynia and manages the port infrastructure and part of the port territory and owns 100% of the shares in each of the operational companies. In Gdańsk, the Port of Gdańsk Authority Co. (Zarzád Portu Gdańsk) has responsibility for the management functions with regards to the port infrastructure and parts of the port territory, owning packages of shares varying in quantity in a small number of the operational companies. A limited number of the operational companies are completely independent and the whole of the share capital belongs to their employees.

The Act on Seaports and Maritime Harbours created a series of totally new organisations that are to manage the ports which have major significance for the Polish economy. In this situation, in the port of Gdynia, in addition to the existing Port Gdynia Holding Co., a new body - the Port of Gdynia Authority Co. (Zarzád Morskiego Portu Gdynia S.A.) - will be established, taking over from the existing body the management of the port infrastructure and territory. The Port Gdynia Holding Co. at least for the time being, will thus be an owner of shares in operational companies. At present it is difficult to foresee the direction of the further evolution of this structure which is still dominated by state ownership. The Port Gdynia Holding Co. is a company that is still fully owned by the State Treasury. In this situation, although the operational companies are legally independent bodies, because of the fact that they are 100% owned by the Port Gdynia Holding Co., they are to a large extent subordinated to the State Treasury. Economic reasons suggest that the optimal decision would be to proceed with fast privatisation of the structure as a whole. However, in direct contradiction to this, by establishing a new port management body in Gdynia, the legislator contributed to the preservation of the existing, state influenced system. If the Port Gdynia Holding Co. was transformed into a port management body, the privatisation process for the operational companies would be considerably easier. However, maintaining 'the status quo' in the operational sphere is the reason for the present structure's existence, presuming that according to the Act, eventually a new port management body will be created. The privatisation of each operational company weakens the power of the Port Gdynia Holding Co., and privatisation of all these companies would make the body almost entirely unnecessary. One can of course, privatise the whole structure of the holding including the Port Gdynia Holding Co. but then the place of the state monopoly in the operational sphere will be taken over by a new private monopoly. Also, some indirect variations are possible consisting of the individual privatisation of a part of the operational companies and the privatisation of the remaining part of the holding as a separate event. The implementation of any of these variants of privatisation, will require considerable determination from the State Treasury as far as resisting the political monopolistic power of the Port Gdynia Holding Co., is concerned.

The situation in the Szczecin-Świnoujście port complex is similar. The existing Port of Szczecin-Świnoujście Authority Co. (Zarzád Portu Szczecin-Świnoujście S.A.) is fully owned by the State Treasury. It has ownership of 45% of the shares in each of the operational companies, whilst the rest of the shares are highly dispersed between numerous small owners so that the Port Authority has effective control of their operations. The subordination of the operational companies to the existing Port of Szczecin-Świnoujście Authority Co. is made more firm by the fact that these operational companies do not own any substantial production property and operate on the principle of property leased from the Port Authority 'mother-company'. The creation of competition for the state monopolist in the operational sphere in Szczecin-Świnoujście may be easier than in the port of Gdynia because of existing territory reserves. However, their utilisation will require a very large capital investment.

The circumstances in the port of Gdańsk are different as far as the above is concerned. At the end of 1997, the State Treasury and the Gdańsk community established the Seaport Authority of Gdańsk Co. (Zarząd Morskiego Portu Gdańsk S.A.). However, far from helping the situation, this created a very complicated legal situation, by which two bodies, the long existing Port of Gdańsk Authority Co. (Zarząd Portu Gdańsk S.A.) and newly established seaport organisation have the responsibility of carrying out highly similar functions, as laid down in their statutory notations. Over a longer time period according to the Act, the newly launched company will become the sole body managing the port infrastructure and at least a major part of the related territories, taking over from the Port of Gdańsk Authority Co. part of its property and most of its employees. However the question of the future of the Port of Gdańsk Authority Co. remains open. Contrary to its equivalents in both Gdynia and Szczecin-Świnoujście ports, the company did not sustain a developed network of operational companies around itself. Whilst in the early stages in preparing to take over the operational functions of the whole port the company managed to develop operational companies which although connected to the centre with capital ties, were still legally independent of their 'mother'. It also sold the relevant production property to these operational companies. As a result of these actions, the statute of the Port of Gdańsk Authority Co. was changed. Providing services to shipping and cargo were excluded, and only functions connected with the infrastructure and port territory management remained. These functions will now be conducted by a new body - the Seaport Authority of Gdańsk Co. (Zarząd Morskiego Portu Gdańsk S.A.). As a result of this highly confusing situation, various ideas have been analysed concerning the future of the Port of Gdańsk Authority Co. (Zarząd Portu Gdańsk S.A.). One of them includes the idea of merging both management companies in the future.

Following from the considerations discussed above, one can draw a number of conclusions that centre around the primary concept that to transform the existing management bodies in the ports of Gdynia, Gdańsk and Szczecin-Świnoujście to ones that also have responsibility for operations, would have been easier to implement than the solution finally adopted which resulted in the creation of these new managing bodies in the ports of prime economic significance.

The management of smaller ports and maritime harbours that are not of fundamental significance to the economy was entrusted by the legislator to the local municipal communities of the respective ports and harbours. The communities will also decide upon the organisational and legal form of their management, i.e. for example, they can establish independent economic bodies if they wish in a fashion similar to commercial companies. However, if a community does not make suitable efforts to carry out port or harbour management, the responsibilities for port infrastructure will be taken over by the director of the respective state maritime office.

Ownership relationships within ports and the rules of their utilisation are the second question of key importance for the port management that is regulated by the Act on Ports and Maritime Harbours. Port territory located within the borders of the three international ports are owned by the State Treasury, the local communities and/or private persons.

In the port of Gdańsk 90.6% of port territory belongs to the State Treasury, 9.1% to the Gdańsk community, and 0.3% is private property. In the port of Gdynia 97.3% of port territory is owned by the State Treasury, 1.1% by the Gdynia community, and 1.6% by private persons. In the Szczecin-Świnoujście port complex 71.4% of port territory belongs to the State Treasury, and 28.6% to the Szczecin and Świnoujście communities.

There are numerous economic bodies located within port territories which have the unlimited right of the user to lands upon which their operations take place. In other words the territories in question are owned by the State Treasury or local communities and at the same time they are utilised by economic bodies located upon the given piece of land.

The unlimited right of user is a form of management close to a property right; however it does not entitle the user to all the rights that the owner has. The right is essentially disposable and it can be sold or brought in as a contribution in kind to companies. The right is granted for a period between 40 and 99 years and it is usually tied in with the necessity to pay fees to the owner, i.e. in the case of port territories, to the State Treasury.

Within port boundaries there are also some pieces of land which remain unutilised and owned by the State Treasury and/or local communities and to which there is nobody with an unlimited right of use. The largest area of this kind is located within the port of Gdańsk where substantial reserves of land that will be utilised eventually, are known to exist. The port of Gdynia is in a less fortunate situation because it does not have many opportunities to acquire new pieces of land which could be used for development purposes.

The structure of port territory ownership in Polish ports, and the structure of an unlimited right of user that comes with it, is a very important issue with regards to the functioning of port management bodies and the possibilities for the advancement of port management skills.

In the ports which are of major economic significance to the economy the State Treasury and local community have the right to make as a payment in kind, only those port territories where the unlimited rights of the user were not established. This means that in the first period of time under the new Ports and Harbours Act, companies managing ports of a primary significance to the economy can become owners only of areas which have not been utilised up to this time. Port management companies will have a direct influence in managing only a part of these port territories. The influence of port management companies in the utilisation of areas given to other bodies with an unlimited right of user will as a result, be minimal.

This is a basic weakness of the Act on ports and maritime harbours but it does ensure that the development of one landlord for territory as in each major port location, does not occur.

The legislator found himself in a difficult situation considering the established ownership relationships for port territories which had been established at an earlier date. Setting up port management companies as sole landlords of port areas as a whole would limit the rights of existing users. It would mean in practice taking away a part of the rights from economic bodies located in ports that were recently granted to them. Considering the need to maintain trust in the law, in existing legal practices and to ensure some sort of stability in the industry, this solution was deemed not to be acceptable.

In the longer perspective, ownership relationships within port territories may change in favour of port management companies. The legislator guaranteed that port management organisations will have the right of pre-emption of property rights or an unlimited right as the user of port territories. If recent owners or users wanted to give up their rights, the port management body would have an opportunity to be the first one to accept their offer, and enlarge its territory with pieces of land of which the body is going to be a landlord. However, it needs to be recognised that the process of establishing a single landlord for the large majority of port territories will take a considerable period of time.

The port management body already set up in Gdańsk - the Seaport Authority of Gdańsk Co. (Zarzád Morskiego Portu Gdańsk S.A.) - is still not an owner of any part of the territory of the port because the State Treasury and the Gdańsk community made only a financial contribution to the account of the share capital of the newly created port management company. In the same way as is the case for ports which are of prime importance to the economy, the bodies managing small ports and maritime harbours will initially have only marginal influence in the management of the port territories previously owned by the State Treasury and which are now utilised by other bodies and with an unlimited right of user. The port management body will have within its cognisance only port territories already belonging to local communities and the ones recently remitted to those communities by the State Treasury. When considering the specific conditions that exist in the smaller ports and maritime harbours, there is also the real possibility of creating a situation when the whole or at least a major part of port territory falls solely within the responsibilities of the various port management bodies rather than those of the State Treasury.

As the state legislator was not able, at least at the beginning, to delegate efficiently the control function over the whole or even a major part of port territory to port management companies, direct state administration supervision over these territories was established. The port water-based industrial and commercial areas and the infrastructure providing access to ports and maritime harbours were all excluded from this activity.

The activities of the port territories located within the borders of the major economic ports of Poland, requires agreement of the Ministry of State Treasury operating in accordance with the Ministry of Transportation and Maritime Economy. The activities of port territories located within borders of small ports and maritime harbours requires the agreement of the Ministry of State Treasury and the opinion of a director of a sufficiently responsible maritime office. The utilisation, leasing or renting of pieces of land belonging to the State Treasury or a local community for a period longer than three years requires agreement from the Ministry of the State Treasury and a supportive opinion from a director of an suitably responsible maritime office.

## The transformation of management operations within Polish seaports

On the whole after the second world war period, and until the end of the 1980s, but excluding the immediate post war phase of 1945-49, operations within Polish ports were characterised by a concentration of port services in each port under the jurisdiction of one state-owned firm, combining economic management with operations, and with the absence of competition in the port services production sphere. The result of adopting this operational model was the full monopolisation of the port services market. Within each major Polish port (Gdańsk, Gdynia, Szczecin-Świnoujście), one state owned economic body existed which provided services for both cargo and ships (concentrating upon the basic ones including loading and storage), and also its duty was to maintain and develop the port infra-structure and suprastructure. In different phases of this period these organisations have adopted various names. In the final period before the fundamental changes in the social, economic and political system in Poland they were known as:- the Maritime Commercial Port of Gdańsk (Morski Port Handlowy Gdańsk), the Maritime Commercial Port of Gdynia (Morski Port Handlowy Gdynia) and the Szczecin-Świnoujście Port Authority (Zarząd Portu Szczecin-Świnoujście).

The process of the transformation of operational organisation and ownership in Polish ports really commenced in the early 1990s together with the transformation of the whole Polish economy. A major goal of the transformation was - according to the requirements of the market economy, and following both European and world standards - on the one hand to separate the operational sphere of activity in each of the ports from the economic sphere, and on the other to lead through the transformation of the operational activities to the privatisation of this sphere (according to the accepted rule that in order to privatise a large state-owned company, then first one has to transform it).

With regard to the fact that state-owned firms were the basic form of organisation to carry out operational activities in Polish ports before 1990, a structure largely unknown in developed market economies, the transformation process in Poland (including that occurring within the maritime ports sector) had to consist of not only a change in the organisation that had responsibility for the economy of the ports but also in changing its legal format - from a state-owned firm into a capital company with all the legal responsibilities that this brings.

A capital, i.e. an indirect, method of port company privatisation was selected. The Maritime Commercial Port of Gdańsk (Morski Port Handlowy Gdańsk), and the Szczecin-Świnoujście Port Authority (Zarząd Portu Szczecin-Świnoujście) were both transformed into capital companies in May 1991 and the port company in Gdynia in November 1991.

In the period before enforcement of these changes by the Parliament of the Republic of Poland on December 20th 1996, the Act on Ports and Maritime Harbours, involving the transformation of the operational sphere of Polish ports, was advanced in a variety of ways and to a varying degree. The process was furthest advanced in the port of Gdańsk.

As a first stage in the port of Gdańsk, over 30 limited liability companies were established carrying out operational, technical, and servicing-auxiliary operations for ports, cargo and hinterland transportation. At the next stage in the middle of 1993, a series of particular companies purchased elements of port suprastructure from the Maritime Commercial Port of Gdańsk Co.

(Morski Port Handlowy S.A.). Meanwhile, the same Maritime Commercial Port of Gdańsk Co. sold its shares in these companies. The only relationships which now exist between the Port of Gdańsk Authority Co. (Zarząd Portu Gdańsk S.A.) (a change of name from the Maritime Commercial Port of Gdańsk Co. (Morski Port Handlowy S.A.)) and these companies stem from lease contracts for the property and other elements of port infrastructure. As a result of these changes, the complete separation of the two spheres of activity in the port of Gdańsk was finally achieved.

In passing judgement upon the transformation achieved within the port of Gdańsk it needs to be noted that the existing operational companies are commonly weak organisations as far as their capital base is concerned. This results in very limited investment possibilities for these companies and a low level of attractiveness for any prospective investors. However, at the same time, there has begun to emerge evidence of advanced diversification in operational activity within the market for certain specific companies. Meanwhile, there remain a number of companies that continue to carry out ineffective and inefficient operational activities, and are beginning to suffer as they meet increasingly fierce competition.

A similar process of change stemming from the transformation effects was adopted in the Szczecin-Świnoujście port complex. Compared with Gdańsk, the number of established exploitation limited liability companies within which the Port of Szczecin-Świnoujście Authority Co. (Zarząd Portu Szczecin-Świnoujście S.A.) has shares, is notably smaller. In addition, the degree of transformation is far less advanced and up to now, operational companies have not invested in any supra-structure elements. Thus in the Szczecin-Świnoujście port complex the process of separating operational activities from management activities has not been completed yet.

A different direction for transformation has been adopted in the port of Gdynia. Operational companies created there have 100% of their shares owned by the Maritime Commercial Port of Gdynia Co. (Morski Port Handlowy Gdynia S.A.) who in return, have made a contribution in kind through production property (i.e. some elements of the suprastructure). The problem of the low initial capital of companies, which has occurred in the process of transformation in the two other major ports has thus been solved. It is presumed that in the future the Morski Port Handlowy Gdynia S.A. will conduct a privatisation process of their operational companies, one by one, allowing the participation of interested external investors. A change in the name of the port from Maritime Commercial Port of Gdynia Co. (Morski Port Handlowy Gdynia S.A.) into Port Gdynia Holding Co. was also a consequence of the new structure.

## Conclusions

The transformation carried out up to now in all three port companies is mainly characterised by a process of reconstruction and has brought about substantial beneficial changes within the operational sphere of Polish seaports. The transformation of ports caused de-monopolisation of the recent system of providing loading, storage and other services in particular ports. Also new operators have emerged within the Polish port services market, constituting a large number of mainly private firms carrying out servicing operations and a series of new port service companies providing loading and storage, manipulation, refining and other activities. These activities are adapted to a large degree to the requirements of the market economy and thus contribute to the improvement of Polish port efficiency and adds to their competitiveness.

Enforced by the Parliament of the Republic of Poland on December 20th 1996, the Act on Ports and Maritime Harbours and the gradually continuing process of its implementation, has presented chances to complete the transformation and privatisation process in the operational sphere of Polish seaports. It is to be expected that as a result, in particular within the larger Polish ports, economically stronger firms will emerge, following the example of developments within ports of the EU, and carrying out a series of diversified operations. This process is highly necessary because Polish ports whilst they function on the edge of the national economy and within a highly competitive international environment, have to meet standards and requirements typically set from the demand side and represented by their competitors' qualities. In addition, it is anticipated that the larger operational companies will continue to create a number of smaller specialised economic units providing a variety of port services.

The transformation process of the operational sector of Polish seaports has not created any barriers for continuing further transformation and privatisation of the port of Gdynia nor the Szczecin-Świnoujście port complex. Some difficulties however may emerge in the port of Gdańsk. It is in this port to a larger extent than the others, that the process of transformation of a substantial number of small service companies needs to be accompanied by a process of financial strengthening, combined with the combination of parts of these operational companies into larger, and thus more robust service groups. In this way, they will become fully operational and more able to function efficiently within the developing competitive market.

# References

K. Dobrowolski and S. Szwankowski (1997) *Procesy restrukturyzacji i prywatyzacji w prywatyzacji przedsiębiorstw portowych i żeglugowych w Polsce (Transformation and privatisation processes of port and shipping companies in Poland)* [in] *Restrukturyzacja transportu morskiego Polski. Studia i Materiały Instytutu Transportu i Handlu Morskiego (The transformation of maritime transportation in Poland. Studies and materials of the Institute of Maritime Transport and Seaborne Trade).* Uniwersytet Gdański, Gdańsk (in Polish).

A. Grzelakowski (1997) *Ocena aktualnego stanu oraz perspektywy rozwoju polskiej gospodarki morskiej (An assessment of the present state and development perspectives of the Polish maritime economy),* Hamburg (in Polish).

*Integracja Polski z Uni Europejski - szanse i zagrożenia polskiego transportu (The integration of Poland with the European Union - chances and threats for Polish transport),* SITK, Warszawa 1997 (in Polish).

S. Szwankowski (1996) *Dostosowanie polskiej gospodarki portowej do wymagań i standardów Unii Europejskiej (Adjustment of the Polish maritime economy to requirements and standards of the European Union),* Wydawnictwo Instytutu Morskiego, Gdańsk (in Polish).

S. Szwankowski (1995) Institutional problems of restructuring of Polish ports, *Bulletin of the Maritime Institute in Gdańsk,* vol. XXII, no. 1, 15, 56.

# 9. Eastern European development and the role of international transport - a case study of Poland

*Michael Roe*
*Institute of Marine Studies*
*University of Plymouth*

## Introduction

This paper provides an analysis of the events that have occurred in Eastern Europe during the last ten years with a particular emphasis upon the maritime sector and its role within the framework of the Polish economy. In so doing, an attempt is made to establish the significance of this most international of transport modes upon the progressive moves of Poland from a developing status to one of development on a par with the rest of Europe and in so doing, to establish whether shipping as a sector has a role to play in the economic progression of a developing state. The paper is based upon extensive periods of research in Poland and the Polish maritime sector, undertaken by the author over the last two decades supported by a mix of European Union funding, the Polish shipping industry and colleagues in the University of Gdańsk in Sopot, Poland.

Over the period from the late 1980s right through to the present day, there has occurred a series of economic, social and political changes in the region of Eastern Europe that have never before been experienced anywhere in the world. The countries previously dominated in all ways in life by the attitudes and policies of the Former Soviet Union (FSU) moved at breakneck speed from a position of a command economy to one where there has been the development of a capitalist market that is attempting to reflect the economic and social situation that exists in the rest of Europe and across most of the developed world.

In many ways the influence of the FSU created a situation not too diverse from that of a series of developing countries who have been suddenly exposed to the market forces that existed elsewhere. As we shall see, the Eastern European states suffered from low economic and social standards, poor infrastructure and precarious political and social structures which were in desperate need of improvement and revitalisation. The area that we shall consider here is that which includes the European countries that were consistently members of the Council For Mutual Economic Assistance (CMEA), excluding the FSU itself. These countries were Czechoslovakia, Hungary, Bulgaria, Romania, Poland and Eastern Germany (DDR). We have excluded the FSU as it presents a special case in itself, albeit one which again would reflect the development of an essentially developing country in the new economic climate of Europe. The CMEA was essentially an economic club, theoretically with voluntary membership of like politically minded countries, all allies of the FSU at the time that Communism was the ruling structure of that state. The CMEA was intended to co-ordinate economic progress and decision-making between these states who were organised along Communist principles with state owned economies dominated by monopolistic producers in a command economy framework. A number of other countries were also members at various times - e.g. Cuba and Mongolia - but for the sake of clarity will not concern us here. In practice, their was no choice of membership and decisions upon policy were dominated by the FSU, who used a system of economic ties and force to impose their requirements on the other members. On its collapse in 1991, the FSU owed enormous sums of money to all the other member states for goods they had received and paid for in worthless 'transferable roubles'. These debts remain largely unpaid today. One major impact of the policies of the CMEA was a consistent failure of the states who were members, to match developments and economic standards of the west. The revolutions in Eastern Europe of the late 1980s and early 1990s dismantled this framework releasing each CMEA country from the requirements of the FSU and thus opening up the possibility of reform and progress towards a more developed status.

In this paper we shall look at the role of the transport sector within this framework and in particular the impact of the maritime industries as part of the international transport economy in contributing towards the development of the Eastern European states as they attempt to move towards the developed status of their neighbours to the west. We shall further concentrate upon the position in Poland as it developed from the mid 1980s through the period of chaotic change and up to the present day. Poland has been chosen for a number of reasons - it represents a major maritime nation of the world with a large, although declining, national fleet, it is a very large supplier of crews for fleets throughout the world for reasons which will become apparent later, and it possesses a major ancillary maritime sector including international ports, brokers, agents, forwarders and logistics specialists. Unlike most countries, it has its own classification society. It also represents a highly interesting country from the point of view of its economy and level of development. In the late 1980s Poland was one of the poorest of all the Eastern European states and closest in many ways to that of a conventional developing country. Incomes were very low, infrastructure poor, and political instability rife. By the mid 1990s, Poland had shown the fastest growth of all the previous Eastern European states and was the first to turn around a declining GDP to one that was positive. Today it remains poor relative to the west but shows a dynamism in its economy and social and political life that is the envy of all the former CMEA countries. We shall not in this paper attempt to claim that this turnaround is due solely to the existence or structure of the maritime sector in Poland, but it does bear close examination whether the strong international transport base that exists has had an effect, and more generally it does mean that Poland presents a highly interesting case.

From this discussion it is hoped that we can identify some of the significant roles that international transport and shipping in particular, might play in revitalising economies, not only in the rather specific circumstances of the former Communist bloc, but also elsewhere in the developing world.


**The old system**

It would be impossible to assess the role of any sector in aiding development processes within an economy, without first assessing the position before changes of the nature outlined here had taken place. We thus begin with a brief review of the structure of the economic process within the CMEA states, using Poland as our main study area. A number of other sources of discussion on this area are available (including for example Chrzanowski, 1977; Krzyzanowski, 1993; Ledger and Roe, 1993, 1995, 1996, 1997; Roe, 1997a, 1997b; Sawiczewska, 1992; Toy and Roe, 1997; and Zurek, 1996). Further reviews of the more general Polish situation also exist (e.g. Fairplay, 1995; Lloyd's List, 1995, 1997; Lloyd's Ship Manager, 1992, 1996).

The impact of the CMEA system throughout the countries of Eastern Europe resulted in a consistent pattern of economic development and structures with features that were consistent across the region. These features can be summarised with particular respect to the Polish maritime situation:

*Ownership*

Ownership was vested almost entirely in the hands of the state in all economic sectors across the region. The maritime sector was no exception. In Poland shipping operators were split into three state owned companies responsible for liners (Polish Ocean Lines - POL), bulk (Polska Żegluga Morska - PŻM) and ferries (Polska Żegluga Bałtycka - PŻB). No private operation of ships was permitted and no competition within Poland existed. In addition, no realistic competition existed with the other CMEA fleets - particularly those of the FSU, Romania and Bulgaria - as the efforts of each were co-ordinated at state level.

*Monopoly status*

Due to the absence of competition, each enterprise operated effectively in a semi-monopoly status competing only on international cross trading routes with operators from elsewhere in the world. Thus, for example, Polish Ocean Lines was guaranteed a CMEA place on the Europe-North Atlantic route but then faced competition from operators from the UK, France, the USA etc.

*Subsidy*

No true costing of any activities took place and pricing was completely artificial. All new equipment was provided by the state, at no charge, including the provision of new vessels, port improvements, payment for crews and officers and bunkering. This had a sizeable effect upon the industry. It made it internationally competitive as fleets could operate at below true costs against free market private operators, thus obtaining market share. It made Polish built vessels popular (in fact a requirement) as only such vessels were free; it made Polish crews the only ones to be used. It encouraged Polish vessels to travel back to Poland, sometimes sizeable distances, to bunker in Polish ports.

*Currencies*

No CMEA currency was ever convertible. Thus there was a consistent and urgent need to earn hard currencies by some means or other by all the CMEA states to provide a means of purchasing desperately needed equipment, food, drugs, arms or whatever else was only available on the free market where only convertible currencies were acceptable. The result was that any international activity paid for its costs as far as possible, in soft, local currency - e.g. Polish złotys - and charged for services provided - e.g. carrying containers across the North Atlantic from Rotterdam to New York - in convertible currency, usually US dollars. CMEA shipping thus became a significant force in international crosstrade shipping services - bulk, liner and ferry - charging US dollars at less than the market rate and sometimes even less than the true cost of providing the service. The criterion used by all the CMEA states was US dollars earned per local currency expended. The more the better.

Shipping was not alone in being used this way as a hard currency earner, and other activities such as international trucking, tourism and even prostitution were organised by the state to pull in resources. The result was an oversized fleet, developed way beyond the needs of the country concerned, and operating economically unfairly (i.e. heavily subsidised) on all major trading routes of the world.

*Co-ordination*

In theory the system should have resulted in benefits emerging from economies of scale and a co-ordinated framework of investment and international trade. In practice, partly because of a high level of corruption encouraged by the structure of targets and rewards that existed, the level of co-ordination was poor. It did result in a process of guaranteed and directed traffic such that rail transport was always favoured over road for the inland leg of a freight movement and that the state operator could rely upon large quantities of freight heading in their direction partly because all aspects of the movement were state controlled, but also because by using national operators, hard currency could be earned from western exporters or importers, or saved when the importer or exporter was a Polish company. Polish fleets (and of course those of other CMEA countries including even land-locked Hungary and Czechoslovakia) thrived as a result.

*Foreign Trade Organisations*

This process of currency conservation and freight co-ordination was organised by a series of state enterprises - Foreign Trade Organisations (FTOs) - through whom all imports and exports to and from Poland had to be agreed and administered. FTOs existed for all commodities and clearly wielded considerable power within the state international transport system.

*Banking*

In all the CMEA states, the banking structure was entirely owned and administered by the state, who used it as a means of collecting together convertible currency revenues of the international trading companies and then redistributing them into the sectors that the state felt was most deserving. Shipping was a high earner but never received in return, anything like its earnings back as hard currency, thus preventing its investment in high quality infrastructure, training or equipment. Due to a combination of the problems stemming from unconvertible currencies, and the political constraints in trade which stemmed from the Cold War, CMEA produced vessels, although free, were poor in sophistication. In banking terms no true mechanism existed for borrowing money either within Poland or on the international market, and thus shipping companies, and the ancillary companies in the industry, were forced to build and buy locally.

The CMEA based system had a mix of advantages and disadvantages for the shipping sector in each country, where the pattern of structure, imposed by the FSU through the economic, political and military ties it had, was almost the same. True, there were no worries about employment, salaries, investment, debt or bankruptcy. However, the technical state of the fleet, and its ability to survive in the real economic world should changes ever take place, were far from satisfactory. The completely artificial nature of the whole market structure is apparent from the above and is the fundamental reason for the failure of the CMEA maritime sector to develop effectively and efficiently, and for the economies of each of the countries concerned to have suffered and eventually failed. By the same logic, a change in these economic structures from those of the command based system of the CMEA to that of the western developed capitalist world should produce a marked effect in moving these economies forward towards a developed status.

We shall now go on to look at the revolutionary changes that did take place within these economies and attempt to establish both whether the Polish maritime sector itself is emerging from its developing status and then what contribution it is making towards the development of the economy as a whole.

## The economic and structural changes

Following the revolutionary developments in the region and the overt failure of the Soviet Union to intervene when Hungary, in particular, allowed travelling East Germans to cross to Austria without the appropriate documentation, there have been massive changes in the way that the economies of Eastern Europe have developed and in particular an attempt to catch up with the rest of Europe in style, approach, quality of life and income. This quite clearly, has had an effect upon all sectors of each of the economies including the international transport sector in general and the maritime area in particular. We will go on to look at this relationship and also the changing role that the maritime sector is playing in the development of the Polish economy as it reacts to the new economic, social and political change.

Immediate impacts were felt in a number of ways:

*Markets*

The substantial, artificial markets were withdrawn almost overnight as the state removed its guaranteed cargo flows opting for modes and routes that were the most efficient or cheapest, and the shipping companies found themselves having to search for new sources of cargo in a market that was unregulated and open to the normal economic pressures of the west. This manifested itself in a number of ways, not the least being the transfer of a large number of shipping routes from the international seaports of Gdynia and Gdańsk to the better connected and located facilities in Hamburg, Rotterdam and Antwerp. Prior to the dissolution of the command planning system, trade was directed through Polish seaports to save the costs and hard currency required when using western ports, even if this entailed long ballast journeys for ships travelling unnecessarily eastwards into the Baltic Sea. The true economics of the situation should have dictated that the majority of long distance and significant shipping services would have operated out of German, Dutch and Belgian ports in providing services across the north Atlantic, to the Far East and beyond. Until the early 1990s, Polish Ocean Lines, for example, provided services to locations all over the world directly from Gdynia regardless of true economic cost, in an attempt to save precious convertible currency, supported by subsidies and guaranteed cargoes. The new regime made this impossible as exporters and importers, state or otherwise became more aware of the true costs involved.

*Subsidies*

Subsidies were withdrawn almost entirely and almost immediately. This affected all parts of the shipping industry and the related sectors. Thus ports, ship operators, and state owned brokers, agents and forwarders all lost their subsidy and were expected to compete and survive in the new market place. The concept of bankruptcy and an accompanying legal framework was introduced and those unable to survive without state support were doomed. In particular, the shipping operators have faced some of the most complex problems. Polish Ocean Lines for example, have reacted by reducing fleet size substantially, not renewing vessels as they would have in the immediate past, abandoning routes, ports and services (for example to Cuba, North Vietnam etc. and slot chartering on the North Atlantic), reducing total employees drastically and restructuring the company to provide a more flexible and sensitive basis for service provision. PŻM in the bulk sector has been less affected in that they were rather more market aware before the changes took place but have still had to restructure the company to survive. PŻB, the ferry company, remains in dire financial straits with a largely very old fleet and severe competition on their Baltic routes.

Overall, very few replacement vessels have been provided since the early 1990s, employee levels have been enormously reduced, services drastically cut and company restructuring has become a necessity rather than a desire.

*Competition*

Previously there was none. Competition in the ship operating sector has slowly emerged both from within the sector itself - for example PŻM, the bulk shipping company, now part owns a Baltic ferry service (Unity Line) with EuroAfrica of Szczecin, an offshoot of Polish Ocean Lines (liners) - and outside. The two most significant invaders of Polish international maritime transport space are Stena Line ferries of Sweden, competing with PŻB and Unity Line on the Baltic Sea between Poland and Sweden, and Maersk Line of Denmark, providing direct container feeder services from Gdynia into their world-wide network of trunk routes. Although some foreign operation of services has existed for many years - for example Andrew Weir's United Baltic Corporation UK-Gdynia service - this has always been in close collaboration with the Polish operators (in this case EuroAfrica) and has not represented any true competitive market.

Competition has also emerged in the ports sector. No new ports have been built in Poland but new developments at existing ports have taken place including the Duty Free Zones now being developed at each of the three main ports of Gdynia, Gdańsk and Szczecin. The transfer of services west to Hamburg and beyond has already been noted whilst the ports of Gdańsk and Gdynia are both actively (and openly) competing for transit traffic to and from the Baltic States, the Ukraine, Belarus and Russia.

In the ancillary industries competition has been even fiercer. In Szczecin for example, where once there was one state freight forwarder, one agent and one broker, there are now more than 30 of each competing for port and shipping traffic including large numbers of new companies based around ex-state employees and even interlopers from other areas who were once Gdańsk or Gdynia based state representatives who used to work in collaboration with their Szczecin counterparts. Thus C. Hartwig Gdynia now trades openly in competition with C. Hartwig Szczecin, for forwarding work within the latter's named port.

*Monopolies*

Monopolies have thus begun to disintegrate and with them has come a freedom to choose a wider range of other decisions. For example, prior to the changes, there was no choice about the flag for a Polish state owned vessel. It had to be registered with the Polish register and employ all Polish officers and crew, commonly in numbers far exceeding those of ships in the west and due to the involvement of the state, the cost of so doing was almost nothing. Local currencies would form the bulk of payments and unconvertible złotys could be printed and distributed at will - and were. Under the new regime, market forces are now beginning to apply and thus the cost of crewing using a well regulated, if still unconvertible currency, has become unsustainable. The result under the new liberalised regulations, has been a rush to leave the Polish flag and its requirements for Polish manning and a move towards much cheaper flags of convenience, especially those of Cyprus and Malta. This has caused some political problems but remains a consistent trend. It also has the sizeable advantage of opening the doors of international finance to the Polish shipping industry, which on the rare occasions when it finds itself able to contemplate renewing the fleet, has been unable to borrow from western based banks if the proposed vessel is Polish (or Romanian, Bulgarian, Russian etc.) flagged largely because under Polish (and others) law, the state and crew have precedence over the bank at times of financial default.

## Hard currency

Hard currency remains a problem as none of the former CMEA countries have fully convertible currencies yet. International shipping remains a good way of gathering convertible currency and from that point of view the decline in the East European operations of shipping companies has been disadvantageous to the countries concerned. However, the shipping companies can now retain all the hard currency they earn thus placing them in a stronger position than many other previously state owned enterprises. This advantage has been largely wiped out by the substantial taxes that they are required to pay as state companies, over and above those of the newly emerging private sector - a sort of penalty for remaining in the state sector.

## Privatisation

Each of the East European states have embraced the concept of privatisation wholeheartedly although not all have progressed with putting the concept into practice as quickly as others. The maritime sector has been affected by this trend as much as any other, recognising the role that the transfer of ownership will have in stabilising the political changes that have taken place and in reinforcing the moves towards a free market economy that appears to be the desire of much of the region. The laggards in general are some of the Former Soviet Union countries and in the region in which we are interested, Bulgaria in particular where little privatisation of substance in any sector has occurred. Elsewhere, progress in the maritime sectors varies from poor to acceptable in comparison with other economic groupings. In Romania, there have been expressions of intent by the state but little else yet. In the Czech Republic, the ex-state operator Czech Ocean Shipping Company was privatised early on, whilst in the Slovak Republic, no such movements can be found. In Poland there has been very chequered progress. The ancillary industries have seen a massive growth in private sector activities with competitors to the existing state companies, or those newly transferred to the private sector, springing up in the broking, agency, forwarding, crewing, logistics and supply sectors. The ports of Gdynia, Gdansk and Szczecin are now populated by small private companies, targeting small sectors of the industry (commodities, sources, single ship operating companies) and making great progress in forming a truly competitive market in the maritime sector.

In ship operations the picture is very different and consistent throughout the ex-CMEA. Poland provides a typical example here. The large majority of two of the three state owned organisations - PŻM and POL - has been restructured into holding companies under which lie a succession of small operating companies nominally transferred into the private sector (and recognised as such by Polish law). These include as examples, in terms of PŻM, Polsteam Tankers (chemical carriers specialising in liquid sulphur); Polsteam Oceantramp (deep sea bulk carriers), Polsteam Shortramp (short sea bulk carriers); Polsteam Brokers (shipbroking), and so on. In terms of POL they include POL Levant (Mediterranean liners); POL America (South American liners); POL Atlantic (North Atlantic slot charterers in the liner trade); POL Asia (South Eastern Asia slot charterers in the liner trades); Polcontainers (container operators); POL Supply (ships supplies); POL Catering (ships food supplies), and so on. Both parent companies have ownership interests in a wide range of other, private companies including Unity Line (Baltic ferries) and a large number of offshore companies based in Luxembourg, Malta, Cyprus etc. used to provide cheap finance, reduce the regulatory regime, or form some sort of protection against ship arrest and loss of assets. A large number of the subsidiary companies also have part ownership of other subsidiary companies making the whole structure extremely complex.

Both holding companies remain state owned and as far as can be anticipated, will remain so for the foreseeable future. Although some ships are owned, neither operate the vessels as this is undertaken by the subsidiaries. It is claimed that all the subsidiaries are independent of the holding companies and all negotiations and transactions are carried out on straight commercial terms. However, there remains some evidence of preferential treatment, and long term tacit agreements with regards to crewing and loans terms that may be suspect.

The third operator PŻB, the state owned ferry company that also owns the port of Kołobrzeg, is in a rather different position in that it has no subsidiary companies and is now being readied for full sale to the private sector in the very near future. It has been implied by the state that only a Polish investor would be welcomed, although there is some doubt as to whether one will be forthcoming.

*Liberalisation*

Most of the effects discussed above have manifested themselves because of the process of liberalisation that has taken place within the Polish economy as a whole and the maritime market more specifically. Thus ships are seen to transfer flag, new vessels never register with the Polish flag, crews are becoming more international, port transfers occur, traditional shipping routes are abandoned, overseas subsidiaries are formed across Europe, local small scale private competitors proliferate particularly in the ancillary sectors and new western competition enters the ferry and container markets.

Other effects not hinted at above have also taken place. The transfer of inland feeder traffic from the traditional rail mode to that of road has been dramatic as industries which were previously required to use state directed modes now have the freedom to choose themselves according to price, quality and flexibility. This has had a number of effects - it has encouraged the moves to Hamburg and beyond by importers and exporters as the costs of moving goods through German and Dutch ports is less than through the Polish ports particularly if time is an issue; it has further damaged the ports industry in Poland as road connections are poor whilst rail are comparatively good; and it has severe environmental disbenefits as typified by the average 14 hour wait to cross the Polish-German border near Frankfurt-am-Oder. Pressures have thus been placed on the Polish economy to invest in port and inland transport infrastructure to support the ailing international shipping industry, but Poland lacks the finances to do this and so the trend continues.

The process of pricing has also become more western capitalist orientated and thus reflecting the concepts of demand and international resource levels. In the old system prices were artificially set for domestic goods and those traded between the CMEA countries which failed to reflect the true cost or value attached to the items concerned. Following the changes, internationally traded goods were immediately subject to world prices and convertible currency transactions, causing extreme problems for the maritime sector, as well as others, in finding sufficient convertible currency to continue trading and meeting the enormous rise in prices that resulted. Domestically, the removal of state controls led to immediate levels of hyper-inflation with clear problems for the maritime sector again. These inflationary problems have now subsided in all but Bulgaria in Eastern Europe, and even here the problem is now easing, but had a marked impact upon the initial survival of the industry and its ability to support employment and reinvest in materials and infrastructure. The continued decaying facilities within many ex-state industries and in the inland transport, port and shipping infrastructure is evidence of the problems faced and which, in most cases, have yet to be resolved. Only parts of the new private sector (and thus the ancillary maritime industries) show any real significant progress.

*Attitudes*

One of the lasting impacts of the old regime that dominated Eastern Europe up until the late 1980s is that of business attitude. It has to be remembered that under the old system of the command economy, decision-making within all enterprises was from the top down with instructions awaited from the management level above. Thus CMEA international policy for the shipping industry was used as the basis for decisions upon investment in infrastructure, not the demands of the market or the potential of new ideas and innovation. Under a free market situation, this is largely reversed so that the market becomes the determinant of policy or change. This requires a completely different attitude by management and the comprehension and absorption of concepts such as consumer preference, choice and a realistic pricing mechanism. Polish shipping management in all parts of the industry have struggled to adapt to this new scenario and in many ways it is only the younger and newer individuals in maritime enterprises that have been able to understand and implement the policies needed.

*Conclusions to the changes*

Overall, the impact of these social, economic and political changes in Eastern Europe has been formidable and there are many more effects to be felt yet as those countries that were dominated by the command economy of the Former Soviet Union continue to attempt to adapt to the new environment. We can now go on to examine two issues that stem from this unique situation. Firstly, whether international transport in the form of the maritime sector has a role to play in the development process as the countries of the region attempt to raise their economic, social and political standards to those of the developed west; and secondly to assess whether the process of change in Eastern Europe, in terms of this desired westernisation and the introduction of free market principles, actually has any benefits in terms of the process of developing an underdeveloped region, or whether the result is actually the reverse, and that the poverty of Eastern Europe or an individual working within it, will be exacerbated by the process of change?

## International transport and development

It is important now to turn to the issue of development and its relationship with the international transport sector. There has been widespread support for the idea that international transport in all forms is a basic prerequisite for the emergence of a country (or region) from a position of underdevelopment - thus forming a fundamental strand in the developing process. However, whilst the support is strong - and one only has to look at recent decisions from DGVII of the European Union in terms of the support for Trans-European Networks to develop, encourage and maintain peripheral regions (including Eastern Europe) - there is little tangible, or even quantifiable to prove beyond doubt that the relationship exists. It would seem to be obvious but how strong is this relationship and does it always hold good?

In Poland, prior to the changes, there was a clear failure of the economic system of the country to sustain development on a par with the rest of western Europe no matter how this is measured. Thus developments in infrastructure, applied science, management skills and structures, technology and so on were all sadly lagging behind by the late 1980s and were matched by the inadequacies of the incomes received by those who lived and worked there and their relative prosperity. Shipping and the wider maritime industries were no exception to this and it is indisputable that the artificial and in some ways archaic system that was applied to the industry prevented its comparative development. By the same token, the renewal of the economic system and the imposition of a free market economy of a style and character similar to that found in Western Europe should provide the circumstances for an increasingly efficient and dynamic maritime sector. If logic holds good, and given that we assume that the combined weight of opinion that economic development requires a modern and well run international transport system sensitive to the needs of its consumers and market demands is correct, then the maritime sector should now begin to contribute towards this progress and play the role expected of it.

The evidence of the growth in GDP in Poland, and the clear moves in terms of average incomes and lifestyles towards a developed state, helps us to accept that international transport has a role to play here - but inevitably, the degree and significance of its role remains unclear. Is it not simply that the Polish economy as a whole needed exposing to the free market and that no one sector in isolation can claim to be any more important than any other?

What is clear is that since the broad liberalisation of the marketplace in Poland, there has emerged with no state force, an increase in competition, predominantly in the ancillary sectors but increasingly in ports and ship operations, and that the free market style of western Europe has encouraged these developments to take place. With it has come a clear recognition of the need to change attitudes, the slow but steady introduction of new infrastructure wherever possible and as we have seen, tangible growth in prosperity - if so far small. Perhaps, therefore, we can be encouraged by this progress and assume what has been commonly assumed for many years, that international transport, in this case international shipping, is a necessity along with many other factors, to ensure economic development and regeneration. The logic appears impeccable if difficult to prove. This transport development need not be shipping - take Switzerland for example for a country rather less dependent on the sea - but transport is always a vital part and without its liberalisation, removal from protectionism, exposure to competition and a fundamental change in structure and attitude, development overall will be inhibited.

So our initial conclusion is most likely to be that the process of liberalisation in Eastern Europe, and in the context of the Polish maritime sector in particular, is not only an inevitable one led by the prompting of supranational western bodies such as the European Union, World Bank, International Monetary Fund and the European Bank for Reconstruction and Development, and the desires and demands of the domestic populations to benefit from the pleasures of western progress, but also one that overall is beneficial to the countries concerned and to the individuals of those countries. In other words, international shipping benefits from liberalisation and in turn prompts the development process at least to a certain extent.

However, one must not forget the dangers inherent in this process of change and development for it is not all individuals who benefit from liberalisation - many of the benefits tend to be concentrated in narrowly defined sectors - and as we shall see, neither is it necessarily the country or industrial sector that is liberalised that reaps all the benefits.

Taking the Polish maritime sector specifically, we have already noted a considerable number of changes that have occurred since the industry was released from the total control of the state. Firstly, following the withdrawal of the large majority of subsidies to shipping companies, the ports and the ancillary industries and combined with the reduction in state guaranteed cargo, there has been a marked reduction in fleet size in all sectors - bulk, ferry and particularly liner. This does not suggest a lessening in cargo traffic world-wide but does reflect a movement of that traffic to other ship operators who can provide a similar or better quality service for the same price, or even a change in mode. This latter process we saw earlier as an inevitable consequence of the process of change. Incidentally, the new truck cargoes are not even necessarily carried by Polish trucks as the newly liberated road freight sector has also encouraged an inflow of German, Dutch, Russian and other operators to compete for this previously subsidised and guaranteed traffic.

Liberalisation has also hit the shipping industry in Poland through the development of new competition. Although this has so far been limited in the operation sector and constrained to Maersk container lines (Denmark) and Stena Line ferries in particular, it will undoubtedly spread and has caused considerable losses of traffic for both PŻB ferries serving southern Sweden and Polish Ocean Lines on their container feeder services to and from north west European ports. In the ancillary sector, competition has been stronger with a considerable number of western based companies entering the marketplace in Poland and competing against Polish based private, ex-state or existing state firms in the brokering, agency and forwarding sectors in particular. Examples include Danzas of Switzerland and Maersk logistics. These interlopers clearly provide employment for local residents but at the same time are manifestations of a loss of profit abroad and, perhaps more importantly, a loss of control and influence.

This issue of influence also raises its head with the decline in the Polish flagged fleet, and thus the loss of Polish seafarer and officer jobs, stemming both from the reduction in Polish owned vessels through the process of subsidy reduction and cargo redirection noted earlier, and more significantly through the deliberate policy of Polish operators to move vessels to flags of convenience both to save costs of employment and to facilitate borrowing arrangements with western banks. Without strong political pressure, and the odd agreement between companies and employees to retain Polish flagged vessels, the economics of the situation would dictate that there would be no Polish flagged vessels left by now. Few will soon remain. Admittedly this is counteracted a little by the popularity of Polish seafarers on vessels of other developed countries - particularly the United Kingdom - but at the cost of Polish domestic based employment and an overall reduction in employment market size. The effect in terms of influence of this fleet decline is perhaps felt most in the forum of international organisations such as the International Maritime Organisation (IMO), the United Nations organisation that is responsible for safety and environmental regulation of the shipping industry. The loss of a Polish fleet would make the influence that Poland could have within that group that much less. The same inevitably follows for the European Union DGVII (maritime) Section, BIMCO, shipping conferences and so on.

Port decline is another feature of this liberalisation process which in turn may have drawbacks for the development of Poland as a whole. We have noted already how the three ports of Gdańsk, Gdynia and Szczecin have suffered through the loss of guaranteed traffic and the decline in the Polish fleet and this has been exacerbated by the problems besetting the Polish economy since the transformation, with a severe economic depression and rampant inflation, and the loss of transit traffic from the old CMEA partners of Czechoslovakia and Hungary whose exports and imports used to pass through Polish ports but have now also transferred either location to Western ports, or mode to trucking. The immediate effect is a loss of prosperity in the Polish port regions with little prospect of recovery as the market has found new ways of transporting freight. This may be ameliorated a little as economies recover but a full return to the levels of the past is not very likely.

Other disbenefits of the liberalisation process include the potential sale of Polish assets and companies abroad with the consequent loss of profit and control (a problem recently recognised by the state in the proposed sale of PŻB); environmental problems stemming from the reduced roles of rail and ship and the increased use of trucking at a time when European policy generally is in an opposite direction; and the decline of at least parts of the shipbuilding sector (notably in Gdańsk) with the loss of guaranteed new buildings and repairs for Polish and other CMEA state operators.

## Conclusions

As always with discussions of international transport and development there can be no absolutely firm conclusions. The situation in Poland is unique and undoubtedly the development of an efficient and well structured international shipping marketplace and industry will contribute to the general development of the region including Poland itself. It will not however, necessarily directly benefit from the broad sweep of liberalisation that is running through the country and which is an inevitable consequence of the revolutionary phase of the late 1980s and early 1990s. The creation of a liberalised maritime industry may, in fact, lead to its own downfall with consequent benefits for international transport users of other modes, based in other countries or using other ports. Overall, the benefits to the state are probably greater than any loss in employment, income or international influence but within the specific sectors and locations associated with the maritime industry the effects can be severe.

One partial solution to this might be a coherent national shipping policy, something that Poland sadly lacks at present, with an attitude of laissez-faire dominating within a broad context of privatisation and liberalisation. Such a policy could at least look at developments, examine their particular impact and assess their benefit both overall and more specifically. Through this the detrimental effects of fleet loss, and the duplicative inadequacies stemming from a free market (for example in facilities being developed in both Gdynia and Gdańsk for freeports and container terminals, some 20 kilometres apart) might be avoided. In addition, a national policy can contribute towards co-ordination of transport modes, carriers, producers, port authorities and ship operators thus facilitating the development of a more efficient transport system with all the benefits this can bring.

Poland will never be served again by the very biggest of deep sea shipping lines on the trunk markets as it was under the old regime stimulated and supported by artificial economic conditions. However, state interest (rather than interference) could encourage the development of smaller, more responsive ports, which in turn would encourage the development of feeder shipping lines to compete with the environmentally damaging, but fashionably popular (at least in Eastern Europe) trucking modes.

Poland continues, along with the rest of Eastern Europe, to suffer from its history and will do so for some time to come yet. Its international transport sector, and particularly its shipping sector, which was so well supported by the state in the past, has suffered more than most from the new economic, political and social climate. It remains to be seen how well it can adapt (or even survive) and go on to contribute to the development of Poland, or whether it will form part of the declining industries of the region as the process of liberalisation and free market forces continue to bite.

## References

I. Chrzanowski (1977) Polish shipping and shipping policy. *Maritime Policy and Management,* 4 (5), 281-292.

Fairplay (1995) *World in focus; Poland.* 11th May.

M.J. Krzyzanowski (1993) The adaptation of the Polish shipping companies to market conditions. *Maritime Policy and Management,* 20 (4), 301-307.

G.D. Ledger and M.S. Roe (1993) East European shipping and economic change; a conceptual model. *Maritime Policy and Management,* 20 (3), 229-241.

G.D. Ledger and M.S. Roe (1995) Positional change in the Polish liner shipping market; a framework approach. *Maritime Policy and Management,* 22 (4), 295-318.

G.D. Ledger and M.S. Roe (1996) *East European change and shipping policy.* Avebury Press; Aldershot.

G.D. Ledger and M.S. Roe (1997) *European Union shipping policy and East Europe.* in M.S. Roe (ed.) *Shipping in the Baltic region.* Avebury Press; Aldershot.

Lloyd's List (1995) *POL still in midst of major transformation.* 26th May.

Lloyd's List (1997) *Poland.* 29th May.

Lloyd's Ship Manager (1992) *Poland special report.* August.

Lloyd's Ship Manager (1996) *Poland special report.* August.

M.S. Roe (ed.) (1997) *Shipping in the Baltic region.* Avebury Press; Aldershot.

M.S. Roe (1997) Developments in East European ports. *The Dock and Harbour Authority,* 78 (876): 43 - 45.

M.S. Roe (1997) *East European shipping.* Oxford Analytica; Oxford.

Z. Sawiczewska (1992) Reconstructing Polish ports and shipping. *Maritime Policy and Management,* 19 (1), 69-76.

N. Toy and M.S. Roe (1997) *The Polish passenger ferry industry in the post communist era.* in M.S. Roe (ed.) *Shipping in the Baltic region.* Avebury Press; Aldershot.

J. Zurek (1996) Restructuring the Polish shipping companies (current state and trends). *Polish Maritime Review,* September 22-25.

# 10. Privatisation of ports - the case of Eastern Germany

*Karl-Heinz Breitzmann*
*Institut für Verkehr und Logistik*
*Universität Rostock*

## Introduction

Since 1990, seaports in the eastern part of the re-unified Germany have undergone a series of deep structural changes. In this region, the collapse of the political and economic system of the former GDR (East Germany) along with the whole of the Eastern Bloc, in conjunction with the consequential economic problems which have stemmed from the transition to a market economy and integration into the Federal Republic of Germany have led to a dramatic shrinkage of cargo handling. Moreover, ports have faced fundamental changes in the structure and technology of transport. As a consequence, state-dominated property rights and organisational structures have had to be adapted to a newly developing and imposed market system.

This paper attempts to analyse these highly interconnected processes and to go on to focus upon some of the problems of privatisation within a rather more narrow definition.

## Structural changes in cargo handling

Seaports along the East German coast of the Baltic Sea – now belonging to the federal state of Mecklenburg-Vorpommern – have prospered twice in history. Once in the Hanseatic period from the 12th to the 15th century and then again as a result of large exports of grain in the second half of the 19th century. Since then, rapid industrialisation in other parts of Germany and the development of alternative competing overseas shipping centres has resulted in the ports of Mecklenburg-Vorpommern falling into relative insignificance.

After the Second World War the GDR leadership decided to establish a series of national ports and a sizeable merchant fleet in the form of the state owned shipping enterprise DSR, in order to become both politically and economically independent and to save and earn hard currency. The most important decision was to construct a new international overseas port in Rostock which was subsequently opened in 1960. Taking together all East German seaports and ferry terminals, cargo handled amounted to more than 33 million tons in 1989 dominated by trade through the port of Rostock.

In 1990, following the 'German Currency, Economic and Social Union' of 1st July, 1990 and re-unification with the Federal Republic of Germany on 3rd October, 1990, these ports were confronted with a severe decrease in business. Cargo handling went down to 16 million tons in 1991, which represented about 59 % of the 1989 level (see Table 10.1).

**Table 10.1**
**Cargo handling in the ports of Mecklenburg-Vorpommern\* 1989 - 1996 (million tons)**

| Year | Rostock\*\* | Wismar | Stralsund | Sassnitz | Mukran | Total |
|------|-----------|--------|-----------|----------|--------|-------|
| 1989 | 21.3 | 3.3 | 0.8 | 4.8 | 3.1 | 33.3 |
| 1990 | 13.7 | 3.0 | 0.8 | 4.2 | 1.9 | 23.6 |
| 1991 | 8.9 | 2.0 | 0.6 | 3.6 | 1.1 | 16.2 |
| 1992 | 10.6 | 1.9 | 0.9 | 3.3 | 1.0 | 17.7 |
| 1993 | 12.4 | 1.7 | 0.6 | 3.0 | 1.4 | 19.1 |
| 1994 | 15.4 | 1.7 | 0.8 | 3.0 | 1.5 | 22.4 |
| 1995 | 16.8 | 1.8 | 0.8 | 2.5 | 0.9 | 22.8 |
| 1996 | 17.2 | 1.9 | 0.7 | 2.4 | 0.8 | 23.0 |
| 1996+ | 19.8 | 1.9 | 0.7 | 4.7 | 1.7 | 28.8 |

Source: Author

* Excluding deadweight of trucks/railway wagons by ferry transport.
** International port; ferry terminal at Warnemünde included.
+ Includes deadweight of trucks/railway wagons by ferry transport.

The changes in cargo handling were a direct result of the structural crisis of the East German economy as it progressed through transformation into a market system. The reduced economic activity in the new federal states went hand in hand with reduced import and export volumes. This was intensified in particular, by the substantial fall in foreign trade with the USSR and its successor countries.

When the German 'Currency Union' came into effect and the administrative procedures concerning provision of directed cargo allocation were removed, the monopoly position of East German ports vanished. Many goods from southern parts of former East Germany and particularly containers, now preferred to take a route to and from overseas regions via German North Sea ports, more specifically those of Hamburg and Bremerhaven.

Commencing in 1992 and continuing through all the following years, an increase of cargo handling could be identified. However, this was not merely a recovery in the amounts of cargo handled, as other manifold structural changes were involved. The most significant ones will be outlined here.

Firstly, the ports have concentrated upon Baltic and North Sea trades whilst deep sea liner shipping for example, has been largely closed down (see Table 10.2).

**Table 10.2**
**Overseas origin and destination of goods handled in the ports\* of Mecklenburg-Vorpommern\*\* 1995 (%)**

| | Origin/Destination | Rostock | Wismar | Stralsund |
|---|---|---|---|---|
| 1 | Scandinavia | 32.1 | 56.4 | 59.5 |
| 2 | Baltic Transformation Countries | 15.5 | 14.4 | 7.4 |
| 3 | Western Europe | 9.6 | 26.0 | 25.0 |
| 4 | Mediterranean/ Northern Africa | 8.8 | 0.9 | 2.2 |
| 5 | Other Continents | 15.6 | 1.2 | - |
| 6 | Germany | 18.4 | 1.1 | 5.9 |
| | Total | 100.0 | 100.0 | 100.0 |

Source : Author

\* Ports of Rostock, Wismar, Stralsund
\*\* excluding ferry transport

In the bulk sector of the port of Rostock, intercontinental transport still plays a role through the import of iron ore and the export of scrap and grain.

Secondly, the structure of bulk handling has fundamentally changed. Whilst ore and metal imports as well as exports of potash shrank considerably, mineral oil and building materials grew to take a new leading role. Grain and fodder – which were almost entirely imported in former times – are dominant exports today. Moreover, large quantities of scrap metals are shipped from Rostock in what is also quite a new trend (see Table 10.3).

Thirdly, the bulk handling sector was linked to the creation of port-related industries at the site. Several sea exporting or importing firms have started their business in the ports or in adjacent areas since 1990. In Rostock, these include a coal power station, a malting factory, several grain traders, oil merchants, a scrap treating company and firms dealing with building materials.

**Table 10.3**
**Cargo handling of liquid and dry bulk goods in Mecklenburg-Vorpommern\* 1995**

| GOODS TYPE | INGOING ('000 TONS) | OUTGOING ('000 TONS) | TOTAL ('000 TONS) | (%) |
|---|---|---|---|---|
| **1. Liquid goods** | 1 692 | 1 682 | 3 374 | 22.1 |
| - Crude oil | 305 | 1 275 | 1 580 | 10.3 |
| - Oil products | 1 359 | 337 | 1 696 | 11.1 |
| - Other | 28 | 70 | 98 | 0.7 |
| **2. Bulk goods** | 6 205 | 3 741 | 9 945 | 65.1 |
| - Grain | 119 | 2 147 | 2 265 | 14.8 |
| - Coal | 720 | - | 720 | 4.7 |
| - Iron ore | 1 260 | - | 1 260 | 8.3 |
| - Scrap | 80 | 645 | 725 | 4.7 |
| - Potash, Soda | - | 330 | 330 | 2.2 |
| - Fertiliser | 671 | 602 | 1 272 | 8.3 |
| - Building materials | 3 272 | 17 | 3 289 | 21.5 |
| - Peat | 84 | - | 84 | 0.6 |
| **3. Break bulk goods** | 671 | 1 288 | 1 959 | 12.8 |
| - Metal | 359 | 734 | 1 093 | 7.2 |
| - Timber | 80 | 447 | 527 | 3.4 |
| - Paper | 214 | 3 | 217 | 1.4 |
| - Goods in bags | 18 | - | 122 | 0.8 |
| **Total** | 8 568 | 6 710 | 15 278 | 100.0 |

Source : Author

\*Ports of Rostock, Wismar, Stralsund; excluding ferry transport

Fourthly, the ferry trade with Scandinavia has gained substantial momentum and as a result, the ferry component of port handling has increased notably. Today's port of Rostock is an important ferry port, adding capacity to Sassnitz and Mukran on the island of Rugia to the east.

In addition, the passenger component of this ferry traffic is very important. The opening of the border with the Federal Republic and the rest of the European Union led to an increase of passenger numbers from around one million a year in former times, to more than three million in 1997. Fifthly, there have been fundamental shifts in modal split. In former times, as a consequence of state policy, hinterland transport was dominated by rail accounting for more than 90 % of the total. Today, road transport has taken over 80 - 90 % of traffic in all ports.

Sixthly, several new smaller ports have opened up business, serving local or regional markets.

In the near future it is possible to identify good opportunities for the ports of the former East Germany to increase their activities. In late 1997, the Institut fur Werkehr und Logistik at the University of Rostock completed a forecast for port developments until the year 2010. It was concluded that there is a good chance of increasing cargo turnover by 20 % until the year 2000 – the base year being 1995 – and by 60 % until 2010. Taking into account an optimistic scenario for both direct and transit trade with Russia and the other former Soviet Republics, it is possible to envisage an increase of up to 90 % of trade. However, this growth will not be achieved by itself and considerable efforts will have to be made in order to benefit from these opportunities.

On the one hand, a prerequisite to achieve this development concerns the public authorities with their obligation to upgrade hinterland connections and to adjust them to the needs of today's dominant modal split characteristics. Here, the leading project is the development of the east-west motorway (A20) which will run a length of more than 300 km, complementing the existing north-south highway between Rostock and Berlin. This new highway is intended to integrate effectively the ports of the German Baltic coast into the West European transport network.

On the other hand, the ports themselves and all the related port industries are presented with the considerable challenge of how actively to draw upon the prospects that these new motorway developments will open up.

This second requirement begins to touch upon the second significant recent development - the changes in property rights and organisational structures that are needed to provide for economic development and success.

## Structural changes of ownership and organisation

When we consider the changes in ownership and organisation in the ports, the term 'privatisation' can only be applied in a very broad context. The actual developments are more comprehensively covered by terms such as liberalisation, de-monopolisation, municipalisation or corporatisation.

In former GDR times, commercial ports were state-owned enterprises with the complete responsibility for both infrastructure and superstructure. Being monopolies, these enterprises themselves organised the entire process of cargo handling, storage and warehousing in the territory of the respective port. In the 1970s, all shipping and port enterprises were put under the single management of a 'Shipping and Port Combine'. Here, the shipping operation was given priority and as a consequence, ports were not independent at all and had very narrowly defined limits within which they could make their own economic decisions.

When the former GDR started the process of transition in spring 1990, the Combine noted above was wound up and ports left the holding in order to regain their independence. The former ministerial functions were abolished and there was a general switch to a more liberal market regime. At the same time, shippers got back their rights to decide for themselves upon all transport issues and decisions.

In going through the process of compulsory corporatisation, all state-owned enterprises had to be transformed into capital companies by the 1st July 1990, the date when the German 'Currency, Economic and Social Union' came into being. Enterprises were obliged to prepare an opening balance in (West) German Marks. At the same time, the so-called 'Treuhandanstalt' was founded as a trusteeship organisation taking over the entire shares of all the state-owned companies. Thus, the privatisation agency became the world's largest holding institution.

The transition process included the community's right to re-claim their former property and to obtain ownership of enterprises which were core service providers for local supplies. As a result, ports in Mecklenburg-Vorpommern entered into a limited form of share-holding with the effect that Mecklenburg-Vorpommern became co-owner in the ports of Rostock and Wismar (see Table 10.4).

Another important port location existed at the railway-ferry terminal in Mukran on the island of Rugia. It was built in the 1980s in order to establish a direct link to the Former Soviet Union and more precisely to Klaipeda in the now independent Republic of Lithuania and in the process, circumventing Polish territory and the political/economic problems that they presented for

116

transit traffic. Ownership lay in the hands of DSR, the former East German state-owned carrier. In 1992, the terminal was reorganised into a fully owned subsidiary company of DSR. One year later, the port was removed from DSR and municipalised into a public port. As the new owner, the small city of Sassnitz was heavily overburdened by the enormous requirements of port development and as a consequence the state of Mecklenburg-Vorpommern stepped in as co-owner.

**Table 10.4**
**Ownership of ports in Mecklenburg-Vorpommern**

| Port enterprise | City ownership (%) | State of Mecklenburg-Vorpommern (%) |
|---|---|---|
| Seehafen Rostock | 74.9 | 25.1 |
| Seehafen Wismar | 74.9 | 25.1 |
| Fährhafen Mukran | 90.0 | 10.0 |
| Stralsunder Hafen und Lagergesellschaft | 100.0 | - |
| Rostocker Fischereihafen | 100.0 | - |

Source : Author

If we now move on to consider privatisation in a more confined sense, we have to leave aside cargo handling and to look into other port related businesses including forwarding, agency, hinterland transport, ship supply etc. These fields were also the responsibility of state-owned monopolies in the former GDR. Forwarding, for instance, was arranged by the company 'Deutrans', meanwhile brokerage and agency services were the responsibility of 'Deutsche Schiffsmaklerei', etc.

The more liberal market regime after 1990 allowed the rapid establishment of a large number of companies by private interests. Table 10.5 highlights the case of Rostock as an example. Frequently, the companies were private successors of the former state-owned firms or they originated from outsourcing functions of former port enterprises. In addition, there were affiliates of West German companies or newly founded companies headed by former East German entrepreneurs.

## Main problems of privatisation of ports

If we now come to port privatisation in a specific sense, a number of very complex questions emerge concerning ownership and organisation. Two representative problems will be analysed here in more detail.

**Table 10.5**
**Enterprises and institutions of port and maritime industries in Rostock 1994**

| | Sector | Number of companies/ institutions | Number of employees |
|---|---|---|---|
| 1. | Port and maritime transport industries | 153 | 4,744 |
| 1.1 | Administration/ Cargo Handling/ Warehousing | 6 | 1,314 |
| 1.2 | Port forwarding, Brokerage/Agency | 41 | 154 |
| 1.3 | Transport | 20 | 352 |
| 1.4 | Pilotage, Towage | 5 | 107 |
| 1.5 | Sea and ferry shipping | 15 | 2,371 |
| 1.6 | Ship supply, Bunkering | 17 | 243 |
| 1.7 | Tally | 8 | 36 |
| 1.8 | Marine insurance, Inspection | 8 | 33 |
| 1.9 | Ship repair and port maintenance facilities | 22 | 107 |
| 1.10 | Other | 11 | 27 |
| 2. | Port related industries | 37 | 1,374 |
| 3. | Maritime Authorities and Institutions | 27 | 1,143 |
| | **Total** | **217** | **7,261** |

Source : Author

*The relationship between port infra and superstructure*

We shall first look into the question of port infrastructure. In defining port infrastructure we shall include harbour entrance channels, marine constructions such as moles or jetties, water basins and quay walls, transport infrastructure in the port territory and construction for the protection of the environment.

A common experience of West German ports and other ports in continental Europe is that port infrastructure generally cannot be developed and managed with full cost-recovery or profitably. A substantial increase in port dues would be necessary in order to achieve cost-coverage. This option is very often limited for example by strong competition between continental ports operating within the same hinterland area.

There is a tradition of considering infrastructure and superstructure separately in western German ports. In Hamburg, Bremen, Emden, Wilhelmshaven and Lübeck the city or the regional state concerned are owners of infrastructure and thus responsible for investment, maintenance and exploitation. As far as sea channels are concerned, these functions are fulfilled by the German Federal government.

On the other hand, cargo handling and warehousing is the responsibility of city owned or private port and stevedoring companies. They have to pay rent for the use of land and infrastructure whilst they also have to invest in cranes, sheds, warehouses, forklifts etc. Of course, their broad economic aim is both to cover costs and to earn a reasonable profit.

Following the transfer of East German ports from the Treuhandanstalt to the different communities, the situation differed fundamentally from that described for West German ports. Here, the port companies themselves were responsible for infrastructure and superstructure.

As a result of careful investigation at the port of Rostock, the decision was taken to divide the enterprise into one firm which should own the infrastructure and a second company for the management and operation of the port (see Table 10.6).

As a result, a fundamentally new solution was found. The infrastructure was placed not directly under the city's administration but instead in the hands of a separate, commercialised, legally private company. By choosing this structure, the focus was placed upon increasing distance from the local authorities and thus this should encourage stronger independence. The advantages were seen as improved flexibility and market presence.

As the European Union is becomingly increasingly involved in port matters (e.g. the recent Green Paper), this model may become even more interesting in future than it is already today. One of the policies of the European Union Common Transport Policy (CTP) is that subsidy is forbidden or at least placed under the strict control of the European Commission. As a consequence of this we can ask, what are the implications for subsidising port infrastructure?

**Table 10.6**
**Ownership and organisation in the Port of Rostock**

| Company | Function | Ownership |
|---------|----------|-----------|
| Seehafen Rostock Verwaltungs-gesellschaft mbH | Owning, developing and operation of land and infrastructure | 74.9 % City of Rostock 25.1 % State of Mecklenburg-Vor-pommern |
| Seehafen Rostock Umschlagsge-sellschaft mbH | Cargo handling, warehousing. Owning, developing and operation of superstructure | 100 % City of Rostock (until 1996) 100 % private (since 1996) |

Source : Author

One thing is certain, transparency is needed. This can be secured in a rather convenient way by applying the Rostock solution. Since the port policy of Europe is on the move, the transition experience from Eastern Germany may possibly be of interest here.

**True privatisation of ports?**

We now come to the remaining and rather more sensitive issue of the role of private investors and private interests in general within the port companies themselves.

Here, developments in the recent past in Rostock have seen the sale of the city-owned stevedoring company to a private investment group. The port infrastructure company however, remains in the public hands of the city and the federal state.

Until very recently, it was the established policy of Rostock City Council not to give any concession to private stevedoring activities over and above those available to publicly owned companies. As a consequence, these activities were reserved for the municipal company or for public/private joint ventures. However, this policy is now changing once again, stimulating a long and controversial debate concentrating upon the advantages and disadvantages of privatisation and the best approaches to handling these issues. The eventual outcome was the sale of these activities to the UK based Kent Investment Group - a step unimaginable only a few years back.

This transfer of ownership and change of privatisation policy generated a number of different issues that needed to be considered. On the one hand, ports are now seen not just as enterprises but rather as instruments of regional development as well. Ports indeed can and do attract investors in industry and trade, which is a necessity especially under the current and recent eastern German economic conditions. One conclusion in these circumstances would be not to privatise the larger ports with their highly complex and substantial commercial relationships to a variety of branches of the economy.

On the other hand, it is indisputable that private companies are commonly more flexible in dealings with the market and efficient in how they operate and what they do. Private investors need to be included in order to establish or strengthen urgently needed links to shippers, brokers, agents, exporters, importers etc. and to open up new fields of commercial activity.

Finally, questions of profitability and finance are high on the agenda. Here, the situation in eastern Germany is particularly complicated. Municipal enterprises in particular, are in a position to obtain high promotional funding for the development of infrastructure. However, only in the coming years, when the objects of capital expenditure have to be replaced, will it become clear what the economic implications are that arise from this policy. At the same time, the municipalities are confronted with conflicting requirements manifesting themselves mainly in high debts, and thus presenting difficulties in approving significant investment in their own ports.

It is necessary to bear in mind the overall situation in eastern Germany when considering the privatisation of ports in the region and one clear conclusion is that the situation needs to be handled very cautiously. At least several alternative models of privatisation should be evaluated in the course of the decision-making process. It is possible to identify at least four different models that might be used all of which have the starting point that port infrastructure and superstructure should be combined into one public company. This latter policy requirement stems from the difficulties identified so far in splitting these two functions in the eastern German scenario.

*Model 1* draws upon the case which is to be introduced in Rostock and reflects the structure to be used there.

*Model 2* would concentrate upon privatising, for instance, those parts of the port's infra- and superstructure which are highly specialised and suited for individual and single user shippers only.

According to *Model 3,* a holding structure would join publicly owned bodies with different private interests in different parts of the ports. These 'daughter operating companies' however, would have to be large enough to allow for synergetic effects and economies of scale to be realised and to allow for competitiveness in the long term.

*Model 4* combines the principles of Models 1 and 3 in that it contains both a public holding company responsible for the superstructure and state investment in the infrastructure of the port. It may be an adequate solution to the problems of ownership, especially for larger ports.

## Conclusions

Should the privatisation of ports in eastern Germany continue to be considered seriously, it is certain that the variety of solutions proposed and worthy of some consideration will continue to grow. The problems outlined here will not just go away and will have to be faced and dealt with as the years pass and the need for the final divestment of state interference which is a legacy from the old regimes, is left behind. The four models proposed here are just a limited number of examples of the diversity of approaches that exist.

## Model 1

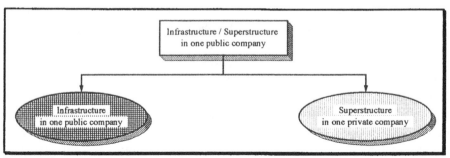

Source : Author

## Model 2

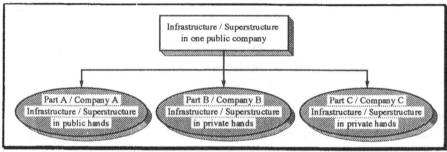

Source : Author

## Model 3

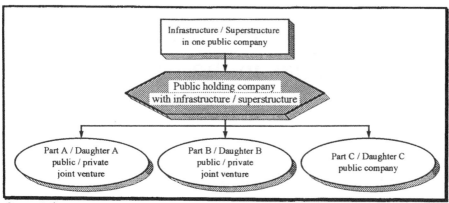

Source : Author

## Model 4

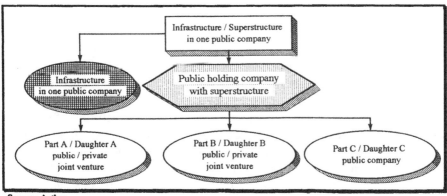

Source : Author

# 11. Managing transition – privatisation and restructuring of former Socialist shipping companies in the Baltic Sea region

*Falk von Seck*
*Institut für Verkehr und Logistik*
*Universität Rostock*

## Introduction

The economic and social collapse of the states in Central and Eastern Europe marked the beginning of the transition process towards market economies. Fundamental changes not only affected the specific production structures in each country in the region but also the existing monetary exchange conditions with other countries. The currency used for foreign trade between Socialist countries was changed almost immediately from the rouble to the dollar. Market prices for raw materials were introduced. The resulting decline in trade volumes caused a drastic decrease in demand for shipping transport. Under these circumstances, Socialist shipping companies were widely unprepared to face the abrupt cutback in government subsidies and state protection that occurred.

This paper addresses the issue of privatisation and restructuring of shipping corporations in the Baltic Sea countries in Eastern Europe. It intends to analyse the basis, problems and results of the far reaching changes that have occurred. The analysis is based upon extensive research and field studies in Russia, the Baltic States, Poland and East Germany. The analysis had to cope with dramatic and complex structural changes in a very short period of time, not to mention an extreme shortage of reliable data.

Aware of the fact that successfully transforming the shipping sector certainly has an influence upon the general speed and route of economic development in transition countries, the paper finally closes with a discussion of the overall results of transforming Socialist shipping companies into market players. The differences and instability of macro economic patterns of production and consumption make little allowance in establishing the definite causes of the very complex transition results which have emerged.

## Starting conditions for transition

Shipping has always been a field of great national interest, not only because of shippers' demand, but also for other economic and political reasons. The shipping sector in Socialist economies was particularly unique because of its strong public goods and services approach. Starting conditions for transition in each of the countries affected, showed strong similarities.

Socialist shipping was commonly defined by state-ownership, heavy centralisation and concentration. State property and state activity in shipping was regarded as necessary as was state protection.

Shipping was generally subject to central planning procedures. With governments setting political and macro-economic shipping goals, only limited possibilities for strategic decision-making and action existed at enterprise level. Factors of production were centrally allocated. Accordingly, manpower, investment and decisions concerning the fields of activity were set administratively and thus severely restricted company autonomy. The political bureaucracy even decided specifically operational matters so that shipping companies were essentially operational units, translating strategic targets into specific structures and then fulfilling them practically afterwards.[1]

All state shipping companies experienced a rapid growth beginning in the 1950s. They all basically started from nothing after World War II. In particular conventional liner shipping gained competitive positions applying international standards and business rules. World-wide networks were installed. A process of international co-operative orientation was characteristic of this time although to a different extent in each national case.

All shipping corporations maintained ownership of large fleets and their enormous sizes often made them the biggest in Europe. Following central government policy, their main task was to transport goods for national foreign trade, to earn foreign currency and to save upon expenses at home.

---

[1] One should not forget however, that business partners from market economies quite enjoyed the participation of central institutions. This was seen as a prerequisite for mutual trust especially where high capital commitment was involved.

Furthermore, military-strategic aims were added to the shipping policy functions. Soviet fleets for example, made particularly strong defence efforts, orientating their liner fleet towards ro-ro instead of the container technology applied world-wide. At the beginning of the transition period, currency rather than shipping functions dominated Polish as well as East German shipping.

**Table 11.1**
**Fleets of Eastern European shipping companies at the beginning of the transition period**

| Vessel Type | | Shipping Company | | | |
|---|---|---|---|---|---|
| | | BSC | DSR | LSC | POL |
| Total | number | 164 | 164 | 104 | 97 |
| | 1,000 dwt | 1,737 | 1,700 | 1,433 | 914 |
| General cargo vessel | number | 67 | 70 | 8 | 46 |
| | 1,000 dwt | 838 | 708 | 22 | 357 |
| Container vessel | number | 17 | 16 | 4 | 36 |
| | 1,000 dwt | 262 | 232 | 33 | 482 |
| Ro/Ro-vessel | number | 36 | 7 | 7 | 9 |
| | 1,000 dwt | 455 | 39 | 38 | 54 |
| Ferry | number | 0 | 2 | 0 | 3 |
| | 1,000 dwt | | 24 | | 10 |
| Reefer vessel | number | 0 | 10 | 27 | 3 |
| | 1,000 dwt | | 56 | 177 | 11 |
| Wood transporter | number | 41 | 10 | 0 | 0 |
| | 1,000 dwt | 182 | 45 | | |
| Bulk vessel | number | 0 | 24 | 0 | 0 |
| | 1,000 dwt | | 558 | | |
| Tanker | number | 0 | 0 | 51 | 0 |
| | 1,000 dwt | | | 1,122 | |
| Gas Tanker | number | 0 | 3 | 7 | 0 |
| | 1,000 dwt | | 17 | 41 | |
| Shortsea vessel | number | n.d. | 21 | n.d. | 0 |
| | 1,000 dwt | | 18 | | |
| Passenger vessel | number | 3 | 1 | 0 | 0 |
| | 1,000 dwt | n.d. | 3 | | |

*data at 31.12.1989; fleet in ownership of the companies or its subsidiaries.
Source: author's investigations on the basis of Lloyd's Confidential Index, div. volumes; Preis et al. 1992

It was not only the aims but also the structures of Socialist national fleets that sought to implement national shipping policy and foreign trade targets of the countries concerned.[2] Thus, the specific structures of the fleets showed a distinct complexity (see Table 11.1).

However, all fleets also showed signs of insufficient investment, and vessels were often very old and obsolete. Transport technologies used were rather backward, e.g. in the case of comparatively large general cargo businesses. Competitive transport qualities were deficient as regards frequency, speed, transit time and punctuality. Socialist shipping suffered from the clear handicap of its prevailing regional orientation of service networks with point-to-point routings instead of global service activity, using for example hub port concepts. The Socialist states guaranteed that their fleet capacity would be used, for example by introducing certain cargo allocation measures. There was a common contractual arrangement that exports would be c.i.f. and imports f.o.b.. There was also governmental price regulation for shipping services although to a differing extent in each national case. The East German DSR, for example, had the freedom to set prices according to market requirements for their international market activities. International freight rates also formed the basis for charging national shippers. Soviet carriers however, broadly followed central ministry price setting.

Contrary to common belief, there was no effectively planned division of labour between the Socialist shipping groups. Institutionalised COMECON shipping institutions never achieved much influence in fact. Instead, Socialist shipping companies were entrusted national or regional monopolies. They were commonly active in liner and charter markets enjoying a large degree of specialisation.

East German shipping, for example, was allocated to Deutsche Seereederei (DSR) alone. In Poland, liner structures were distinct from the bulk sector and from short sea shipping. Liner sector activity was carried out by Polish Ocean Lines (POL). The Polish chartering business for the bulk sector formed part of the Polish Shipping Company (PŻM). The Polish Baltic Shipping Company (PŻB) was the company active in the short sea business.

In the Former Soviet Union, shipping structures followed mainly geographical criteria defined by sea basins, home ports and cargo specialisation. Shipping companies working from the Baltic Sea base included the Baltic Shipping Company Leningrad/St. Petersburg (BSC), Estonian

---

[2] It has to be pointed out that such close ties are not uncommon in international shipping. After World War Two this was customary also in market economies. However, this changed in that former close bonds between foreign trade and the national fleets have since largely disappeared.

Shipping Company Tallinn (ESCO), Latvian Shipping Company Riga (LSC) and Lithuanian Shipping Company Klaipeda (LISCO).

The fleet stationed in Latvia was particularly active in reefer and liner shipping. The Lithuanian fleet with its home port in Ventspils was very active in liquid bulk transport. The Estonian Shipping Company worked particularly in conventional liner shipping to African ports and the short sea business from Tallinn. In contrast, the Leningrad based Baltic Shipping Company concentrated on international liner shipping as it was one of the leading Soviet companies in that specific field.

Generally, Socialist shipping companies were characterised by their rather deep organisational and production structures. They were part of vertically integrated maritime conglomerates which combined a huge variety of services and support activities. A typical feature was the integration of seaports into these complex corporations. In the GDR, for example, the 'maritime transport and port industries conglomerate' incorporated ports and other maritime support enterprises. The East German sea carrier Deutsche Seereederei, functioned as the core company business. Polish ports however, always stayed outside such conglomerates. It was the USSR, which created the highest level of integration, with even ship repair yards included in the shipping groups.

These highly integrated structures and the resulting concentration of resources, certainly opened opportunities to transform scale-effects into competitive advantages.[3] Some of the Socialist shipping companies were in a position to translate these into international competitiveness. In most cases however, Socialist particularities eased the pressures from international markets so that technology and ship size increasingly lost pace. Lack of efficiency and of certain managerial know how became characteristic features at company level.

The downward trend in economic growth and productivity already turned out to be a major problem in the Socialist countries from the early 1980s. Worsening and inadequate supply chains and insufficient technical and social infrastructures forced the Eastern European shipping companies to increasingly seek self-sufficiency to secure their inputs. Likewise, shipping businesses had to fulfil a variety of social obligations and provide services for

---

[3] However, western shipping companies at that time showed already strong tendencies towards organisational decentralisation, beginning in the mid 1980s. These developments were strongly linked to the revolution of computer technology. It allowed for intelligent flexibility of concentrated and often centralised economic structures. Socialist shipping enterprises however, could not achieve this urgently needed flexibility through communication networks due to lack of investment.

the community or the region. These included housing, education, the provision of medical assistance and other items. In principle, enterprises were overstaffed with seamen and shore personnel.

In the same way as the Socialist network structures lent stability to the economic system, the massive interruptions and disturbances of the existing economic equilibrium could do nothing else than result in a chain reaction leading to the breakdown of the whole system. This complete collapse became the starting point for transition towards new structures.

## Changed policy framework for shipping

### Central aspects of change

These deficiencies of centrally planned shipping described above had to be changed fundamentally during the transition processes. Accordingly, all transition economies initiated swift and comprehensive liberalisation. In addition to reforming the currency as regards convertibility, the abolition of the state's monopoly on foreign trade went in hand with an end to the transport monopoly. Shippers gained freedom to choose their carriers. Moreover, foreign carriers gained access to formerly restricted transport markets in the countries in transition. Only cabotage markets remained partly protected.[4] It was the OECD which became very active in formulating multilateral shipping principles with transition countries. This culminated in a pact signed in 1993 including *inter alia* national treatment of foreign carriers as regards port fees and charges.

Liberal changes encompassed far more than foreign trade. Deregulation also enlarged the scope for economic decision-making at company level. Central management and controlling functions were replaced by allocation through markets and prices. Former restrictions on participation in the international division of labour were abolished and negative restrictions on competition lifted. State conglomerates were broken up. Their former, mostly vertical networks were replaced by mainly horizontal links involving contractual co-operation with business partners and clients.

Altogether, liberalisation and deregulative processes supported a third core aspect of transition, the commercialisation of businesses. Aiming at international competitiveness, budget limits for shipping companies were

---

[4] In practice, restrictions on cabotage trades play a role in Russia only.

swiftly hardened and state subsidies cancelled. Generally, profit aims replaced former product maximisation behaviour. Firms gained economic autonomy as well as strategic and operative responsibility. They were assigned the basic freedom to decide upon fields and conditions of activity. Here, the generally long-standing experience of Socialist shipping and its ability to work in international markets was as important for managing transition as was the highly qualified manpower. Companies active in liner shipping had a particularly reputable record of working in international markets. In contrast, the bulk sector was often characterised by the charter monopoly of Socialist states which dominated in bilateral trade. The companies had only marginal commercial charter activity.

These elements of transition lessened the state's interventionist power and have created a very complex interplay with each other. Privatisation however, is the fourth factor which has a great influence on change.

Indeed, foreign trade related aspects of liberalisation have been supported by deregulation/commercialisation objectives; pressure to rationalise and increase efficiency facilitates better service and lower transport costs for national foreign trade. Moreover, liberalisation, deregulation and commercialisation can proceed without necessarily implying privatisation. Privatisation however, cannot develop to its full advantage without liberalising, deregulating and also commercialising economic structures. In contrast, these three factors together – to a certain degree – can be seen as substitutes for privatisation.

Depending on the level of influence that governments decide to exercise upon economic structures, different strengths of each of the named factors finally add up to the total transitional framework. As it is clear that governmental interests will not be suspended with privatisation but will still aim at a certain interventionist potential for influencing socio-economic structures, the relevant mix of these four change factors is a very sensitive matter.[5]

Except in the case of Germany, the retreat of the states was accompanied by a gap in government shipping policy. The former direct state influence on companies was generally stopped. Indirect positive and negative links between the governments and national shipping as well as structures to balance interests were urgently needed. Yet new targets and policy tools were not readily available. The process of taking a position as regards functions and

---

[5] However, the actual course of transition has made any calculated decision-making on individual transition factors or even weighted intervention difficult, if not impossible.

the extent of national fleets is still under way.[6] As developments have proved, finding an adequate shipping policy for transition has certainly not been a trouble-free process.

## Implications of Soviet disintegration

*The division of the Soviet fleet and changes in shipping policy*

The political disintegration of the Soviet Union brought about the problem of distributing the Soviet fleet among the newly independent states. National allocation of vessels was decided merely in accordance with the former Soviet home ports of shipping operators (see Figure 11.1).

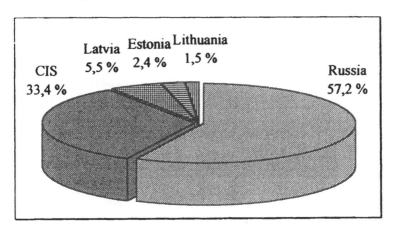

**Figure 11.1**
**Fleet division between the independent states of the former Soviet Union**
Source: author's calculations after ISL 1992, p. 216ff

Here, the economic division of labour following former Soviet objectives of national shipping policy had resulted in asymmetries and heavy specialisation. The partition led to very specific structures for the newly established national fleets. As a result of the split, nearly all the total transport capacity for oil and

---

[6]As far as can be seen as yet, there are signs of a Polish approach reflecting primarily upon the status of the national ports. The Baltic States appear to be developing a distinct focus upon self-sufficiency and independent maritime activity also focusing upon ports. Shipping is left to the market.

oil products was located in the North Western economic region and that of reefer tonnage in the Baltic Republics. Russia remained with ten large shipping companies and the 'Sovcomflot' special shipping corporation. It found itself in a position of holding a radically diminished and overaged fleet hampered by desperate structural problems. The withdrawal of the fleet was particularly severe in reefer tonnage, wood transporters, small and medium tankers as well as in passenger vessels. In contrast, container and ro-ro tonnage were comparatively strongly represented in Russian shipping (see Table 11.2).

It was this Russian ro-ro and container tonnage which was relatively sound in terms of age structure. Yet, in all other groups more than two thirds of the vessels were older than 10 years at the end of 1992. In particular the general cargo fleet was antiquated (see Table 11.3).

**Table 11.2**

**Tonnage structure by country following the division of the Soviet fleet (at 1.7.1992 in 1,000 dwt)**

| Vessel Type/ Country | Russia | CIS[7] | Latvia | Estonia | Lithuania |
|---|---|---|---|---|---|
| Total ('000 dwt) | 13,649.6 | 7,976.7 | 1,301.1 | 572.0 | 348.6 |
| (share %) | 57.2 | 33.4 | 5.5 | 2.4 | 1.5 |
| General Cargo | 3,923.9 | 3,065.2 | 39.5 | 257.2 | 120.0 |
| Tanker | 3,908.9 | 1,165.7 | 892.9 | 8,0 | 3.4 |
| Bulk | 3,116.6 | 2,610.2 | 0 | 259.7 | 160.2 |
| ro-ro | 1,103.2 | 466.7 | 52.8 | 38.9 | 40.5 |
| Reefer | 1,055.1 | 350.9 | 297.6 | 7.6 | 24.5 |
| Container | 484.6 | 145.8 | 18.3 | 0 | 0 |
| Chemical Tanker | 32.8 | 20.8 | 0 | 0 | 0 |
| Passenger | 24.5 | 12.0 | 0 | 0.6 | 0 |
| Liquid Gas Tanker | 0 | 139.4 | 0 | 0 | 0 |

Source: author's calculations after ISL 1992, p. 216ff

---

[7] Fleets from other countries in the Commonwealth of Independent States. Except for the Russian fleet this concerns the fleets of Azerbaijan, Armenia, Belorussia, Kazakstan, Kirgizstan, Moldova, Tadjikistan, Turkmenistan, Uzbekistan and the Ukraine.

A very distinct and problematic case of dividing the Soviet fleet arose from the 'Sovcomflot' shipping company which was established in 1986. Two years later, Sovcomflot was already converted into the first joint-stock company in Soviet shipping. Its remit clearly lay outside the transport function but with the state's hard currency interests. Here, Sovcomflot's core aim was to procure the tonnage needed for Soviet shipping. It took responsibility for buying and selling vessels for its shareholders in international markets. Likewise, the company fulfilled holding functions for subsidiaries and managed capital interests of the Soviet maritime sector world-wide.

**Table 11.3**

**The Russian Federation's cargo transport merchant fleet –**
**age structure by tonnage group\* (%)**

| Vessel type / Age | <5 | 5-9 | 10-14 | 15-19 | 20-24 | ≥25 |
|---|---|---|---|---|---|---|
| ro-ro | 12 | 45 | 20 | 19 | 4 | 0 |
| Container | 19 | 25 | 25 | 20 | 11 | 0 |
| Dry Bulk | 4 | 24 | 38 | 23 | 8 | 3 |
| Tanker | 15 | 19 | 18 | 16 | 14 | 18 |
| Reefer | 8 | 13 | 12 | 12 | 27 | 28 |
| General Cargo | 7 | 7 | 11 | 21 | 28 | 26 |

\*at 31.12.1992
Source: author's calculations after Holt 1993, p. 147

Since being founded, Sovcomflot had acted in a liberal and often deregulated economic environment. It had enjoyed the distinguished position of making strategic decisions quite independently from ministerial structures. Foreign currency income has been allocated to the firm itself for re-investment. The company has had the freedom to deal directly with clients whilst placing vessel orders with foreign shipyards. To do this, Sovcomflot has had access to international credit markets backed by Soviet financial security.[8]

Following Soviet disintegration, Sovcomflot became increasingly active in setting up joint ventures with Western European partners, founding one-ship companies and allocating ownership rights to companies abroad, especially in Cyprus. The introduction of Western bookkeeping and accountancy rules has

---

[8] About 75 % of the Sovcomflot ships had been flagged out during Soviet times. Since 1992, all seagoing vessels have been sailing under foreign flags.

supported a reorientation towards international markets and has increased the acceptance needed for expanding business in this area. In view of these special circumstances, the Soviet disintegration and the Russian transition crisis affected the company comparatively little.

The disintegration however, led to serious conflict concerning share ownership and the division of vessels among the several Sovcomflot shareholding companies. Thus, the company regained management of the vessels formerly allocated to carriers in the newly independent states which had previously operated the tonnage. The Estonian Shipping Company, for example, was particularly badly affected by this decision. Here, conflict over Sovcomflot's tonnage claims resulted in the arrest of several Estonian ships and caused further economic problems there.[9]

Sovcomflot's signed-up share capital of at least US$ 800m had to be decided upon during the division. The controversy was resolved through the take-over of 88 % of Sovcomflot shares by the Russian Ministry of Transport whilst re-valuing the company's balance. The other 12 % remained with BSC, LSC, NOVOSHIP, FESCO and BLASCO.[10] The subsequent division of shares is shown in Table 11.4.

**Table 11.4**
**Sovcomflot – division of shares 1988/1992**

| Shareholder / Year | 1988 | 1992 |
|---|---|---|
| Ministry of Sea Transport | 51 % | 88 % |
| Black Sea Shipping Company | 18 % | \| |
| Novorossijsk Shipping Company | 14 % | \| |
| Latvian Shipping Company | 11 % | 12 % |
| Far East Shipping Company | 3 % | \| |
| Baltic Shipping Company | 1 % | \| |
| Soviet Danube Shipping Company | 1 % | - |
| Sakhalin Shipping Company | 1 % | - |

Sources: Seatrade 1990, p. 9; Interfax News Agency 1992a

The company still holds the position of largest Russian shipowner, with more than 70 vessels totalling about 3 mil. dwt. It transports about 32 mil.

---

[9] See also: Fairplay 1993, p. 10; Fairplay 1993a, p. 6.

[10] See: Interfax News Agency 1992a.

tonnes of goods annually (about half of the goods transported by all Russian carriers under the Russian flag).[11]

Although the privatisation of Sovcomflot was considered, these plans were dropped in mid 1995. Then it was agreed to continue Russian state ownership in the company. This decision was explained by problems with privatising the Baltic Shipping Company and especially with the broad and largely unloved foreign shareholdership established there.[12]

The special circumstances of dividing Sovcomflot did not visibly affect the general framework changes in shipping policy, which were based on liberalisation and deregulation. However, conditions were re-established to allow for comprehensive state influence of the firms after 1992.[13] The law concerning equity capital companies, for example, provides that:

> ... the statutes must include additional provisions which ... guarantee the participation of state authorities in the administrative management of these joint stock companies...[14]

The transport ministry retained the right to assign the management in such joint stock companies and made use of this privilege.[15] Moreover, the direct responsibility of the directors of the ten biggest Russian shipping companies to the ministry was decreed at that time.

In practice, the political disintegration led to the conversion of former Soviet sea carriers into competing sovereign market players. There also were new competitors from river shipping and the fishing fleet, particularly in Latvia and Russia. Competitive pressure was added by the entrance of foreign carriers into formerly Soviet domains of foreign trade and transit markets following liberalisation. Here, the abolition of government price setting for transport in the foreign trade segment resulted in a linking of the company

---

[11] National statistics provide Sovcomflot data separated from the national fleet under the Russian flag and also separated from the national fleet outside the shipping companies' balance sheets (for example foreign subsidiaries). The author (if not stated to the contrary) refers only to the Russian fleet under the national flag here and in the following sections.

[12] See: Fairplay 1995, p. 10.

[13] '... Ministries were told to stop meddling in managerial decisions but were left with responsibility for the performance of the enterprises within their authority.' See: Rodnikov 1994, p. 8.

[14] See: GKI 1992, §2 as well as art. 5.

[15] See: GKI 1992, art. 5.; and for the implementation EBRD 1993, p. 23.

price policy to international markets. It can be assumed that positive signals also affected transport segments with continued cabotage reservation schemes and government price setting.

Similar liberalisation processes as those affecting shipping companies applied to all monopolistic structures in state maritime industries. 'Sovfracht',[16] the former Soviet charter monopoly for example, gained economic and legal independence from governmental authorities within the context of being converted into a equity-capital company in 1991. Though subsequently privatised in 1994, 49 % of the shares remained in state ownership. Sovfracht's profile in international markets has increased and the client base has been broadened from Russian and CIS carriers to third party interests. Today, in particular, Greek shipping companies form a group of strong and regular customers, accessing Russian tonnage via Sovfracht. Subsidiaries in London and the United States have been allotted more weight by becoming active in NVOCC markets.[17] Sovfracht still holds the position of largest Russian shipbroker and shipping agent. It retains the formal status of a holding company for the country wide network of 'Inflot' Agencies.

*Economic framework changes*

Evidently, the starting conditions for implementing a market system in shipping were rather difficult. It was not only the specifics of the tonnage taken over as a result of splitting the fleet that had a decisive influence on the transition framework. The factors of strongly diminished transport demand, costs and competition also required a new order for the Russian maritime transport industry.

*Firstly,* the economic breakdown with further shrinking in production[18] and lower trade[19] resulted in a clear decrease in national cargo transport from

---

[16] It was already set up in 1929 as a state company within the Ministry of Sea Transport.

[17] NVOCC- 'non vessel owning (operating) carrier' - transport activity without vessel ownership.

[18] By the end of 1994 Russian GNP had fallen to about half of the 1990 level. The investment volume assigned to the transport and communication sectors decreased from 12 % of the total investment volume for the periods in question in 1986-1990 to 6.4 % in the first half of 1994. See also: IWH 1994, pp. 3-15; p. 64.

[19] Lacking actual information, many companies based their production decisions in this phase of liberal self-discovery upon experience from decades of state-planning. Thus, the results were often inappropriate to market requirements. See also: Winiecki 1993.

136

1990.[20] Considerable influence upon this development also has come with fundamentally changed political conditions for settling foreign trade. The abolition of cargo allocation schemes in the Socialist block and the termination of the central state's monopoly in foreign trade has led Russian shippers to more often go for c.i.f. imports and f.o.b. exports.

*Secondly,* the complete disintegration of traditional patterns changed the former foreign trade cargo flows via the Baltic States into transit cargoes through newly sovereign states. The results had a particularly severe influence on the Baltic Sea shipping companies, especially because of the close relationship between the shipping company resident in a certain port and the cargo volumes running through this port. In 1991, the final year of the Soviet Union, cargo volumes accounting for about 30 % of the total Soviet sea transport were still being transported via Soviet Baltic Sea ports and thus dominantly by shipping companies resident there. In this context, an accountable share of total Soviet sea freight was transported via Latvian ports, amounting altogether to around 11 %. Estonian and Russian ports participated with 4.4 % each. Lithuania represented nearly 2 %. The Latvian route accounted for at least 25 % of the total Soviet liquid bulk exports. About 15 % of metal exports and about 17 % of the imports of machines and equipment passed through Lithuanian ports. Estonian ports were the corridor for about 80 % of the Soviet grain imports and stood for more than 50 % of the wood exports as well as for 25 % of all seaborne reefer imports in the Former Soviet Union.[21]

*Thirdly,* besides facing the situation of what were former national cargo flows converted into transit flows, pressure from inflation and a lack of liquidity among Soviet transport clients resulted in Russian sea carriers having only a minor interest in working with national shippers. Far reaching obsolescence of infra and superstructure, insufficient reliability of the ports, missing hinterland connections and frequent examples of bad management

---

[20] The Russian foreign trade volume shrank by 15-20 % annually. See: Bolz/Polkowski 1993, p. 9. Formerly, about 60 % of the total Soviet foreign trade volume was achieved in partnership with COMECON countries. The foreign trade volume between Russia and COMECON shrank to 25 % of the original level by 1992. Only 3 % of the total Russian foreign trade volume was carried out with this country group by then. See also: Christiensen 1994, p. 38.

[21] See: Levikov 1993.

caused a further decrease in calls of the Soviet fleet at national ports. Increases in port charges encouraged such developments.[22]

*Fourthly,* with liberalisation, foundations for an increased integration of Russian shipping companies into the world-wide division of labour were laid. Facing the decrease in transport demand, a strong strategic orientation towards foreign markets started, e.g. via crosstrades. For Russian shipping companies, the share of crosstrade increased from 30 % to 53 % of the total transport between 1990 and 1992. The share of cabotage transport however, shrank from 28 % in 1988 to 19 % in 1992. Yet, the shipping companies were not in a position to offset the breakdown of national transport markets by undertaking international activities. Total Soviet sea transport shrank to 75 % of the 1988 level by 1992.[23]

## Implications of German unification

### The adoption of the West German shipping policy framework

It was the abolition of political regulation for East German shipping at the end of 1989 which set up a widely liberalised economic environment for DSR. The practice of orientating foreign trade contracts on c.i.f. export and f.o.b. import was also discontinued then. The former monopoly carrier DSR experienced the complete opening of market and price relations, and independent economic decision-making started.[24]

Yet, there was no clear government policy positioning towards East German Shipping. The definition of its role in the now all German fleet was lacking.[25] Instead, DSR had to struggle with West German carriers merely for its right to exist.

---

[22] State pricing for federal ports officially continued yet has not been implemented in practice; the situation was equivalent to free price setting.

[23] For further reading see: Von Seck 1996.

[24] However, the deregulation of the markets for manpower caused severe problems following the brain drain of qualified staff leaving for the West.

[25] After all, about 70 % of the Federal Republic of Germany's foreign trade is conducted by sea transport. See: VDR 1995, p. 3; Hinz 1996. About 10,000 jobs on board German vessels are complemented by about 44,000 jobs in the shipbuilding sector and by another 76,000 jobs in subcontracting sectors. See: Huth 1997; Commission 1996, p. 40ff.

At the same time, the obligatory introduction of the West German shipping policy framework became an essential element of transition. It contained the following broad policy targets:

1. securing competitiveness of the German fleet and Germany itself as a shipping location;[26]
2. intervening positively in competition and market structures;[27]
3. intervening positively in the seaworthiness of vessels and safety of maritime transport.[28]

Accordingly, DSR has been integrated into the German system of federal shipping aid which draws on the following means for support:

1. tax allowances by beneficial depreciation rules;
2. assigning losses through the limited partnership model;
3. allocating tax advantages to income from shipping activities;
4. state financial support;
5. the German International Sea Shipping Register.

Taking first tax allowances by beneficial depreciation rules, German carriers may claim special depreciation for seagoing ships amounting to about 40 % of the original price within the first year and the following four years of use. A prerequisite for this is that the vessel was sailing at least four years under the German flag. The possibility of linear depreciation also existed and would bring the total depreciation to about 48 % in the first year and about 82 % within five years.

Meanwhile, the second element consists of lowering tax liability by assigning losses through the limited partnership model. In this case, a partner with private liability enlists limited partners for a loss generating limited partnership company which is participating in ship funds. Taxable losses for the limited partners are generated by using special depreciation rules. The partners can offset these losses against positive income from other sources.

---

[26] This includes the extent of the national fleet; profitability of national shipping; influence through a national fleet on the transport costs in international trade; personnel development and employment functions of the national fleet; research and development. Finally, German shipping policy aims at complete improvement of the framework conditions for the maritime industry. See further: Hinz 1993, p. 95.

[27] This includes the basis for competition rules; institutions for ensuring competition; external relations.

[28] This includes aligning with international agreements; the accession to conventions and institutions; registration of ships; standards; port state control systems; environmental protection of the sea.

About 40 % of the total capital investment of German owners in sea-going ships was raised by such fund companies in 1996 (see Table 11.5).[29]

**Table 11.5**
**German tonnage investment through fund companies (mil. DM)**

| Position / Year | 1989 | 1990 | 1991 | 1992 | 1993 | 1994 | 1995 | 1996 |
|---|---|---|---|---|---|---|---|---|
| Total investment (in mil. DM) | 1,320 | 1,430 | 1,460 | 2,210 | 3,030 | 4,440 | 6,000 | 7,500 |
| including ship funds | 510 | 480 | 630 | 830 | 1,120 | 1,630 | 2,180 | 3,000 |
| number of vessels placed | 41 | 42 | 52 | 53 | 76 | 109 | 156 | 175 |

Source: Dobert 1997, p. 15

The third strand is the allocation of tax advantages to income gained from shipping activities. At the same time in Germany, the income generated from operating merchant ships in international trade is treated as foreign income and thus tax favoured: 80 % of the profits are taxed at only half the ordinary tax rate. Also profits from selling vessels are usually taxed at this preferential tax rate. Like any other East German enterprise, DSR has been relieved of paying trade tax on capital. All the tax advantages within the context of income and capital taxation are linked to the German register and to flying the German flag.

State financial support. Cash contributions from the German Federal Government were granted to shipping companies originally as interest-free loans and have been given as subsidies ever since 1987. Such subsidies are linked to a requirement that ship management is for predominantly a full year under the German flag and thus partially to jobs for German seamen. By the end of 1996, the basis for measuring the eligibility for support was the remaining book value of the vessels using straight line depreciation. Thus, tonnage older than 14 years was not supported.[30] Owing to budget policy

---

[29] Other sources suggest up to 80 %. See Lloyd's Shipping Economist 1994, p. 25; Drewry 1996, p. 63.

[30] For German shipping companies these state grants meant an average release of about 200,000 DM per vessel in 1996. If one sees these state subsidies in relation to the total number of German seamen, each job at sea was subsidised by about 100,000 DM annually. Moreover, each training place for an apprentice was supported with about 35,000 DM.

considerations the DSR fleet did not receive financial contributions although largely operating under the German flag and thus eligible for cash assistance. However, it was allocated 25 mil. DM twice as so called 'restructuring help' in 1991 and 1992.

The years 1992 and 1997 saw attempts to change the government's aid policy. Only reduced support volumes were made available (see Table 11.6).[31]

**Table 11.6**
**Government cash aid to German shipping, 1990 - 1997**

| Year | 1990 | 1991 | 1992 | 1993 | 1994 | 1995 | 1996 | 1997 |
|------|------|------|------|------|------|------|------|------|
| Cash aid (in mil. DM) | 131.7 | 80.0 | 40.0 | 110.0 | 100.0 | 100.0 | 100.0 | 30.0 |

Source: synopsis from diverse publications of the German Shipowners Association VDR

A new tax system for shipping operations will be in place from January 1999. Shipping companies active in international business are then allowed to decide to use a lump sum tonnage tax system per vessel instead of the recently introduced profit taxation. One condition for this is predominant registration in a German register each year and headquarters and ship management being located in Germany. Moreover, employers are allowed to keep 40 % of the wage tax otherwise transferred to the state.

Finally there is the German International Sea Shipping Register (ISR). German carriers can reduce their original personnel costs by about 40 % without losing their right to receive subsidies by additionally registering with the German International Sea Shipping Register which was established in 1989.

In addition to the system of federal shipping aid the special support schemes for the German shipbuilding industry contributed to the generally positive development of the German fleet (see Table 11.7).

German shipowners had a share of about 2.4 % of the world merchant fleet at the end of 1996 and thus held the ninth position by world standards.[32]

---

[31] It becomes clear that the recent situation of reduced subsidies in Germany reasonably differs from the conditions of comprehensive state subsidy which were characteristic since 1987. It would be wrong to neglect this fact whilst applauding the abolition of the state subsidies for transition shipping. And: 'No European government renounces supporting the fleet under its flag.' See: VDR 1996, p. 19.

[32] See: ISL 1997. Here for merchant ships ≥1.000 GT/BRZ at 1.1.1997.

141

German carriers lead especially in the field of container shipping where they control about 9 % of the total world container tonnage as beneficial owners.[33]

**Table 11.7**
**Total German merchant fleet, 1991 - 1996***

| Year | 1991 | 1992 | 1993 | 1994 | 1995 | 1996 |
|---|---|---|---|---|---|---|
| Under the German flag | | | | | | |
| number | 388 | 322 | 287 | 695 | 644 | 620 |
| mil. GT/BRZ | 4.608 | 4.229 | 4.152 | 5.323 | 5.231 | 5.705 |
| Under a foreign flag | | | | | | |
| number | 289 | 354 | 404 | 695 | 772 | 814 |
| mil. GT/BRZ | 3.228 | 3.889 | 4.346 | 5.270 | 6.108 | 7.207 |
| *including ships additionally registered in Germany* | | | | | | |
| number | 102 | 153 | 200 | 497 | 565 | 564 |
| mil. GT/BRZ | 0.729 | 1.092 | 1.484 | 2.387 | 2.968 | 3.170 |
| Under the economic influence of German shipowners | | | | | | |
| number | 677 | 676 | 691 | 1390 | 1,416 | 1,388 |
| mil. GT/BRZ | 7.8 | 8.1 | 9.6 | 10.6 | 11.3 | n.d. |
| mil. dwt | n.d. | n.d. | 16.3 | 16.0 | 17.0 | 17.2 |
| Share under the German flag of the total fleet of German shipowners (by GT/BRZ) | | | | | | |
| share (%) | 59.0 | 52.2 | 43.2 | 50.2 | 46.3 | 44.0 |

*excluding coastal vessels, the fishing fleet, pleasure craft and passenger vessels without cabins, data at 31.12.; vessels ≥300 GT/BRZ, from 1994 onwards vessels ≥100 GT/BRZ.
Sources: VDR (several publications); ISL (several publications); Hansa 1992, p. 836; DVZ 1995, p. 3; VDR 1996, p. 3

---

[33] Thus, the developments in international liner shipping have an enormous importance for German shipping: 51 % of the German shipping income of about DM 10 bln. annually originates from the container fleet which has been largely grown by using the 'funds' model. However, the volume of newbuilding tonnage did clearly ease the economic link between transport demand and supply. The value function of the vessels became stronger. Also the speculative function (successfully played by Greek shipowners for generations) grew. Even the German shipowners association warned about this before the fleet got 'out of hand' and indicated the negative results of such artificial separation between demand and supply with other factors increasingly determining the newbuilding activity. See: VDR 1996, p. 31.

The shipping policy of the Federal Republic of Germany increasingly reflects the embodiment of the single market policy of the European Union.[34] Yet, whilst the European shipping policy of the 1980s has notably achieved outward effects by implementing liberalisation, distinctive inner effects in the European as well as in the German context have failed to develop. This is particularly true for the national flag and employment effects of the fleet.[35]

*Economic framework changes*

The beginning of transition was characterised by the consequences of German monetary union and especially by shrinking transport demand subsequently leading to tense economic pressures.

*Firstly,* the monetary, economic and social union went in hand with the acceptance of market prices and cost structures as well as new bookkeeping and balancing standards. The basis for this was the inter-state treaty of 18.5.1990.[36] From 1st July 1990 East German enterprises have been governed by rights and duties of independent commercial decision making.[37] The treaty obliged companies to issue DM opening balances within a period of three months. Assets had to be re-valued based on book values. Claims and debts had to be re-valued from two GDR Marks to one DM. Operating costs like salaries prevailed unchanged at 1:1.[38]

A notable dilemma arose from the structure of the DSR balance sheet with its large amounts of old loans from the East German National Bank.[39] According to East German accountancy regulations, a newly built vessel bought from a foreign shipyard before monetary union was balanced with an internal re-valuation factor (Richtungskoeffizient, RIKO).[40] The practical result was that an original investment of one DM was booked with an

---

[34] See further: Commission 1996, p. 58; Commission 1996a, p. 3; Commission 1996b.

[35] See further: Böhme 1995, p. 32ff.

[36] See: GBl. DDR I, 1990, No. 34, p. 331 (from 25.06.1990).

[37] See: GBl. DDR I, 1990, No. 34, Chapter III; Article 11, Article 14 (from 25.06.1990).

[38] See: GBl. DDR I, 1990, No. 34, Attachment 1, Article 7, §1-3, p. 342; as well as GBl. DDR I No. 64, p. 1909ff.

[39] Argument that these book debts against the state should have been classified as the capital resources of the enterprises rather then evaluating them as real bank credits did not gain the government's support. See also: Willgerodt 1990, pp. 311-323.

[40] The RIKO describes the assumed amount of DDR marks to be spent to earn one DM. Here, the decreasing profitability of the East German economy became obvious by increasing the RIKO from 2.2 in 1975 to 4.4 in 1989.

equivalent of about four GDR Mark. The particular modus operandi of the monetary union now resulted in having the same vessel in the books with more than double the original real DM new vessel price (depreciation not considered here). In late 1990, DSR had debts of about 250 mil. DM to the privatisation agency calculated on the basis of the former compulsory RIKO standards.[41]

*Secondly*, there was a close link between monetary union and the shrinking of shipments for the foreign trade segment. The practical over-valuation of the East German currency by about 400 %[42] accelerated a massive decline in production (see Table 11.8). The first two months after the currency union saw a halving of East German industrial production;[43] industrial output for example, dropped to about one third of its original level.[44]

Altogether, the breakdown in foreign trade and the general shrinking of economic activity in the new Federal States totally undermined the existing transport basis for shipping in the Eastern part of Germany (see Table 11.9).[45]

---

[41] On the other hand, evaluating hard currency income gained from the former extensive crosstrade activities by RIKO created a book advantage by re-arrangement here as well.

[42] Before the background of cost and sale problems the quotation of the then president of the Federal Bank of Germany Pohl is relevant: 'We introduced the DM with practically no preparation or adjustment, and, I would add, at the wrong exchange rate ... So the result is a disaster, as you can see. I am not surprised, I predicted it.' Cited after: Jeffries 1993, p. 399.

[43] About half of all industrial sites in East Germany were closed between 1990 and 1993. See: H. Böckler Stiftung 1994, p. 26; H. Böckler Stiftung 1994a, p. 24. The research capacities in the industrial sector shrank by three quarters. See: Reissig 1993, p. 16. The number of industrial jobs in East Germany sank to about 600,000 in 1994 from 3.2 mil. so that the relevant share of the total employment is merely 10 % now. See: Deutscher Bundestag 1994, p. 265ff. Similar data can be found in Breuhl 1994. In the total German context East German industrial production holds a share of merely 2-3 %. See: Deutscher Bundestag 1994, p. 488.

[44] The comprehensive breakdown of production in East Germany did not go in hand with an equivalent decrease in demand. Instead, annual transfers accounting for a volume of about three quarters of the East German GNP rather facilitated an increase in demand. In fact it was a function of the long-standing division of the economic cycles in Germany, industrial breakdown and transition crisis in the East and economic boom caused by the unification in the West. See further: Ghaussy/Schaffer 1993. For the first time, a growth of 7.8 % compared to the previous year was experienced in 1992. However, there has been a lower growth of the gross national product in East Germany compared to West Germany since 1996/97, further widening the gap between East and West.

[45] Here, the cutting of the link to former foreign trade partners in the Soviet Union had particularly damaging effects. The seaborne trade of goods between the GDR and the states of the former USSR originally represented about 55 % of all East German seaborne imports and 8 % of all seaborne exports.

**Table 11.8**

**Development of the German Gross National Product, 1990-1997\* (percent of previous year)**

| Year | 1990** | 1991** | 1992 | 1993 | 1994 | 1995 | 1996 | 1997*** |
|---|---|---|---|---|---|---|---|---|
| GNP East Germany | -21.5 | -30.0 | 7.8 | 8.9 | 9.9 | 5.3 | 2.0 | 2.0 |
| GNP West Germany | 5.7 | 4.5 | 1.8 | -1.9 | 2.2 | 1.6 | 1.5 | 2.5 |
| GNP Germany Total | n.d. | n.d. | 2.2 | -1.1 | 2.9 | 1.9 | 1.5 | 2.5 |

\*Prices from 1991; \*\*East Germany with actual prices; \*\*\*preliminary data
Sources: DIW 1996, p. 699; Deutscher Bundestag 1993, p. 330f.; ibid. 1996, p. 56

**Table 11.9**

**DSR - Development of goods transport 1989-1993**

| Year | 1989 | 1990 | 1991 | 1992 | 1993 |
|---|---|---|---|---|---|
| Goods transport (in mil. tons) | 14.033 | 13.094 | 8.061 | 6.402 | 6.187 |

Sources: Maritime Conglomerat of the GDR, several issues; Interviews of the firm

*Thirdly,* the shrinking in transport volumes resulted in severe economic pressures for the shipping companies. The first six months after monetary union had already caused a decrease in the company's income of about 50 %. Ocean freight income generated from East German foreign trade, shrank to 15 % and income from third party business went down to 80 % of the original level.[46]

Faced with the threat emerging from a background of the universal breakdown of transition companies, parliament legislated the remission of debts for companies entrusted to the privatisation agency.[47] Here, the possibility of re-evaluating debts was also opened. Where an enterprise was regarded capable of being restructured and the privatisation process had not

---

[46] Thus, shipments for the East German foreign trade now generated only about 10 % of total DSR income.

[47] At the time of legislation, in September 1990, about 90 % of all Treuhand enterprises were threatened with insolvency. See: Treuhandanstalt 1994, p. 4.

been started yet, an application for the remission of old debts and the handing out of cash loans was feasible.[48]

Under the circumstances described, DSR was required to cover losses amounting to 204 mil. DM alone in the second half of 1990 and about DM 200 mil. in 1991. Finally and in essence, the finance necessary was raised from the company's own funds. It remained the duty of DSR itself to restructure. The privatisation agency became merely active in 'balance sheet restructuring'. Within this context, guarantees of the agency secured a short loan volume with commercial banks taking the maximum of about DM 120 mil. by the beginning of 1991.[49]

## Privatisation as the core of transition processes

### General aims, methods and results of privatisation

*The aims of privatisation* Market economies are characterised by dominantly private structures of ownership. Thus, privatisation must be regarded as the most decisive basis for transition.

Privatisation within the context of transition, fundamentally differs from world-wide privatisation processes omnipresent today. Key transformations of ownership structures and efficiency criteria *of* the whole national economies are typical here instead of distinct microeconomic changes by reforms merely *within* existing structures. Transition implies fundamental reconstruction of the total socio-economic systems which then forward new social structures. Thus, privatisation is most comprehensive here.

Two main targets of privatisation can be identified under transition circumstances. *Firstly,* privatisation focuses on systemic change by establishing private property as the basis of a market economy.

The primacy of privatisation as the core of systemic change towards new economic patterns was defined right at the beginning of transition. Here, shipping with its strong capital base and its considerable contribution to national income was given generally high ranking. In Latvia, for example, the

---

[48] Enterprises with a relatively strong capital base however, had to pay back liabilities to the state. It was the privatisation agency which decided the individual level case by case taking the average capital volume of the relevant West German sector as the basis. See also: Breitzmann 1993; as well as: Breitzmann/ Von Seck 1994.

[49] Loans were handed out with annual interest of 10-11 %. Moreover, the privatisation agency received a broker's fee for its financial services from the recipient transition company.

contribution of the state carrier LSC to the GNP amounted to 8.5 % in 1993. Moreover, the very sizeable employment in shipping made privatisation generally important. The necessity of simultaneously installing the missing market conditions and sound social structures replacing the planned economy structures made the system creating function of privatisation particularly challenging. In order to keep the social system functioning, much effort and careful commitment was needed.

*Secondly,* there are efficiency functions of privatisation at micro and macroeconomic level. This is an important aim of privatisation with the major objective to increase efficiency. Inefficiencies in state owned enterprises are assumed to be caused *inter alia* by the far reaching division between ownership and management and by conflicts of interest arising from these. The bringing together of both functions within the context of privatisation should support the establishment of efficient incentive and controlling systems. Accordingly, privatisation should result in strategic changes that can positively influence efficiency functions at enterprise and macro level.

At *company level* the fundamental aim of privatisation is to minimise the state's influence on economic decision making. With orientation towards policy making, privatisation implies a chance for increased productivity. Considering the generally poor financial capabilities, privatisation is seen as a meaningful way of supporting capital investment, technology, management know-how and integration into international economic networks. Moreover, the private sector is generally assumed to provide for sound cost consciousness. It is the private owner himself who is considered to be the better executor of necessary adjustment processes. He is supposed to be better suited to reducing the widespread over-employment that is commonly found. Generally, privatisation is assumed to increase the competitiveness of transport suppliers and thus to work to the advantage of transport clients, too.

At *macro level,* privatisation aims at aggregate gains and benefits for domestic welfare. On the basis of macro-considerations, the decisive question for privatising must be whether a comparative advantage of remaining in the state sector no longer exists. The question here would be whether privatisation leads to a shrinking of total economic costs in the provision of shipping services. In this context, prospective productivity potentials under state and private ownership must be compared, establishing the rationalisation potential that privatisation could set free. Or, as Genberg puts it: '..it has to be weighted between privately profitable and socially damaging effects...'.[50]

---

[50] See: Genberg 1992.

The extremely high socio-economic importance the shipping corporations had in the regional and national context led privatisation in shipping to have great influence upon macro level developments. Economic advantages, for example, from integrating the transition economies into the international division of labour and particularly from extending the European Union, can only be realised if surplus benefits are not offset by additional transport costs. Here, shipping can undoubtedly contribute significantly.

It has to be pointed out that privatisation is by no means unanimously accepted as sufficient for gaining improvements in efficiency. Whilst one view puts private property as the crucial factor in increased allocative and operative efficiency,[51] the opposite approach recognises the chance of achieving visible efficiency potentials already within the context of commercialisation under state ownership.[52] The latter view is supported by the fact, that state-owned firms can be placed on a commercial rating list that ranges from very bad to very good. Examples from the European and world shipping scene show that public company status does not necessarily lead to defective competitiveness or lack of profitability. Hence, a compulsion for privatisation certainly cannot be derived from the mere existence of state ownership.

Approaches to privatisation are frequently accompanied by philosophical reflections. Yet one has to recognise that where philosophy enters the scene, ideology tries to get in the backdoor. It seems to be rather ideologically burdened to consider state ownership and active market participation of the state as generally unsuited for micro efficiency reasons.[53]

From the above it becomes clear that efficiency considerations are not easy to apply. The example of Eastern Germany proves how incomplete and one-sided a picture can be drawn when comparing just the income from privatisation activities with the financial expenditure for the actual privatisation processes. It clearly is not just a macro-economic loss of about DM 260 mil. which marks the final balance of privatisation in East Germany. At the same time, this spending must be recognised as a state subsidy to the private sector.

---

[51] See for example: Kikeri 1992 p. 3; Albach 1993 pp. 57-58; Deutscher Bunderstag 1993, pp. 202-204; Eberwein 1992 p. 76ff.

[52] See for example: Propp 1964 pp. 20-26, 147-155; Matzner 1992 p. 83; Blanchard et al. 1992 p. 29; Vernon-Wortzel 1989 p. 633ff.

[53] See: Williamson 1992.

At micro level, the example of privatising DSR underlines this fact. The company was sold for a price of DM 10 mil. The privatisation contract provided cash restructuring subsidies of at least DM 200 mil. Moreover, the company was originally equipped with readily disposable assets accounting for a market value of clearly more than one and a half billion DM.

In fact, many arguments pro-privatisation can be countered with contrasting positions. Thus, privatisation can certainly support the elimination of former monopoly positions of shipping companies. Yet, no causal link between competition and privatisation could be established in the course of the author's research. Increased competition from both the shipping sector and from other modes of transport, stemmed mainly from changes in the other core elements of transition and did not necessarily require privatisation.

To assume efficiency gains by re-uniting managerial and ownership functions is not universally accepted. Widespread shareholdership as well as tendencies towards multinational shipping structures support the preservation of such division after and beyond privatisation. Moreover, considering the common separation between ownership and management in any multinational firm, the validity of arguments concerning the rise of productivity based on establishing effective private control seems even more questionable. Mere privatisation (except in cases of a clear MBO) can hardly bring managers' incentives equal to owners' true interests. In addition, effective management control does not come free. Any new 'incentive' has to be paid for by someone, adding to the macroeconomic debit side of privatisation.

Even though a private owner is likely to execute urgent corrections in overstaffing and fundamental restructuring more successfully than the state could do, empirical research carried out shows that reduction in employment (for example) has been completed comparatively slower during the active privatisation phase than at the pre-privatisation stage.

Not least, privatisation opens the opportunity not only to foster economic development but also supports ecological aspects too. Yet, transition shipping failed to encounter any practical incentives for environmentally friendly technologies or patterns of production. Neither the use of resources nor the minimisation of polluting emissions were part of privatisation considerations. Here, high additional costs of intervention must be expected in the long run.

Altogether, privatisation within a system that creates efficiency functions at company as well as at macro level is a very sensitive factor of transition. Since transition has gone hand in hand with large income losses, budget deficits and economic collapse for entire regions, privatisation brings dangers. Individual or grouped opposition from people long accustomed to values of equality were widely present so that the necessary balancing of interests has to be ensured and very cautious consideration needs to be applied. Evidently, the methods of handling privatisation are of utmost importance for the outcome of the transition process.

*Methods of privatisation* Privatisation concerns the transfer of national ownership and possession of productive property from the state to private legal entities and private persons. In its narrow sense, privatisation includes the transfer of existing enterprises either one hundred percent and thus in total, or in part (distinct functional units, company assets or shares). In its wider sense, it also includes the independent expansion of the private sector, i.e. setting up new firms.

In all, privatisation cannot be regarded as a straight and clear-cut procedure. It rather works as a trend within a highly dynamic process (see Figure 11.2).

Having decided to privatise and not to municipalise or liquidate, there remains a wide range of means for implementing this step. The author differentiates selling and giving away for free as the two basic privatisation methods applied.

*Selling* of state property to the private sector is based upon government decisions in favour of accepting a certain net present value of a privatisation through receipt of a single payment and giving up prospectively continuous financial streams of income from that organisation.

Selling has been the privatisation method most frequently used in transition economies. Its prevailing application dates back to the Thatcher government in Great Britain during the 1980's privatisation campaign.[54] The countries in transition followed this principle.

The sales method allows for specific participation of the management and/or employees. Here, sales may occur in a conditional or unconditional manner. *Conditional selling* places limitations upon prospective buyers participating in the privatisation procedure by defining certain contractual arrangements, for example by applying open or closed tenders. In contrast, *unconditional selling* addresses a comparatively larger group of interested parties in a rather unrestricted way, e.g. through finance auctions.

---

[54] See also: Wiltshire 1987 p. 20; Ott et.al. 1991 p. 12; Littlechild 1989 pp. 15-26; Nikpay 1993 p. 16.; Foster 1992.

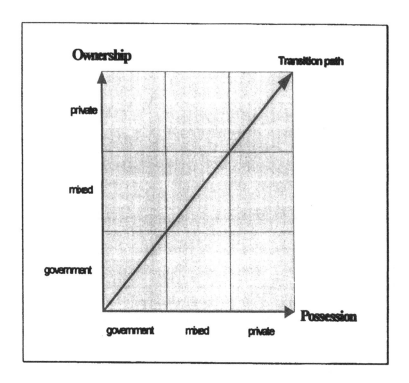

**Figure 11.2**
**The main components of privatisation under transition**
Source: author's graphic

Objections to selling particularly centre on speed, fairness and the implications for the capital and finance markets. Thus, the selling procedure itself is rather time consuming because of the need to evaluate the organisation to be privatised and to find buyers also willing to accept possible conditions of sale.

Selling raises arguments as regards fairness. Accordingly, sales favour those who wish to acquire an even larger stake in national assets which tend to belong to the wealthy already. Another argument is that national buyers possibly consist of the former Nomenklatura or those who have made their fortunes on the black markets. In East Germany for example, capital restrictions narrowed the group of potential buyers basically to West Germans. Finally, about 80 % of the buyers were resident in West Germany.

The practical selling procedure of the privatisation agencies clearly underlined the dominance of system creating functions. Although the over-supply of firms at one period and the deficiency of functioning stock-markets led to low prices, these were supported by book valuations which were additionally discounted in anticipation of future losses.[55] The formally applied method of selling thus acted almost like the assets were given away for free with very complex implications for both the capital and finance markets.

To *give away* for free these assets means waiving the income from privatisation. This method is said to foster the establishment of a new (national) class of owners.

Financial capital in the transition countries had principally been nullified by inflation and re-evaluation. The income of East Germans for instance, from savings or capital assets equalled almost zero. What existed was a relatively low level income from employment only. In all transition countries, foreign interests were normally not included in primary privatisation allocation. Here, people's fears of economic control and foreign domination had to be taken seriously. In Poland in particular, historical experiences contributed to a deliberate blocking out of foreign participation. The solution lay obviously in a gift-based approach in the circumstances of a widespread lack of capital.

The practical experience of the transition economies makes it possible to differentiate between two types of giving away for free:

1. ownership certificates. Such certificates represent vested rights to receive a certain absolute value from the state property to be privatised. Ownership certificate schemes were widely discussed but not implemented in the research area.

2. voucher system. The basis for a voucher system used in giving away property for free is the allocation of coupons to the citizen with a printed nominal value. These vouchers entitle the holder to receive a certain part of the state property to be privatised. Yet, the face value of the vouchers and its true purchasing power will be determined by the market in course of the privatisation itself and according to supply and demand. Voucher systems were widely applied in Russia, the Baltic States and Poland but not in East Germany.

The 'free' approach (be it in the form of ownership certificates or vouchers) has the advantage of a quick and largely popular transfer of ownership by

---

[55] The fact that any valuation under these circumstances must have been highly subjective, added to perceptions that companies were given as gifts to distinguished friends.

avoiding the costly and time consuming procedure of valuation. Giving away for free can thus be comparatively easily implemented. It does not however, add in itself to the equality of distribution. Yet because the spreading of wealth is relatively broad, it makes private and especially foreign investment generally more difficult to obtain. Opponents also argue the inability of the many recipients to appreciate economically what has been obtained freely and has not been paid for. Moreover, the key problem of effective controlling structures under circumstances of scattered ownership is not tackled at all. Clearly, the multitude of small shareholders will face more costs than benefits from attempts at control, thus freeing management even more from outside control.

Another typical element of transition is so called *'spontaneous privatisation'*. Basically, this form can be included in the category of giving away for free because no price is paid for transferring property rights. Spontaneous privatisation works in that government officials, directors or managers of state enterprises initially obtain private rights of possession of the relevant enterprises, assets or future income. These rights are subsequently converted into *de jure* private ownership. The new private owners gain their legitimacy for example on the basis of company statutes. The former public owner however, neither initiated nor explicitly agreed with these processes of spontaneous privatisation. However, at least responsibility rests here with the legal framework which allowed this.

In addition, *restitution* has been generally important as another method of privatisation. In shipping however, the specifics of being state companies from its origins made restitution irrelevant. Nevertheless, in some cases restitution claims concerned the land upon which company units were built.

*General results of privatisation and institutional support structures* Using these methods of privatisation – and in Poland frequently also the setting-up of small firms – all transition countries considered in this paper, established extensive private sector participation in their national economy with both the speed and extent of the changes being unique (see Table 11.10).

To a certain extent, the share of private enterprise contribution to the national product exceeds that in established market economies. The public sector turnover in Austria for example, stood at 82 % of the total turnover at the end of the 1970s, in Italy at 52 % in the mid 1980s. The public sector share of national income in The Netherlands accounted for more than 70 % in the 1980s and remained at over 60 % despite reduction still in 1993.[56]

From the above, it becomes clear that the concept of a market economy does not necessarily imply the extent of privatisation actually experienced in the countries of transition. However, if one wishes to utilise the advantages of incentives and improved efficiency in allocating resources by market mechanisms, privatisation as a fundamental element of transition certainly must be generally comprehensive.

Before the privatisation process began, state property had to be assigned a clear status. In particular, the disintegration of the USSR had left a legal void in regard to this issue which had to be overcome. In Latvia, companies were nationalised before privatisation. In Poland, major problems arose from collective and employee ownership being set up in the 1980s. Here again, nationalisation was on schedule as a precondition for privatisation.

**Table 11.10**
**The Status of the private sector in transition economies**

| Criterion | RUSSIA | ESTONIA | LATVIA | LITH. | POLAND | DDR |
|---|---|---|---|---|---|---|
| Enterprises privatised/liquidated of those listed for large scale privatisation* | 55 % | 74 % | 46 % | 57 % | 32 % | 89 %** |
| Contribution of the private sector to GNP *** | 58 % | 60 % | 58 % | 65 % | 58 % | n.d. |

*data mid 1996; **data at 1.1.1997; ***data end of 1995, Latvia: share of industrial production.
Sources: The World Bank 1996 p. 7; BMWI 1997; information by the Treuhandanstalt

The necessity to define the framework for privatisation supported the concentration of responsibility into special agencies under the control of the government. Thus, former responsibility of branch ministries with special

---

[56] See: Wright 1994 p. 109; 202.

154

knowledge was changed into primarily political control.[57] In East Germany, the 'Treuhandgesellschaft' was founded in 1990. Russia established its State Property Funds and Privatisation Committees in 1991. A comprehensively responsible privatisation agency was set up there in 1994. In Poland, the year 1991 laid the foundations for the first governmental privatisation body. In 1996, responsibility for state assets was concentrated in a 'Ministry of State Property'. In Latvia, the year 1993 marked the establishment of the Latvian Property Fund. One year later, the Latvian Privatisation Agency was set up. Here, the integration of both organisations characterised the final centralisation of privatisation in 1995. There are signs that the administrative bureaucracy of privatisation is generally developing a specific persistence: this is no surprise since bureaucracy practically has to abolish authority itself.

Although privatisation was commonly given high ranking, its concepts followed different national targets. The East German original motivation to privatise for example, aimed at real participation of the people in national wealth. Initially, existing systemic principles were not questioned at all. This, however, changed fundamentally. The economic, currency and social union from 1.7.1990 defined the so called 'social market economy' with its typical private ownership as a common economic basis of a reunited Germany. Later, the treaty of unification detailed the roles for the process of merger.

Assessing privatisation as the best way of handling the conversion process, the trustee holding and privatisation agency 'Treuhandgesellschaft' decisively influenced the outcome of transition. Companies were structurally separated from the government sector by compulsory capitalisation. The splitting-up of existing conglomerates was followed by sale or liquidation. Here, the Treuhandgesellschaft was granted the monopoly of sale for approximately 8,000 state enterprises employing some 46 % of the entire East German workforce.

Owing to fears of political hindrance which could slow down the transition process altogether, privatisation was speeded up. In December 1994, privatisation was officially completed with the closing down of the privatisation agency. Up until then, 68 % of all enterprises within the responsibility of the agency were privatised or re-privatised. About 28 % of all enterprise stock had started liquidation procedures. However, another 11 % of

---

[57] It generally was the privatisation agencies – backed by the executive units of governments – who gained the freedom to not only decide upon privatisation but upon strategic and also operational aspects of shipping. Such was particularly the case in Russia but Germany and Latvia were close followers. Up until now, Polish shipping has resisted such tension and primarily follows guidelines issued by the maritime department of the Transport Ministry.

the original number of enterprises allocated to the Treuhandanstalt remained with the Treuhand successor BVS (Bundesanstalt für vereinigungsbedingte Sonderaufgaben) in early 1997. It has to be underlined that the speedy process was largely supported by the existence of the stable social and economic system of West Germany.

The German approach to privatisation differed widely from other transition countries. In Poland, for example, changes in the eighties had already resulted in the establishment of broad public participation. With several years of experience of real mass participation in economic decision making, fundamental systemic change was addressed immediately, running ahead of all other transition economies investigated. Here, Poland and the Baltic States could rely for example on former civil codes set aside after World War Two. In contrast, lack of experience with private property proved difficult particularly in Russia.

Polish privatisation aimed at more clarity in possession rights, at increased competition and also at social elements. Restructuring was explicitly included here. The Russian privatisation concept addressed efficiency aims at company level, lowering of burdens on state finances and also social components. Privatisation in Latvia mainly centred on establishing capable economic structures independent from Russia. Here, the use of resources, social aims, investment, restructuring and the elimination of management defects were addressed.

From the studies undertaken, it is clear that mass privatisation (and here of small and medium enterprises primarily) dominated the beginning of transition processes in all the countries examined. The mass approach took into account the extent of property to be privatised. The vast number of organisations to be privatised required adequate handling at government level and thus mass privatisation schemes in one form or another.

The approaches to handle the demand side of privatisation were slightly different but generally required the involvement of the public. East Germany made a clear exception insofar as it did not pursue a policy of mass public involvement. Here, privatisation followed personal and often informal negotiations. In Russia and Poland the intended active participation of citizens in the privatisation process was achieved by using tradable vouchers and the system of employee participation.[58] Latvia completed broad, open tenders and

---

[58] In the end, Russian companies – after an initial period of comprehensive selling to insiders – also left only minor shares for truly public sale.

later decided sales through the Riga stock exchange.[59] However, in Russia as in the Baltic States, permission to participate in the privatisation process was closely linked to questions of nationality and citizenship.

Since 1994, the Baltic states and especially Estonia and Latvia have reflected the influence of the TOB (Treuhand Osteuropa Beratungsgesellschaft) and thus the German privatisation policy. From that time, the selling of enterprises and production units have been governed by case decisions and no longer are based on mass involvement for demand or supply.

## Results of privatisation in transition shipping

*Privatisation in shipping – a synopsis* Generally, privatisation in shipping focused upon supporting systemic change by establishing private property as the basis of a market economy. Again, the other main reason for privatisation was the need to increase the efficiency of shipping companies.

Privatisation in shipping is characterised by state responsibility and central political decision-making structures. The practical privatisation of shipping followed the rules of 'large scale privatisation' referring basically to the size of the businesses concerned. Here, the Baltic States and particularly Latvia and Estonia followed a strong sector specific approach with shipping being dealt with separately. In some cases it was even completely removed from the general privatisation laws.

Privatisation in shipping followed the privatisation of small and medium enterprises. It thus proceeded rather slowly compared to other branches of the national economy. Important factors here were the historical experiences with shipping and its classification as a strategic sector.

Privatisation in shipping mainly relied upon the re-distribution of existing property. Correspondingly, the establishment of new shipping companies was addressed only secondly, partly in Latvia and Russia and even less in Poland and in East Germany. Here, high capital requirements required market shares and know-how in markets with only marginal profits whilst the competitive situation in world-wide shipping made grass-root developments often unrealistic.

Before a shipping company commenced the process of privatisation it often underwent conversion into a capital company or a company with limited

---

[59] For shipping, the amount of capital tied up especially in vessels, was a reason at least officially to involve the broad public in the privatisation processes.

liability.[60] East German companies were compulsory capitalised in line with the West German capital company model beginning in March 1990. DSR had been converted into a capital company with limited liability in June 1990. Russian shipping companies were obliged to become joint-stock companies beginning in October 1992. In Poland, capitalisation started in 1993 for the Polish Baltic Shipping Co. The liner company POL however, still has the status of a 'company of the Treasury' having not undergone capitalisation yet. The Baltic States saw the capitalisation of the Estonian and the Latvian shipping companies in 1995.

First arrangements for privatisation were seen in the USSR when property transfer for BSC and LSC was initiated in 1990. In 1991 however, the process was stopped for LSC whilst it was being nationalised. Here, the preparative stage for selling ended only in 1997. The intended spread of shares through voucher schemes was revised and the company prepared to be sold for cash with at least 35 % of its shares to go to a strategic investor in mid 1998. Polish shipping started partial privatisation of subsidiary companies in 1991. Parts of PŻM were privatised in 1993. In the case of POL, management approved privatisation only in 1994. Although the company remains in state ownership, full privatisation is pending. Russian shipping companies experienced extensive privatisation between 1992 and 1994. Since then, secondary distributions have gained momentum. The East German DSR was privatised by signing the selling contract in May 1993 and complete ownership passed to two Hamburg businessmen. About eight interested parties participated in the preceding bidding process and the final decision was made against the Bremer Vulkan concern and in favour of the Hamburg bidders.

More detailed analysis of privatisation in shipping requires viewing ownership rights and rights of possession separately. For the former, one has to distinguish between the share and structure of private ownership. Moreover, the structure of the rights of possession and the allocation of economic risk have to be considered.

The *share of private ownership* and thus the dominance of private share capital is often seen as the decisive criterion for successful privatisation. State ownership in fact, often lasted for a minority shareholding. Whilst DSR went for full privatisation right from the beginning, Russian shipping was given the

---

[60] Sometimes this process is referred to as organisational privatisation or capitalisation. The formal conversion of a state owned enterprise into private structures is characteristic here. Despite the profit orientation and financial independence of that firm, the final control rests with the state as owner. The capitalisation often went in hand with the fundamental commercialisation of that firm.

possibility of staying with up to 51 % in state ownership until the year 2005.[61] 29 % of the BSC for example, remained in state ownership after the primary privatisation phase. The Latvian LSC originally strived for a state ownership share of 50 % and later for 25 %. Finally, it was listed for full privatisation, too. The Estonian government retained 30 % of the ESCO shares sold in mid 1997.[62] The 'so-called' private subsidiaries of POL however, are often majority state owned. Parts of the Polish Shipping Company (PŻM) are also characterised by such quasi-privatisation.

Moreover, a comprehensive evaluation must consider the *structure of ownership* rights. Being majority privately owned, the original scattered distributions of shares were often thought to help overcome possible opposition to manager or state commercial decisions which were necessary and unloved in the transition context. However, splitting ownership amongst numerous individuals - particularly employees - resulted in conflicts of interest and often hindered restructuring processes.[63] The primary distribution in Russia for example, led to an allocation of about half of all titles to employees and management. In the case of BSC, shares were distributed to about 17,000 individuals. The part-privatisation in Polish shipping ended with an allotment of about one third of the shares to employees and management. With a figure of 5 %, the LSC finally decided for only limited employee-ownership and thus for limited dispersity. The only notable decline in the number of owners per abstract unit of property has been reached in the case of privatising DSR where two persons bought the company.

As experience proves, it is not sufficient to take private ownership structures resulting from the first phase of distribution as a basis for making conclusions upon privatisation altogether. The outcome of the primary phase proved to be very unstable, results have often been reversed by secondary distributions in a short period of time. Here, the broad distribution of shares has been revised to accumulations favourable to insiders. These processes of redistribution are still not settled nor are the ownership structures.

---

[61] See: President of the Russian Federation 1994, Art. 2.6; 2.7.; President of the Russian Federation 1993. For all federal privatisation objectives see Russian Federation 1992, art. 2.3.11.

[62] The Lithuanian Shipping Company LISCO however, revealed figures of about 20 % of the shares being held by the employees whilst about 70 % should remain in state ownership until the year 2000. See: Fairplay, November 1995, vol. 326, No. 5843, p.33ff.

[63] Beyond this, the general dispersal of ownership caused enormous macro-economic transaction and controlling costs, for example in the course of secondary accumulation. See: Vickers 1988.

Likewise, specific rights of possession are characterising privatisation results. In the field of shipping, liberalisation and deregulation resulted in an original decentralisation of these rights to the management, employee-councils and decentralised institutions of the state. Especially in Poland and Russia influential employee-self-government structures were established. However, a subsequent concentration and centralisation of possession was experienced. Income streams of Russian shipping companies for example, are often controlled by the possession rights of the management quite independently of relevant ownership structures. This was supported by employee-shareholders often working at sea and not being in a position to execute their rights. The management's possession rights were subsequently completed by a highly convoluted process of accumulated ownership titles.

As it seems clear that the linking of management and ownership functions can positively support principal-agent theoretical considerations, the clarity of property rights in shipping must be recognised as limited by the existing divergent level of privatising ownership and possession. From this, incentives to restructure materialised inadequately. DSR is again the only example, where ownership and possession were almost equally concentrated, although the division of management and ownership also continued here.[64]

Another important criterion characterising the results of privatisation is the allocation of economic risks. There was an obvious tendency to spread these risks at the same time as privatising ownership and possession. This is particularly true for DSR but also for Polish shipping where multiform costs remained with the state over and outside of privatisation. In other cases, future risks have been settled by concluding privatisation contracts with soft conditions and easy prices. Here, the renewed part-nationalisation of DSR-Senator Lines to Bremen City or the actual re-nationalisation of the already privatised BSC in late 1996 impressively underlines the readiness of the state to shoulder this burden.

It seems appropriate here to review the privatisation of selected shipping companies in more detail.

---

[64] It should not be overlooked however, that today's world shipping industry experiences rather a continued division of ownership and possession rights. Owners and managers are increasingly distinct from operators. The clear proof for this is the increase in number of vessels under chartering contracts. Moreover, globalisation brings geographical differentiation between the domicile of owners and the places of management or regions of operation. From this, it becomes clear that it is obviously not a specific issue of transition companies to address controlling functions and incentives along increasingly dividing business lines.

**Table 11.11**

**Course of events in privatising selected transition shipping companies**

| Year / Co. | 1989 | 1990 | 1991 | 1992 | 1993 | 1994 | 1995 | 1996 | 1997 | 1998 |
|---|---|---|---|---|---|---|---|---|---|---|
| DSR | | | | | | Privatisation | | | DSRS to Hanjin | |
| BSC | | First arrangements | | Primary Distribution | | | Secondary Distr. | Bankruptcy | | |
| LSC | | First arrange. | | Nationalisation ... | | ... | ... | ... | ... | Tender begin |
| POL | | | | Privatisation of subsidiaries | | | POL Group still fully state owned | | | |

Source: author's investigation and graphic.

161

*Privatisation in shipping - case studies* The *Russian Federation*, acted as a forerunner in privatising shipping and applying voucher schemes. In late 1994, privatisation was already regarded as finished in about eight out of ten Russian shipping companies. It was generally carried out before restructuring.

There were basically three types of privatisation in Russia. The first phase included the privatisation of company shares to insiders and showed clear signs of mass privatisation. Although a sales procedure was applied, payment with vouchers resulted in privatisation taking in practice the form of 'giving away for free'.

In *variant A*, up to 51 % of the shares are allocated to employees and management in closed subscriptions for a price of 1.7 of the nominal share value to be paid in vouchers. 5 % of the shares are allocated to a share fund for company employees to be privatised to insiders at a later stage. The rest remains in state ownership.

*Variant B* of the Russian privatisation model includes the voucher sale of 20 % of the shares to certain groups of management and employees for a price of 0.7 of the nominal share value. There is an option for another 20 % to be bought later. 10 % of shares go into the share fund and the rest remains in state ownership.

*Giving away for free* is the third variant practised in this first phase of privatisation. Here, about 25 % of shares are freely assigned to enterprise insiders as stock without voting rights. Another 10 % of shares can be bought for vouchers at a price of 0.7 of the nominal value. Another 5 % of the shares are reserved for sale to the management, 10 % remain with the share fund, the rest with the state.

The decision on the privatisation method was largely made by the management. It generally followed a managerial strategy primarily of maintaining ownership and possession rights with insiders. The decision on the actual privatisation variant supports the finding that management was anxiously trying to gain controlling blocks of shares through all phases of the privatisation.[65] Consequently, it was *variant A* which was preferred although the employees received a relatively large amount of 51 % of the shares (see Table 11.12).

By extensively applying *variant A*, it can be assumed that shareholding employees did not execute a valid controlling function as regards the

---

[65] See also: Lloyd's List 1996, p. 2.

management.[66] Existing possession rights of the latter were thus not threatened by the considerable share of employee ownership. Moreover, the comparatively low sales of stock by finance auction connected with this variant made it possible to avert external interests. The comparatively high price of the shares with this variant was lowered by general undervaluation of companies. Moreover, book profits could be used here as means of payment for shares taken from the share fund. Here again, the management was clearly privileged by being ahead with information.

By applying the variant of *giving away*, only low level capital expenditure in the form of vouchers is necessary for realising privatisation. At the same time, it is rather unlikely that third party majority participation could be established. This variant was applied in two Russian shipping companies.

By applying the *variant B* of selling the enterprise basically through a MBO/EBO, the management was in a position easily to gain majority shares during the primary distributions. However, the obligations when using this variant (such as prevention of bankruptcy) meant it was not applied in shipping.

Independently of the privatisation variant chosen, the management gained advantages in allocating shares to themselves in several ways. During the primary distribution phase requests were already being made to the employees to contribute certain share volumes to certain funds named by the management. The press reported deliberate shifting of shareholder meetings to remote places and determined minimum blocks of the broadly spread shares necessary for authorisation to vote.[67]

Ambiguous legislation allowed the management to offer shares of certain subsidiary companies to fulfil the required volume of overall stock to be sold at public auctions. The controlling capital for a number of certain strategic enterprise units was thus blocked.[68] In other cases, decisive increases in capital were made by the management purely to their private advantage.[69]

---

[66] Seamen particularly are not in a position to represent the controlling interest arising from their rights as owners. The work at sea, far away from the scene and especially the lack of information also bolstered the management's strong position.

[67] See further: The Economist 1995, p. 93.

[68] Interview by the Author 1994e. The legal basis for this had often been established by the management itself for example through the company's statutes. See also: Seatrade Review 1993, p. 31.

[69] According to Russian legislation, even normal bank loans were recognised as a means of increasing capital if they were used for investment purposes. Here, focused insider privatisation was supported. See further: Rau 1994, pp. 11-13. Taking the case of the Sakhalin

Considerable secondary redistribution processes are typical although there was a sound private sector established already. As the primary distributions of ownership rights were unstable and changing, secondary distribution resulted in accumulated shares for the management and in some foreign participation. Secondary accumulation has generally been dealt with very discreetly with detailed information rarely available. Even the Russian transport ministry in its position as shareholder in most shipping companies, has been refused information about actual shareholder structures.[70]

Secondary accumulations were typically based upon the sweeping sale of freely tradable shares by the poorly and irregularly paid work force.[71] In the case of BSC, a decline in ownership numbers from 17,000 down to 10,000 individuals within one year was estimated.[72] About 20-30 % of all BSC stock arrived within secondary markets by the end of 1995. Here the British ownership consortium, Maritime Investors Ltd. was in a position to accumulate 23.3 % of all shares (see Table 11.13).[73]

---

Shipping Co. as an example, the management had implemented a capital increase by re-valuing the balance sheet without the consent of the shareholding private parties and even against the votes of the Russian state which held 25.5 % at that time. The result was a clear accumulation of ownership rights by the management who gained majority shares. See: Wolkow 1995. Similar transactions were reported from Primorsk Shipping Company where the management issued shares for subsidiary companies, again without asking the shareholders. The result then was the doubling of equity capital in favour of certain shareholders. See also: The Economist 1995, p. 93.

[70] See: Russian Federation Department of Sea Transport within the Ministry of Transport 1995. A copy of the book of the shareholders of the Sakhalin Shipping Co. was reported to have attained a price of US$ 30,000 on the black market. See Wolkow 1995.

[71] Over a longer period, the re-distribution was severely hampered by technical problems. In the case of BSC, the capacities of registration of the new owners allowed for only 70 to 80 transactions per day. As the decisive proof of ownership was signing in the shareholders book, the supervision of that document by the BSC management itself over a long period did not make the process more trustful.

[72] Interview by the Author 1995a; Interview by the Author 1994f.

[73] See also: Interfax 1995a; Lloyd's Ship Manager 1995, p. 5.

**Table 11.12**

**Primary share distribution in large Russian shipping companies by variant of privatisation***

| Company / Shareholder | Employees | State | Public Sale[74] | Privatisation Variant |
|---|---|---|---|---|
| BSC[75] | 61.0 % | 25.5 % | 13.5 % | A |
| FESCO | 51.0 % | 20.0 % | 29.0 % | A |
| Kamchatsk Shg Co. | 49.0 % | 51.0 % | none | A |
| Murmansk Shg Co.[76] | 49.0 % | 51.0 % | none | A |
| Northern Shg Co. | 36.3 % | 20.0 % | 43.7 % | to give away |
| Novorossijsk Shg Co. | 49.7 % | 45.0 % | 5.3 % | to give away |
| Primorsk Shg Co. | 61.0 % | 26.4 % | 12.6 % | A |
| Sakhalin Shipping Co. | 51.0 % | 25.5 % | 23.5 % | A |

*by Dec. 1994

Source: Interview by the Author 1994c.

Following the first phase of 'closed subscription' voucher privatisation and redistribution, the second privatisation phase of public voucher auctions started. Here another 17 % on average of the shares of the combined 83 companies in the sea and river shipping sector were sold by July 1994.[77] A third phase of privatisation began with the auction of one quarter of the shares on average in national loan auctions for cash. Here, the primary aim was to finance the state's budget deficit.[78] It remains unclear however, to what extent the 'loan for shares' schemes resulted in true private ownership and what share of finance from these auctions was of immediate benefit to the shipping companies. Yet without doubt, the governmental share in the companies and at least the state's possession rights were further reduced as a result (see Table 11.14).

---

[74] On no account can the shares distributed in public selling be unequivocally classified as belonging to the private sector. Here, the public sale of shares for example of the Sakhalin Shipping Co. resulted in a 10 % participation of foreigners but also in share ownership of the regional government amounting to 13.5 %. See: Interfax News Agency 1992b.

[75] Interview by the Author 1994d; Lloyd's Ship Manager 1994, p. 10.

[76] Interview by the Author 1994a.

[77] See: IWH 1994, p. 85.

[78] See for example: Boycko 1995, p. 170.

165

**Table 11.13**

**Distribution of share ownership in the BSC, 1994 – 1996 (%)**

| Share volume | by | | |
|---|---|---|---|
| Shareholder | 12/94* | 12/95** | 7/96*** |
| Russian interests, among them: | 100.0 | 76.7 | 70.4 |
| GKI (Russian Privatisation Committee) | 25.5 | 25.5 | 25.5 |
| Property Fund of St. Petersburg | 4.2 | 4.2 | 4.2 |
| Employees and management | 51.0 | 32.4 | 39.0 |
| among them: management | n.d. | n.d. | 12.3 |
| among them: Morflotinvest | n.d. | 3.7 | 7.0 |
| Reserve stock (for AfBU, third parties and auctioning) | 14.3 | 14.5 | 1.0 |
| Foreign interests, among them: | 0.0 | 23.3 | 29.6 |
| Maritime Investors Ltd./ Tufton Oceanic (U.K.) | 0.0 | 23.3 | 26.3 |
| Others (not clearly assigned) | 5.0 | 0.1 | 0.7 |

Sources: *Priwalow/Tschernakov 1996, p. 42; **St. Petersburg Times; slightly differing data in Trade Winds 1995, p. 3; ***Interview by the author 1996; similar results in Priwalow/Tschernakow 1996, pp. 42-46; Trade Winds 1996, p. 13

Nevertheless, fundamental and considerable state ownership in Russian shipping companies remains. At the beginning of 1997 only the Primorsk Shipping Co. had completely eliminated state participation. On average, shipping companies are characterised by a 25 % minority participation by the Russian state.

**Table 11.14**

**Loan auctions in Russian shipping companies**

| Company / Share | Former state share | Loan auction |
|---|---|---|
| NOVOSHIP | 45.0 % | 20.0 % |
| FESCO | 34.0 % | 14.9 % |
| Murmansk Shipping Co. | 49.0 % | 25.3 % |
| North Western Shipping Co.* | 25.5 % | 25.0 % |

*originally river shipping company only, now active with river-sea vessels in sea shipping also.

Source: Orlova 1996, p. 100ff

The possession rights linked to this government ownership however, can be assigned to third parties. Normally, individuals from the ministry or from the company management are assigned these rights to exert them in their interest.[79]

The president of BSC announced the company's inability to meet its liabilities in a shareholder meeting on 13th June 1996. The Russian tax authorities alone claimed outstanding tax liabilities of about US$ 80 mil. Accordingly, all BSC national bank accounts were frozen. Vessels were arrested and sold at public auctions. More than 7,000 employees registered pay claims of a total of US$ 4 mil.[80]

Referring to the national interest of the Russian state in the further existence of a capable Russian transport fleet, a presidential decree obliged the Russian government to secure and stabilise BSC.[81] However, no practical results of the decree were obvious for a long time. The company's insolvency was officially declared on 25.12.1996. According to the Russian legislation, this formal declaration opened the possibility to access state loans again. The Russian government stood as security for the company and all its debts. A plan was agreed for the repayment of liabilities to the state and tax rebates were arranged.[82] BSC however, lost its status as a commercial, independent economic entity and a state trustee was put in charge of the remainder of BSC.[83] The Russian state's capital and financial commitment to the company cemented the worthlessness of private ownership titles. It is safe to assume that this process marked the renewed nationalisation of BSC.

In East Germany, ownership of the national shipping corporation lay with the Treuhandgesellschaft from March 1990. Trusteeship was performed by authorised representatives. These however, were called back by the newly reoccupied Berlin headquarters of the privatisation agency. A supervisory board was established and new directors and managers were appointed. The

---

[79] See: Frydman 1993, p. 80.; Holt 1993, p. 134; Smith 1993, pp. 8-24. 'Despite progress in privatizing some transport operations, there is evidence that the system continues to operate under old rules and to reimpose them where market forces are starting to break them down.' See: Holt 1993, p. 1.

[80] See: Borisova 1996a.; 1996b; 1996c

[81] See: President of the Russian Federation 1996.

[82] See: Moloney 1996, p. 1; Badkhen 1996.

[83] The trustee placed by the Russian government was the former BSC president. Members of the government and the Russian Central Bank as well as the deputy transport Minister were accredited to the board and shareholder bodies. Monthly reports to the ministry were then demanded.

direct influence of the Treuhand upon company decision making increased remarkably from late 1992. The privatisation policy applied was clearly dominated by the Treuhand and particularly in contrast to confirmed business concepts. Members of the DSR board stepped down in protest against the lack of transparency in the Treuhand's privatisation negotiations which were carefully channelled past them.

A selection process for the new owners was undertaken yet decision-making power lay only with the Treuhand board. This group recommended the complete sale of DSR to the Rahe/Schües investment group on 18.5.1993, thus preferring what was called a 'middle-class solution'.[84] It is impossible for non-insiders to identify criteria which were decisive behind the decision governing this primary phase of privatisation.[85]

With the consent of the Treuhand supervisory board, both bidders bought DSR as a largely restructured company with diverse activities[86] on 28.5.1993 and dated back to January 1.[87] The reported sale price was DM 10 mil.[88] In return, DSR bought different companies of the two new owners which thus brought 24 vessels and the relevant number of employees into DSR.[89]

The privatisation contract with the privatisation agency required a general commitment of three years. The new owners had for example, to provide 1,600 jobs at sea until the end of 1995, manage at least 60 vessels with 900,000 dwt until late 1997 within the DSR group, co-operate with Senator Lines Bremen, evaluate possibilities of co-operating with Hamburg-Süd and

---

[84] See: Treuhandanstalt 1993.

[85] It can be assumed that considerable subjectivity and private decision-making powers contributed here. Even parliamentary investigating committees were refused permission to examine the files on the basis that they constituted a 'core area of executive decision-making powers'. See: Deutscher Bundestag 1994a, p. 97.

[86] The company owned about 900,000 m$^2$ of land with an estimated market value of about DM 500 mil. at 1.7.1990. See: Hanusch 1993, p. 60f.

[87] The approval of the Federal Ministry of Finance of the privatisation contract came on 16.7.1993. See Deutscher Bundestag 1994a, attachments, p. 721.

[88] See: Wirtschaftswoche 1993, p. 10.

[89] It is appropriate here to refer to evidence given before the parliamentary Treuhand Investigation Committee concerning common practices in privatisation. In these documents it says that '... it was by no means unusual that companies that were sold and paid their purchase price from their own assets ... in the way that the sum needed was raised by a loan which was secured on the basis of an encumbrance signed, e.g. for a plot of land privatised in advance.' See Kruger-Kneif, H., in: Deutscher Bundestag 1994, p. 297.

last but not least save Rostock as the shipping location.[90] The new owners promised investments amounting to DM 1.1 bln. per contract and later invested this amount.[91]

Although DSR did not receive large extra sums from the German government for preparing for privatisation, the privatisation contract itself agreed on several positive support measures. With privatisation, the new DSR owners received cash reconstruction subsidies of about DM 200 mil. and considerable indirect improvements in loan repayment conditions. Moreover, all the remaining fleet was at their disposal. Additionally, assets and real estate with an estimated total market value of at least DM 1.5 bln. were available. For all shore-based investment (about half of the total sum of DM 1.1 bln.), the company had access to regular state financial support which could represent about 50 % of this capital expenditure.

An important step in transition involved the complete merger of the world-wide liner activities of DSR with Senator Lines which was supported by targeting market-share and scale effects.[92] The contract for the inauguration of DSR-Senator Lines GmbH was signed on 28.7.1994 and dated back to January 1. The importance and extent of DSR activities brought in to the new company linked the transition of DSR closely to the development of DSR-Senator.

For DSR itself, DSR-Senator Lines represented a mere 50 % shareholding which was completely consolidated in the total balance sheet after 1995. Thus, the autonomy of DSR-Senator clearly limited the risks of this business field against the entire assets of DSR.[93] It also became obvious that liner shipping was not supposed to play a decisive role in the development strategy of the now privatised company.

Massive secondary distributions of ownership and possession rights in the DSR shipping sector started in December 1995. Thus, the Hibeg public

---

[90] The importance of Rostock as a location for shipping was intended to be secured by a divided head office of DSR-Senator Lines in Bremen and Rostock. As regards the problem of maritime location see: Breitzmann/Knauer 1992, pp. 116-129.

[91] It is problematic however, that this investment volume was not explicitly linked to the new owners but to the DSR company itself which finally met the requirements from its own asset base.

[92] Originally, it was only the RTW service and the Europe-Middle East-Asia (EMA) service [later America-Middle East-Asia (AMA)] which were intended to be brought in. The complete integration of DSR liner shipping (e.g. also conventional lines and the existing joint services with Stinnes) was decided after privatisation.

[93] See also: Schües 1994, p. 18.

industrial holding company of Bremen bought 50 % of the DSR-Senator shares for a nominal value of DM 50 mil. in order to provide liquidity for the Bremer Vulcan conglomerate. Later, 5 % were sold to Commercium, a subsidiary of Commerzbank.

The acquisition of shares by the city-state of Bremen was not just an ordinary purchase. Instead, it was a matter of renewed nationalisation of the crucial parts of DSR liner shipping in hand with a nationalisation of losses again. It called into fundamental question the aims of DSR's privatisation regarding efficiency improvements and hard budget constraints. Whilst pure private ownership was originally declared as indispensable for DSR competitiveness, the process of renewed semi-nationalisation passed off rather quietly.

The abovementioned developments were not sufficient to prevent comprehensive losses at DSR-Senator in the ensuing years. In order to protect the company from collapse, capital rich partners were urgently needed. Through a cash injection of DM 100 mil. the South Korean Shipping Company Hanjin had increased the equity capital of DSR-Senator to DM 200 mil. by 25.2.1997. The increased funding was immediately used to strengthen the company's balance sheet.[94] As a result, Hanjin became majority owner in DSR-Senator, holding about 75 % of the shares.[95] Shares held by Commercium were taken over and share ownership of Hibeg diminished to less than 10 %.[96] Deutsche Seereederei remained a minority shareholder in DSR-Senator with about 10-15 % (see Figure 11.3).[97]

The privatisation of DSR-Senator Lines was undoubtedly the decisive process in the transition of East German shipping. Nevertheless, privatisation processes in other businesses of the total company were of importance, too.

Here, Euroseabridge GmbH Fährdienste (ESB), the wholly owned subsidiary of Deutsche Seereederei, has represented the ferry and ro-ro

---

[94] Hanjin Shipping Co. has at its disposal a fleet of about 50 vessels with a joint capacity of 150,000 TEU and is particularly active as crosstrader between Asia and the North American West Coast with vessels of 5,000 TEU. Hanjin accounts for about half of all container transport carried out by Korean shipping. It differs from the DSR-Senator ownership approach in that it maintains its own agency and sales organisation and activities in hinterland transport. The conglomerate also includes two shipyards.

[95] The real purchase price thus lay clearly below the nominal share value. The net asset value of the company was still given at DM 240 mil. in late 1996. See: Roland Berger, cited after: Dobert 1996, p. 32.

[96] See further: Achilles 1997, p. 10; DVZ 1997, p. 1.

[97] The company was renamed Senator Linie in 1998.

business of the company since late 1993. In the course of secondary redistribution and individual and separate allocation of certain businesses from the DSR group to both owners, ESB was assigned to Laeisz shipping in late 1997. The latter sold 50 % of the shares to the Danish state ferry company 'Scandlines AS'. Deutsche Fährgesellschaft Ostsee (DFO), a subsidiary of the state owned German railway, and the thus enlarged Danish shipping company later merged activities to form 'Scandlines AG'.

Passenger shipping became part of the comprehensive shore based tourism sector and thus assigned to the second owner-partner on 1st January 1998. It also included the real estate reserves of the group in form of Immobilien GmbH. The manifold service activities of the Daten & Dienste GmbH underwent secondary privatisation during the course of a management buy-out (MBO).

The far reaching release of Deutsche Seereederei GmbH from holding functions marked the provisional end of DSR's privatisation in its primary as well as secondary phase in late 1997.

*Poland* First attempts to privatise shipping companies date back to 1991. Functional units of the Polish Baltic Shipping Company (PŻB) as well as of the Polish Shipping Company (PŻM) began privatisation in 1993. Following the original management rejection of the proposal to privatise, the Polish government and POL management agreed to a cautiously delayed privatisation of the whole POL group.

In order to break the influence of the Workers' Council and to initiate decisive commercial reforms, it was already intended in 1991 to convert POL into an equity capital company.[98] Against this background the transport ministry assigned a temporary administrator to POL in April 1993. The administrator had far reaching authorisation for initiating structural and strategic changes and represented the state's ownership and possession rights. A visible result of the changes initiated was the multitude conversion of subsidiaries into capital companies on the basis of geographically determined business activities and liner services. Privatisation of functional units from the liner company POL started. Although no progress was recorded in converting the entire POL into a capital company or in privatising the total group for a long time, the part-privatisation of subsidiaries gained momentum.

EuroAfrica Shipping Lines Co. Ltd. took a leading position here. It was founded as a capital company on the basis of the Szczecin POL regional office

---

[98] See further: Zurek 1991, p. 100ff.; Bascombe 1994, p. 55.

in September 1991. Management and employees of not only the company but also of POL obtained 11 % of the EuroAfrica shares within the first 16 months.

Beginning in 1993, the parent company POL sold considerable volumes of shares to the private sector - for example, about 10 % to the Port of Gdynia - and also to forwarders and container logistic firms, to small sea carriers and shipyards. The direct shareholdership of POL in EuroAfrica shrank to 27.7 % in the course of a capital increase in 1994. Thus, the block of shares diminished to 34.9 %. By late 1996 however, state ownership in EuroAfrica had risen again to 45 %. This increase was caused by a secondary re-allocation of shares to the parent company POL from private legal persons. In this context, shares held by the Port of Gdynia were acquired again by POL (see Table 11.15).

Although several capital subsidiary companies were privatised, real classification of these businesses as belonging to the private sector is often hardly justified. For POL-Seal Ltd. for example, a substantial quantity of capital interlinking brings the 49 % of state ownership claimed by the company, to at least 71.9 %.[99]

In contrast to the part-privatisation of certain subsidiaries, the privatisation of the whole POL group of companies has been characterised by a considerable number of conflicting interests and thus is proceeding very slowly. Largely unchanged since its establishment, the holding company POL remains in complete state ownership as a 'one man Treasury company'. First steps to privatise the holding were in theory initiated in 1996.[100] For this reason, the condition of temporary state management through an assigned administrator has been prolonged until June 1998.

Accordingly, POL will be privatised following the Polish mass privatisation programme under which about 600 large enterprises should voluntarily declare their participation as will POL. After conversion into a capital company, 60 % of the shares will be allocated to different investment funds. In this case, 33 % of the shares go to a 'so-called' majority fund. The remaining 27 % have then been distributed evenly between another 14 funds.[101]

---

[99] See: Zurek 1994, p. 9; Interview by the Author 1994b.

[100] See: Bray 1996, p. 2.

[101] See: Sereghyová 1993, p. 23ff.

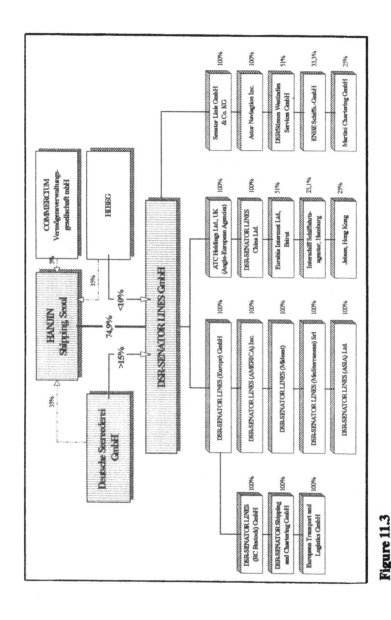

**Figure 11.3**
**DSR-Senator Lines ownership and shareholdings (Feb 1997)**

Source: author's investigations and interviews in the company; DVZ 1997, p. 1

The majority fund with 33 % of the shares, acts as the holding for the corporation concerned. On average 25 % of the total shares remain in direct state ownership from where 15 % of the shares can be allocated to the mostimportant business partners. Another 15 % of shares (originally 10 %) are freely distributed to the employees (see Table 11.16).[102]

**Table 11.15**
**EuroAfrica Shipping Lines Co. Ltd. Shareholdings 1992–1996\* (% and share number)**

| Year/ Owner | 1992 No. | % | 1993 No. | % | 1994 No. | % | 1995 No. | % | 1996 No. | % |
|---|---|---|---|---|---|---|---|---|---|---|
| Total Shares | 25,000 | 100 | 25,000 | 100 | 35,000 | 100 | 35,000 | 100 | 35,000 | 100 |
| POL | 12,175 | 48.7 | 9,686 | 38.7 | 9,686 | 27.7 | 9,686 | 27.7 | 15,386 | 44.0 |
| Port of Gdynia | - | - | 2,500 | 10.0 | 2,500 | 7.1 | 2,500 | 7.2 | - | - |
| Port Szczecin-Świnoujście | 250 | 1.0 | 250 | 1.0 | 250 | 0.7 | 250 | 0.7 | 250 | 0.7 |
| private individuals | 2,695 | 10.8 | 2,695 | 10.7 | 2,978 | 8.5 | 2,528 | 7.2 | 2,528 | 7.2 |
| a.t. employees POL | 1,689 | 6.8 | 1,689 | 6.7 | n.d. | n.d. | n.d. | n.d. | n.d. | n.d. |
| a.t. employees EuroAfrica | 1,006 | 4.0 | 1,006 | 4.0 | n.d. | n.d. | n.d. | n.d. | n.d. | n.d. |
| private legal entities | 9,700 | 38.8 | 9,700 | 38.8 | 19,586 | 56.0 | 20,036 | 57.2 | 16,836 | 48.1 |
| others | 180 | 0.7 | 169 | 0.7 | 0 | 0 | 0 | 0 | 0 | 0 |

Source: author's calculations after information given by EuroAfrica Shipping Lines Ltd

The actual results of privatisation in the research area and the selected case studies make it possible to conclude that privatisation, although the core of transition processes, cannot be regarded as sufficient necessarily to achieve transitional success. The examples used here, especially the bankruptcy of BSC at the end of 1996 and the take-over of crucial parts of the privatised DSR (in form of DSR-Senator by South Korean Hanjin Shipping in 1997) call for further consideration. Consequently, transition must go beyond the 'system creation' function of privatisation with efficiency being of utmost importance.

---

[102] The division of shares to be assigned to employees and management follows company internal rules. In most cases, the criteria for this have been established by the management according to the employee's years at work, age and position in the hierarchy. See further: Sadowski 1991, p. 54.

For this reason, this paper now goes on to further examine elements of restructuring in more detail.

**Table 11.16**
**Share distribution according to the Polish Mass Privatisation Programme**

| Shareholder | Share |
|---|---|
| Employees | up to 15 % |
| State (possibly 15 % for major business partners) | 25 % |
| Leading Investment Fund (Majority Fund) | 33 % |
| Equally distributed to further 14 investment funds | 27 % |
| **Total** | **100 %** |

Source: Karziewicz 1995, p. 14f

### Strategic reorientation and company restructuring

Within the context of transition, privatisation cannot be separated from a series of fundamental restructuring needs that exist. The breakdown of economic structures in connection with liberalisation and deregulation in all countries concerned had led to a drastically changed situation in transport markets. Core changes in the shipping companies became essential. However, the sequencing and speed of these changes with regard to privatisation was and is still a matter of discussion and focuses on three approaches:

1. privatisation *before* restructuring. This aims at establishing irreversible systemic foundations for further reforms. Here, the dominant opinion is that the future private owner should decide about restructuring himself;
2. privatisation *after* restructuring. This takes into account the necessity of 'defensive' changes in preparation for property transfer. Such action is often needed to prevent the breakdown of firms before the private owner can step in;
3. restructuring *by* privatisation. Aims at rehabilitative restructuring by way of privatising itself. Although privatisation can often be seen as a necessary precondition, it is by no means a sufficient factor to ensure the success of the restructuring needed. Within this approach, privatisation is actually an aim in itself with a rather speculative outcome.

There was a substantial difference of opinion about the sequencing of privatisation and restructuring in the transition of the German shipping industry. The legal framework for privatisation allowed the Treuhand Agency to apply a general strategy of speedy privatisation whilst restructuring was not imperative at all. The continued existence of DSR was placed into question by a general declaration that privatisation was the only alternative to closing down the company altogether. The major interests of West German competitors was to seek a quick solution through the latter scenario. Thus, the transition process of DSR with its three year period of focused restructuring before privatisation can be regarded as a rare exception in the whole German transition process.

The Polish shipping industry preferred a generally gradual approach by setting a long phase of restructuring before privatisation. Similar incremental policies were also applied in the Baltic States. The Latvian Shipping Company, for example, never disputed privatisation but, nevertheless, upgraded its commercial activities in the meantime. The Russian shipping companies however, implemented privatisation largely before the necessary restructuring took place. Here, a first phase required the trust of the Russian people and especially of the relevant employees before the economic necessities of restructuring were rather hesitatingly addressed.

Having carefully analysed transition processes in shipping companies in the research area, the following aspects can be distinguished, representing the core fields of restructuring: fleet reorientation and tonnage renewal, market reorientation and portfolio changes, and co-operation and organisation.

*Fleet reorientation and tonnage renewal*

Since former fleet strategies followed a centrally planned trade pattern and the resulting flows of goods, the drastic decrease in national demand for sea transport required fundamental shifts in fleet structures and strategies as well as repositioning in the markets based upon a renewal of tonnage.

Transition fleets were largely obsolete. Outworn technologies had not kept up with advancing international quality requirements. The generally old vessels with a high need for repair and maintenance led to considerable costs. The same tonnage however, represented a widely financially unencumbered and readily available asset, forming an extensive capital base even by international standards. The DSR's opening DM balance for example, named ship assets with a book value of about one billion DM. The BSC retained tonnage worth about DM 800 mil. at market prices even in 1995. The LSC had been certified fixed assets worth DM 600 mil. in mid 1996.

The reservoir and resource functions of the fleet arising from this situation were of utmost importance in the transition process. Widespread inflation resulted in considerable importance to be attached to the capital tied-up in vessels, being internationally both stable and mobile and thus of interest to

176

speculators through its reservoir function. Additionally, it was the vessel's proximity to liquidity which strengthened resource functions.

In order to ease cost pressures and to free urgently needed capital, shipping companies generally undertook far reaching liquidation of vessel assets. Whilst the possibilities of laying up were not used, older tonnage as well as modern ships were sold in large numbers. All the shipping companies scrutinised in this research showed a decrease up to between 60 and 70 % of their original tonnage in the period between 1990 and 1995.

DSR for example, sold almost the whole fleet or liquidated it through fund companies by 1997. Only small interests of about 4-5 % per ship survived. The number of vessels in operation was reduced to one quarter of the former Socialist state. The dead-weight of the Russian fleets shrank by almost one quarter between 1991 and 1996. The BSC lost about 60 % of original capacity in the same period. The Polish fleet had already undergone a decline of around 10 % during the phase of structural adaptation in the 1980s.

**Table 11.17**
**Development of selected transition fleets***

| Company/ Year | | 1989 | 1990 | 1991 | 1992 | 1993 | 1994 | 1995 | 1996 |
|---|---|---|---|---|---|---|---|---|---|
| DSR | | 164 | 139 | 120 | 78 | 49 | 63 | 56 | 41 |
| BSC | no. | 164 | 161 | 167 | 152 | 138 | 135 | 85 | 65 |
| LSC | | 104 | 103 | 104 | 105 | 100 | 83 | 70 | 72 |
| POL | | 97 | 93 | 85 | 70 | 54 | 46 | 43 | 47 |
| DSR | | 1,700 | 1,509 | 1,417 | 1,141 | 927 | 1,102 | 1,022 | 751 |
| BSC | '000 | 1,737 | 1,809 | 1,886 | 1,884 | 1,562 | 1,697 | 1,042 | 779 |
| LSC | dwt | 1,433 | 1,432 | 1,350 | 1,334 | 1,416 | 1,152 | 1,359 | 1,242 |
| POL | | 914 | 888 | 816 | 675 | 481 | 386 | 349 | 451 |

*data contain vessels under operation and only under ship management as well as own tonnage and tonnage of fund companies (especially in the case of DSR since 1994).
Source: author's calculations based on Lloyd's Confidential Index, div. volumes

Between 1990 and 1995, Polish capacity went down by another 25 %, and for POL by 60 %. The Latvian LSC lost about 13 % of its capacity and nearly one third of its former vessels (see Table 11.17).

The bulk of the remaining fleet has generally been brought under foreign flag. DSR for example, completely flagged out between 1993 and 1997. At least 17 % of Russian tonnage was sailing under foreign flag by 1996. The

Polish Steamship Company revealed a figure of about one third flying a foreign flag, POL about 50 %. The Latvian LSC was running about 43 % of its vessels under foreign flag in late 1996.

Reasons for flagging out considerably differed from the usual motivation in established market economies. Cost aspects played a substantial role in East Germany only. In the other transition companies, domestic low cost structures - particularly in the employment sector - made outflagging rather pointless in this respect. However, as a consequence of the commonly unstable legal and political environment in transition economies, international banks generally required the security of reputable foreign flags for granting loans. Meanwhile, the importance of the security function of the aged and largely liened fleet diminished substantially over time. Consequently, it must be assumed that considerations of physical transfer of capital by flagging out played a role as well. Often, flagging out went hand in hand with essential changes at least in the rights of possession of income from these vessels, thus adding to the incentive for spontaneous privatisation.

Viewing fleet development, privatising shipping companies in transition economies has much to do with a process of public dis-investment as opposed to the private investment push intended by privatisation. Private investment realised did not match the volume of public assets withdrawn. The situation remains marked by a lack of capital and problems of liquidity and finance. There is a lack of interest on the side of national as well as foreign investors.

Only a few shipping companies achieved fleet renewal. DSR, for example, was in a position to renew its fleet selectively. Contracts for the delivery of six new full container vessels of 2,700 TEU and for six coastal vessels were signed in 1990. Here, the way the tonnage investment was made was clearly different from the former hundred percent ownership approach. Also the deployment of about 10 chartered vessels of 4,500 TEU through German fund companies was realised by only about 5 % equity capital share.

Likewise, the Polish PSC was capable of implementing a rather comprehensive renewal programme based upon yielding shipping operations in the late eighties. Moreover, an intelligent and timely loan policy contributed positively here, as much as did the income from selective diversification. The Latvian LSC made only limited tonnage investment, primarily through second hand purchases. Nevertheless, fleet structures remained as stable here as in Russia, a symptom of the inertia of the former orientation.

In Russia, a challenging fleet renewal programme was set up in 1992 by presidential decree 'for the revival of the Russian fleet' with at least one third of the total investment needed provided by the state.[103] The need for investment was set at US$ 12 bln. and additionally rouble 50 bln. by the year 2000.[104] On the one hand the programme is based upon the demand for fleet replacement. On the other hand it draws upon forecasts of national cargo flows and upon the intent to increase the share of Russian sea transport conducted by the national fleet. Here, hard currency considerations aim at cost savings from refraining from using foreign sea transport services.[105]

The programme aims at about 600 vessel newbuildings with 8.5 mil. dwt by the year 2000 and thus replacing about one third of the existing fleet. Accordingly, a fundamentally renewed Russian fleet should then consist of 808 vessels with 12.1 mil. dwt.[106] In particular the assumed second phase of the programme (1996-2000) was designed to bring extensive construction activity in the field of smaller tankers, wood transporters and also general cargo vessels.[107]

The implementation of the programme however, instantly failed mainly because of lack of finance. Only 11 % of all planned investment in rouble-terms was made in the period 1993-1995. In dollar-terms, about one third of the planned volume was reached. The programme has been postponed until the year 2005 without changing its contents.

The above analysis shows the generally dramatic decline of tonnage and the ineffective programmes for restoring national fleets. A lack of fully containerised tonnage remains. Moreover, existing vessel sizes often prove too small to compete. Although the surrender of fleet ownership might

---

[103] See: President of the Russian Federation 1992. As well as subsequently: President of the Russian Federation 1993a. For further considerations see also: OECD 1993 p. 47.

[104] The source here is Sojusmornijprojekt Moskau. Other sources quote the total volume of the programme at US$ 14.5 bln. and rouble 6,000 bln. (prices at 1991). See DVZ 1993. According to Seatrade, the volume reached US$ 19.5 bln. See: Seatrade Review 1993a, p. 67. Se also: Interfax News Agency 1992c.

[105] However, Holt refers correctly to hard currency expenses arising from the need to buy new vessels at foreign shipyards (the opposite case to the then lower sale of steel at world market prices as well as to the lower income from national shipbuilding). There are for example, also negative expenses from increased fuel demand (and thus lost income from lower sales of oil at world market prices) which create effects opposite to the balance of payment effects. See also: Holt 1993a.

[106] Interfax News Agency 1994.

[107] See also: attachement No. 1 to the decree No. 996 [President of the Russian Federation (1993a)], issued by the Council of Ministers of the Russian Federation 'Concerning the implementation of the deccree concerning measures for the revival of the Russian fleet' 8.10.1993; as well as: Lloyd's Ship Manager 1994a. p. 7.

originally have positively contributed to raising finance, to shortening planning horizons and to increasing flexibility, funds were soon consumed and opportunities of raising loans on the security of vessels were lost. This might become disadvantageous inasmuch as shippers and partners alike rate a certain degree of shipownership essential for trustworthy long-term commitment.

The capital necessary for achieving comprehensive tonnage renewal could only have been raised by largely involving foreign interests. Such capital engagement however, was factually dependent upon the continued existence of protection in the markets. The success of transition in this regard is heavily influenced by the very complex relationship between privatisation and liberalisation. Thus, the comprehensive liberalisation before privatisation often resulted in the retreat of investors. The interest of private parties in participating in privatisation procedures diminished in the same way as state protection was withdrawn and the markets were opened. As the case of Russian shipping makes particularly clear, lack of private finance and also the results of mass privatisation did not abolish the need for active state support. Subsequently, economic decision making according to competitive advantage/ market potential remained restricted both under private ownership and market conditions.

Against this background, the competitive activities of transition carriers as well developed and advanced shipowners must be ruled out, at least in the medium term.

*Market reorientation and portfolio changes*

Deep transitional crisis in the former Socialist economies required shipping companies to reconsider their market orientation and portfolio structures. Not only markedly reduced fleets but dramatically shrinking transport demand and far-reaching changes in cargo flows have led to specific product/market decisions. Reactions included cutbacks in the shipping sector as well as diversification into maritime linked industries with varying activities ashore.

The shipping sector of DSR for example, experienced a halving of the original cargo volumes of those before privatisation in 1993. In 1996, the Russian BSC moved only about 47 % of the cargo transported in 1992. The total Russian fleet transported about two thirds of the former level respectively. Forecasts assume a further shrinking to 55 % by 2000.[108] In

---

[108] Interview by the author 1997.

1995, the transportation of the LSC under Latvian flag accounted for only 41 % of the year 1991 whilst Polish Ocean Lines accounted for 74 %.

The shrinking processes went along with adjustments in product policy and geographical service patterns. Transportation of certain cargoes was suspended as were services to certain areas. Extensive market exiting was typical. Deep sea lines were abandoned and route changes in favour of North Sea ports were implemented. Idle tonnage was partly placed on charter markets before commonly being sold.

Moreover, facing the steady diminishing transport demand from national foreign trade, activities in liner shipping were expanded into international crosstrade and transit markets. Here, the early advantages of earning foreign currencies were supplemented by the poor infrastructure in national ports and their hinterland, excessive port costs and, particularly in Russia the unstable legal framework and the progressive insolvency of national shippers. In this situation, fleets with originally strong links to national foreign trade were at a disadvantage in comparison with established crosstraders.

The Polish example shows an increase in crosstrade from 18 % of total sea transport in 1980 to 53 % in 1994.[109] LSC's tanker business today (1998), for example, is purely crosstrade. The share of crosstrade in Russian shipping increased from 53 % of the total goods transport in 1992 to an enormous 77 % of the total transport in 1995 showing stable volumes since.[110] However in particular, the cabotage share shrank from 19 % in 1992 to about 9 % in 1997 (see Table 11.18).

It remains to be seen whether the extensive crosstrade orientation can be successfully continued. The long term competitiveness of transition shipping in the crosstrade segment appears to be rather limited. Here, inadequate financial backing, dwindling capital resources, incomplete or inadequate network organisation and the need for a global presence must be considered. The actual position of transition shipping seems to be characterised by toleration from other competitors rather then by their own competitive strength. In many cases, the owner's operational activity in transition shipping has been given up already in favour of mere slot chartering.

In view of the above, changes have included a general shift away from all-service-providers towards geographical and product niches. The only notable

---

[109] However in the case of Polish shipping, increased crosstrade activity had already begun in the early 1980s and was not associated with the process of transition.

[110] The true share of crosstrade is slightly lower because the Russian statistics include here also transport of national foreign trade paid by foreign shippers.

exception here was DSR, seeking to catch up with global container markets by joining the RTW-concept and seeking global alliances through DSR-Senator.

Generally, the interests of big carriers have determined niches for transition shipping. Their mainport concepts opened perspectives for shortsea trades and lines on the periphery of global service networks. LSC, for example dropped deep sea lines in favour of niche orientations in the Baltic trades, especially on the basis of transit flows from and to the Former Soviet Union. It continued niche activities in the tanker segment with ice-going tonnage in the Far North. Long-term special relationships with clients were established in the reefer segment.

Market orientation also included the establishment of long-term relationships with shippers. In particular, the large potential of Russian raw material corporations opened chances for entering into the so called 'special shipping' markets based on long-term commitments. The Murmansk Shipping Company, for example, joined with LUKoil, the largest private Russian Oil extracting company, to found the shipping subsidiary 'LUKoil Arctic Tanker' which intends to employ about 50 tankers on the sea routes in the Far North.

Core elements changing market orientation within the process of transition include the distribution channels and sales structures. After the abolition of the state's foreign trade monopoly, the shipping companies also gained formal independence from the national (monopolistic) agency firms.

Moreover, it is the agency system with its strategic positioning at the periphery of shipping companies, controlling the link to clients which receives considerable interest. Strengthened crosstrade for example, heavily relied upon upgrading this interface.

Developments in the agency sector in the successor states of the Soviet Union were characterised by three partly overlapping processes. Firstly, this included the original demarcation from the Soviet system of Sovfracht agencies. Secondly, it was followed by widespread transfer of agency units to insiders, particularly to managers. The privatised agencies often surrounded the shipping groups with a cover of business contacts, insider knowledge and thus effectively controlled vital economic links. Consequently, even the presence of lasting state ownership in shipping did not hamper private profiting. In the context of organisational restructuring, profitable transactions were increasingly transferred to these strategically located and insider backed private entities. This process can be described as a specific form of spontaneous privatisation. The third process had its roots in the growing influence of agencies. Informal networks and the management *in persona* supported the entry of agencies into active shipping operations.

Polish shipping also integrated the agency system into company structures, mostly by capital shareholding. Only DSR separated from an originally in-house agency system in the process of shrinking to core activities. Income shortfalls and rising costs however, led to a revision of the DSR-Senator approach shortly before the company was taken over by Hanjin.

This far reaching liberalisation allowed the shipping companies to adopt international trends and to enter formerly closed business fields. Against this background the splitting of crew and ship management into different functioning units should be mentioned. Examples of such development can be seen partly in the GDR but also in Polish and Russian shipping companies. In particular activities in the field of crew management have been supported by the existing surplus of qualified seamen. More than 6,000 highly qualified Soviet crew were available for employment on foreign vessels by the early 1990s. Several crew management companies have been set up abroad, particularly in Cyprus.

Generally, the transition carriers quickly took the opportunity of extending their activities into selected shore businesses. The reasons for doing so in the Eastern transition countries most probably included structural deficits within upstream industries as well as the lack of inputs needed for offering high standard services. Diversification led to an inclusion of transport chain elements into company structures despite original steps to reduce the depth of production.

The field studies conducted within the context of this research proved that transport bottlenecks often caused a tendency of re-integration into the shipping concerns. In particular ports, although important links in the transport chain, rely on strong national linkages and had severe difficulties in meeting the requirements of the new market economies. For shipping companies, this meant hindering the intended increased flexibilities and implied considerable losses in quality. Processes of re-integrating ports into the newly structured shipping companies were common in Russia. The BSC, for example, actively pursued the conversion of former ship and repair yards into private seaports. With shipbuilding integration, diversification was much broader here than in other transition countries. This was regarded necessary to get access to tonnage construction contracted under national currency conditions. The Latvian Shipping Company also still owns a repair shipyard. Moreover, both companies are active in container manufacturing.

**Table 11.18**

**Sea transport of the Russian fleet under Russian flag 1992 - 2000***

| Year | | 1992 | 1993 | 1994 | 1995 | 1996 | 1997** | 2000** |
|---|---|---|---|---|---|---|---|---|
| Total | total | 88.62 | 82.7 | 69.8 | 62.5 | 60.0 | 57.7 | 48.7 |
| (mil. tons) | liquid | 39.09 | 37.96 | 31.5 | 28.9 | 26.9 | n.d. | n.d. |
| | dry | 49.53 | 44.74 | 38.3 | 33.6 | 33.1 | n.d. | n.d. |
| cabotage | total | 17.15 | 12.0 | 7.9 | 6.7 | 5.6 | 5.1 | 4.5 |
| (mil. tons) | liquid | 3.67 | 2.7 | 1.4 | 1.3 | n.d. | n.d. | n.d. |
| | dry | 13.48 | 9.3 | 6.5 | 5.4 | n.d. | n.d. | n.d. |
| international | total | 71.47 | 70.7 | 61.9 | 55.8 | 54.4 | 52.6 | 44.2 |
| trades | liquid | 35.42 | 33.7 | 30.6 | 27.6 | n.d. | n.d. | n.d. |
| (mil. tons) | dry | 36.05 | 37.0 | 31.3 | 28.2 | n.d. | n.d. | n.d. |
| out of this Russian | total | 24.2 | 16.4 | 8.3 | 7.8 | n.d. | n.d. | n.d. |
| foreign trade*** | liquid | 12.34 | 9.0 | 2.8 | 3.5 | n.d. | n.d. | n.d. |
| (mil. tons) | dry | 11.86 | 7.4 | 5.5 | 4.3 | n.d. | n.d. | n.d. |
| out of this | total | 47.27 | 54.3 | 53.6 | 48.0 | n.d. | n.d. | n.d. |
| crosstrade **** | liquid | 23.08 | 24.7 | 27.9 | 24.1 | n.d. | n.d. | n.d. |
| (mil. tons) | dry | 24.19 | 29.6 | 25.7 | 23.9 | n.d. | n.d. | n.d. |
| transport performance (bln. ton-miles) | total | 218.7 | 195.2 | 168.0 | 150.8 | 145.0 | 142.7 | 115.8 |

*excluding bareboat-chartering-in, foreign subsidiaries, foreign flag, AKP Sovcomflot
**preliminary data; *** Russian shippers only; **** incl. foreign shippers active in Russian foreign trade
Source: Interview by the Author 1997

The restructuring processes generally went in hand with an extension of activities into multimodal transport segments. This was supported by an increasingly widening logistical approach on the shippers' side. However, conditions of inadequate transport safety (particularly in the Russian hinterland) often hindered truly multimodal transport solutions. Containers are frequently unpacked after unloading in the ports and the contents conventionally transported then by truck further into the hinterland. Shipping companies reacted by a re-entering trucking markets. The Russian BSC owns a fleet of trucks for hinterland transport as does the Latvian Shipping Company. The Polish liner company POL for example, maintains close capital links to the forwarder and transport firm 'Hartwig'. DSR-Senator Lines bought in hinterland services from third parties yet later decided in favour of an in-house capital based commitment.

Transition processes opened ways of exploiting the enormous financial turnover generated by operational shipping in other ways too. In many cases, today's profits from Eastern transition shipping are reported to come from financial operations linked to shipping rather than from operational activities. It was the introduction of convertible currencies which went in hand with the building-up of company intern banking activities. In-house banks of shipping companies often re-collected the money paid out to their thousands of employees at low interest.

There is also an obvious focus towards the real estate sector and the hotel and restaurant business. The Polish shipping companies, for example, possess large congress and hotel capacities. Russian shipping companies like the BSC run hotels in Russia and abroad.

After the expiry of contractual commitments to the privatisation agency, the East German DSR changed its previous approach and focused on the extension of business fields. Today, one must accept the far reaching retreat of Deutsche Seereederei from deep-sea liner shipping. Whilst in 1994 about 90 % of total turnover of the group originated from shipping, the aggregate came down to a mere 80 % in 1996.[111] The shipping sector's total was programmed to shrink to about 50 % in medium term. With the sale of DSR-Senator to Hanjin, this component decreased even further. Figure 11.4 outlines DSR's tendency of change from their own capital/commercial management to loan based capital/investment activities which can be observed for the liner sector located in DSR-Senator and for the whole DSR group of companies alike.

Commercial management which was principally based on the operating side of the shipping business, upon marketing and chartering, describes the core shipping business as it was inherited from DSR. This activity was dramatically reduced. The result of privatisation and restructuring is a diversified service enterprise with minority shareholding in international liner shipping via DSR-Senator and a shrinking residue in Baltic and Shortsea trades. Here, it is the remainder of a 50 % shareholding in the Euroseabridge ferry company.

For DSR-Senator, the positioning as a commercial management provider with heavy reliance upon outside capital (placed in the upper-left corner of

---

[111] Here, the sea tourism and cruise sector with the vessels 'Aida' and 'Arkona' account for the large part of shipping income.

Figure 4) was certainly influenced by strategy decision-making in the Deutsche Seereederei Holding.

At the same time however, an obvious increase in technical management activities like shipmanagement, crew management and chartering business were observed. The function here is to guarantee the services on board and the relevant controlling activities on shore, including insurance, crew, maintenance and repair. Nevertheless, these activities put rather less stringent requirements upon special maritime knowledge and operative know-how than for example, commercial line management. Yet, the very strength of former DSR lay with operational liner shipping. Here, a world-wide network, know-how, markets and trained human resources were valuable resources which certainly could be rated as a competitive advantage for the privatised firm. From this point of view, one could have expected to concentrate upon the ship operating side while elements of technical and investment management could have been allocated to capable third parties or competitors.

Besides the technical focus, there was an overwhelming orientation towards investment-management. Here, the inherited vessel base dominated. It was used to raise liquidity by minimising the capital base. At the group level, a comprehensive amount of capital was subsequently placed into shore businesses, especially into tourism and real estate where the focus lay on high returns on capital. It is not inaccurate to conclude that the remainder of East German shipping is still distant from transforming towards long-term competitiveness and profitability. Yet, this happens no longer within the structures of DSR but under the majority ownership of Hanjin Shipping Company of South Korea.

The case of DSR supports the finding that it is a common feature of all transition companies researched, that activities in shipping and diverse commitments to outside businesses are only loosely connected. Synergy potential did not yield much for the restructuring process. Rather, conglomerate aims and economic independence dominated. Specific interests were particularly linked to the companies' asset base and thus also played a decisive role for choosing business fields and the relevant activities.

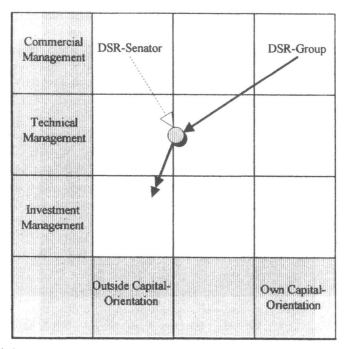

**Figure 11.4**
**Management-Orientation of the DSR-Group of Companies\***
\*trend line with one arrow representing developments in course of transition undergone already, double arrows represent new directions.
Source: author's graphic

*Co-operation and organisational restructuring*

Besides changed market orientations, co-operative structures had to be re-evaluated. Political and economic disintegration changed former partners into competitors. Established co-operative structures between formerly Socialist shipping companies had generally been broken up, joint services were closed down and only in some cases continued by individual partners. After largely losing fleet ownership and market shares, chances for integration into efficient and powerful co-operations narrowed. However, since the companies showed serious financial and competitive weaknesses and were facing increased international competition, co-operative decisions and the joining together with other carriers became an absolute necessity.

Generally, companies focused on business partners from developed market economies. There were however, differing efforts to affiliate with international co-operative structures. Unlike others, DSR continued broad co-operational orientation. Here, the co-operative focus was nothing new. Especially since 1988, DSR had been in a position to find wide access to international liner consortia. Moreover, close co-operation with POL in the EACON Service to the Far East developed, where both companies formerly maintained competing lines. In late 1989 it was already clear, that more close co-operation would be necessary to achieve market power, synergy and economies of scale and scope. Consultations and negotiations with the German carrier Hamburg-Süd failed. Hapag-Lloyd persistently took a position of fundamentally questioning the mere right of existence of DSR. Senator Lines Bremen, however, was itself in a position to seek suitable partners. Here, talks about possible co-operation were held from late 1989. In January 1990, a five-year-co-operation contract was concluded with Senator-Lines Bremen, including *inter alia* mutual slotchartering on the DSR's EMA and on Senator's RTW service. At the same time, co-operation talks were held between DSR, Senator-Lines, POL, CMA and Cho Yang. In spring 1990, a letter of intent was signed between these companies to create the basis for a prospective alliance. However in summer 1990, it became clear that POL and CMA would not join the club and would go their own way. Subsequently, the Eacon Service to Far East was suspended in October 1990.

In early 1991, DSR started active partnership with Senator Lines and later-joining entrant Cho Yang with upgraded frequencies in the now bi-directional RTW service and also participation in the end-to-end EMA service. The strategic partnership with Senator-Lines Bremen was extended to a full merger of the liner sector in early 1994. A co-operative arrangement with Hanjin Shipping Company of South Korea was concluded in 1995 for the Far East trades. Besides bringing scale and scope effects, this link to Hanjin opened up chances of increased global operations. Later, the cooperation was extended also to the Saudi based United Arab Shipping Company (UASC).

Polish shipping maintained a broad pro-co-operative line although the transition companies' specialisation in the markets has been broken up with the beginning of transition and entry intó cpmpetitive markets and thus increased competition followed liberalisation. POL for example, focuses on Baltic and shortsea trades but soundly broadened its activities into the ferry business as well. Nevertheless, early offers from carriers from developed market economies to link up, also in capital affairs - were rejected by POL just as LSC did in another context. Instead, flexibility was achieved by decentralising practical co-operation to the level of subsidiary companies, working together on a case by case basis. In contrast, the Russian BSC pursued approaches fundamentally opposing co-operation, with the aim of sustaining independence.

The complexity of transition called for fundamental organisational restructuring. At the beginning of transition, rigid economic structures prevailed with centralisation mirroring central state ownership. With this background, organisational restructuring aimed at adjusting enterprise and management structures to frame conditions. It started with comprehensive disintegration and abolition of supporting business fields. Highly integrated structures of maritime combines were broken up and the supremacy of shipping in those structures overcome. Formerly functional sectors of the combines like ports, repair yards and forwarders gained their legal and economic independence from the shipping companies. Outsourcing and closing down of activities were common. There was a tendency to free the top management from functional and operative duties and to decentralise these activities to the middle and lower management by setting up profit centres. The fundamental drive behind such moves was commercialisation. In most cases the lack of finance and the abolition of subsidies triggered fundamental organisational change.

The speed of organisational restructuring differed widely. Polish shipping started changes in the early 1980s by locating tonnage with independent subsidiaries. Soviet shipping saw an early break-away of port companies. The Latvian LSC took a different approach in that it remained to a large degree unchanged with manifold social structures in place yet widening its diverse shareholdings.

Above all, organisational restructuring was closely linked to privatisation processes. Privatisation in fact, had to be facilitated by organisational changes. It was fundamental to define, structure and value assets in order to create a clear basis for re-allocating ownership and possession rights. Thus, the formation of legally independent units by capitalising subsidiary companies backed the structural determination and demarcation of property for later privatisation. Here, limited unit sizes were supposed to support saleability.[112]

Following years of organisational change, the widespread setting-up of holding structures was observed. Besides intentions to spread risks and to meet fiscal considerations, this also supported capital acquisition aims.

---

[112] Nevertheless, massive concentration processes with distinct influences upon economies of scale effects and competition play a major role especially in international liner shipping. Increasingly concentrated shippers require logistical concepts and long term commitment only from few container carriers but with global coverage.

Interlinked subsidiaries allowed for privatising parts of companies without jeopardising controlling majorities.[113]

It became obvious that the original process of breaking up company organisations was followed by re-institutionalising former network structures on a contractual basis often using capital linkages. In Russia, this was supported by law. Yet, it should not be overlooked that inadequate and contradictory legal frameworks as well as insufficient controlling measures also partly contributed to the establishment of criminal organisation structures.

The personnel side of shipping was another important aspect of restructuring. Even though equipped with highly qualified labour, shipping companies were largely overstaffed. Eventually, there was a dramatic shrinking everywhere. By 1996, the Latvian LSC shrank employment to 57 % of the Socialist state. POL as well as DSR implemented crucial reductions of staff before privatisation started: POL employment shrank by one third of the former level even by 1989, DSR released about 70 % of the workforce by 1993. In 1996, the total DSR group employment accounted for merely 25 % of the original level and for 51 % in the case of POL. However, the very special circumstances associated with adapting the well-tried social net of the Federal Republic to East Germany does not make it possible to draw valid comparisons with other country cases.

The Russian BSC for example, showed comparatively little decline in employment to 75 % of the 1990 level. Here, reduction was taking place at a comparatively lower speed because the results of mass privatisation and regional-economic effects of the shipping combines were inducing important social constraints. Broad employee shareholdership, inadequate social networks and the lack of infrastructure as well as the employment function of the fleet were reasons for largely maintaining the number of people employed.[114] However, Russian companies still enjoy a comparatively low share of labour as a part of total costs.[115]

---

[113] However, in many cases the return of management power to central holding units was obstructed by the consolidated independence of the individual firms.

[114] Russia publicly aimed at maintaining the personnel number of the merchant fleet and at increasing employment in the seaports by 12,000 people until the year 2000. Interview by the author 1994g.

[115] Generally low crew costs however, can certainly not be sustained in the long run: Russian shipping companies in transition are confronted with an increasingly international employment market for seamen. Considerable increases in employment costs are to be

## Conclusions

About nine years ago (and even fifteen years ago if one takes the Solidarity-reforms in Poland as a milestone) the former Socialist shipping companies started offering services under market conditions and left behind the narrow process of central planning and regulation. Comprehensive changes in ownership and possession rights have occurred since then and products and markets as well as operations within them have changed significantly.

The analysis of these processes above, makes it possible to draw a number of conclusions and to make the following generalisations:

*Firstly,* the shipping companies in transition could not rely on an established transition theory in their process of changing into commercial companies in market economies. Decisions have rather been dictated by specific national framing conditions. They often have been day-to-day reactions to short term changes. Decisions have been largely influenced by sudden developments in supply and demand and by private interests.

*Secondly,* the transition countries examined showed several common characteristics but also distinct differences. Particularly the East German transition processes developed as a special case differing from the others in many respects. Here, recourse to the operational system in the Federal Republic of Germany must be regarded as a decisive advantage.

*Thirdly,* changes in the political framework of shipping and the market transition of the shipping companies concerned did not match each other nor did they run synchronously. Although liberalisation and deregulation led to sudden and strong competition and to the abolition of former far-reaching state protection very early on, the installation of new adequate shipping political frameworks was (and sometimes still is) pending. Transition shipping thus had to undergo essential changes under circumstances of widely absent state support otherwise common in the shipping sector in market economies. The more the need to carefully promote the competitiveness of Eastern shipping might have been overlooked, the more the state's help will be necessary in the long run when policy makers in transition countries might decide in favour of the existence of national fleets.

*Fourthly,* from a systemic point of view, privatisation certainly is the most decisive factor for successful transition. Privatisation must also be recognised as the core of the transition processes in former Socialist shipping companies

---

expected at least from the complete opening of this market towards the West and the resulting competition for qualified crews.

which were originally large by national as well as by international standards. Here, the newly structured ownership and possession rights in the relevant shipping companies and the incentives arising from them can lead to commercialisation, company restructuring, increased efficiency and profitability.

*Fifthly,* the process and results of privatisation are decisively influenced by choosing new owners. Particularly important selection criteria include their social legitimacy, the restructuring concept and the capital strength.

Social legitimacy is an important pre-condition for stability in the transition processes. The holistic integration of value systems, morality and cultural as well as national historical experiences is needed here. Analysis has made clear however, that the failure of controlling and incentive structures was rather omnipresent. In particular the former Soviet shipping companies were characterised by biased decision-making, by signs of private money-making and clear symptoms of criminality.

An attractive restructuring concept is needed which allows the company to stop successfully the general destruction of the capital base, as the reconstruction contributes to efficiency improvements. In many cases however, concepts focused on ownership and possession rights and primarily supported short term privatisation aims. Decision-makers often sought to maximise control and minimise restructuring costs.

The capital strength of the new owners is decisive for the transition companies' capacity to implement restructuring and innovations necessary to survive. In view of the often insufficient national capital inflows and considering the comprehensive investment needed, the choice for the private owner also became a core element for success in this context.

*Sixthly,* transition has proved to be a lengthy process filled with conflicts. Even today, the results do not allow for final evaluation. Some companies have just started privatisation, others are still involved in the process of secondary re-distribution. Even dominantly private ownership structures cannot be regarded as sufficient to declare privatisation finished.

Evidently, the success of transition does not rest with the complex aspects of privatisation but requires sound restructuring. It becomes clear that mere change in ownership does not initiate automatically guaranteed improved competitiveness. The latter however, must certainly be considered as a core criterion for successful transition. In the end, competitiveness must be recognised as a precondition for stable socio-economic structures at the macro-level in society.

*Seventhly,* former large and very complex equity capital oriented shipping companies were reduced to medium scale service enterprises with outside finance. The survival of shipping companies in transition is largely dependant on the success of fleet renewal. As practice has proved however, this is not a direct function of privatisation. In contrast, the capital fixed in the fleets was frequently liquidated and only eventually re-invested in other branches. Consequently, transition shipping companies fall further behind international standards and degenerate to mere niche carriers, often giving up their own operational activity, and being sold or liquidated.

*Finally,* the implications of these transition results are of utmost importance for world shipping. Competitors can recognise and take advantage of the fact that transition shipping in Baltic Sea countries has largely lost touch with globally active and market decisive players although it has undergone broad privatisation and restructuring.

# References

Achilles, G. (1997) Hanjin übernimmt Mehrheit. *VerkehrsWirtschaft*, no. 1, p. 10.

Albach, H. (1993) *The transformation of firms and markets: a network approach,* Berlin: Edition Sigma/WZB-Wissenschaftszentrum Berlin für Sozialforschung, pp. 57-58.

Bascombe, A. (1994) Holding on, *Containerisation International* 27, no. 9/September p. 55.

Blanchard, O., Layard, P.R.G. and Grosfeld, I. (1992) *How to privatize.* In: Siebert, H. (ed.) *The transformation of Socialist economies,* (Symposium/ Institut für Weltwirtschaft a.d. Univ. Kiel, 1991), Tübingen: Mohr, pp. 27-43.

BMWi-Bundesministerium für Wirtschaft (1997) *Wirtschaftslage und Reformprozesse in Mittel- und Osteuropa,* Sammelband, (Dokumentation No. 420). Bonn a.o..

Böhme, H. (1995) *Weltseeverkehr im konjunkturellen Aufschwung,* (Kieler Diskussionsbeiträge 249). Kiel: Institut für Weltwirtschaft.

Bolz, K. and Polkowski, A. (1993) *Aktuelle Entwicklungslinien, Problemfelder der Wirtschaftspolitik und ordnungspolitische Veränderungen in der Wirtschaftsregion St. Petersburg,* Hamburg: HWWA-Institut für Wirtschaftsforschung.

Boycko, M. et al. (1995) *Mass privatization in Russia,* in: OECD *Mass privatisation, an initial assessment,* Paris: Centre for Co-Operation with the Economies in Transition, OECD. pp. 153-166.

Bray, J. (1996) FESCO criticises Moscow over policies and taxes, *Lloyd's List*, v. 13.11, p. 3.

Breitzmann, K.-H. (1993) *Transition from a planned to a market economy*. In: Gwilliam, K.M. (ed.) *Current issues in maritime economics*, Dordrecht a.o.: Kluwer. pp. 22-35.

Breitzmann, K.-H. and Knauer, M. (1992) Schiffahrtsstandort Rostock. *Schriftenreihe der Deutschen Verkehrswissenschaftlichen Gesellschaft B* 153. Bergisch-Gladbach. pp. 116-129.

Breitzmann, K.-H. and Von Seck, F. (1994) *Market transition and privatization in East Germany - the shipping case*, in: Breitzmann, K.-H. (ed.) *Shipping, ports and transport in transition to a market economy*, (Rostocker Beiträge zur Verkehrswissenschaft und Logistik 3), Rostock: University. pp. 5-26.

Christiensen, B.V. (1994) *The Russian Federation: external developments*. Washington D.C. International Monetary Fund.

Commission of the European Union (1996) *Auf dem Wege zu einer neuen Seeverkehrsstrategie*, (Mitteilung der Kommission. KOM (96)81 endg.), Brüssel.

Commission of the European Union (1996a) *Die Gestaltung der maritimen Zukunft Europas*, (Mitteilung der Kommission. KOM (96)84 endg.), Brüssel.

Commission of the European Union (1996b) *Die Verkehrspolitik der Europäischen Union*, in: *EU-Nachrichten*. (Dokumentation No. 6, v. 25.9.1996: Europäische Kommission - Vertretung in der Bundesrepublik Deutschland), Bonn.

Deutscher Bundestag (1993) *Jahresgutachten 1993/94 des Sachverständigenrates zur Begutachtung der gesamtwirtschaftlichen Entwicklung*, (Unterrichtung durch die Bundesregierung: Drucksache 12/6170), Bonn: Bundesanzeiger.

Deutscher Bundestag (1994) *Beschlußempfehlung und Bericht des 2. Untersuchungsausschusses 'Treuhandanstalt'*, (Minderheitsvotum des Berichterstatters der SPD-Fraktion. Drucksache 12/8404), v. 31.8.1994, Bonn.

Deutscher Bundestag (1994a) *Beschlußempfehlung und Bericht des 2. Untersuchungsausschusses 'Treuhandanstalt'*, (Drucksache 12/8404. v. 31.8.1994), Bonn.

Deutscher Bundestag (1996) *Jahresgutachten 1996/97 des Sachverständigenrates zur Begutachtung der gesamtwirtschaftlichen Entwicklung* (Unterrichtung durch die Bundesregierung: Drucksache 13/2600), Bonn: Bundesanzeiger.

DIW – Deutsches Institut für Wirtschaftsforschung (1996) *Die Lage der Weltwirtschaft und der deutschen Wirtschaft im Herbst 1996* (Gemeinschaftsdiagnose der Wirtschaftsforschungsinstitute), Wochenbericht, No. 43-44.

Dobert, J. (1996) DSR-Senator: Eine Vertrauensfrage, *HANSA-Schiffahrt-Schiffbau-Hafen* 133, No. 9, p. 32.

Dobert, J. (1997) Schiffsbeteiligungen – eine Rekordwelle bricht, *VERKEHRSWirtschaft*, No. 3, p. 15.

Drewry (1996) *Shipping Finance*. (Drewry Shipping Consultants), April.

DVZ – Deutsche Verkehrszeitung (1997) 51, No. 25, v. 27th February, p. 1.

DVZ – Deutsche Verkehrszeitung (1993) 47, No. 122, v. 14th October, p. 29.

DVZ – Deutsche Verkehrszeitung (1995) 49, No. 18, v. 11th February, p. 3.

Eberwein, W.-D. (1992) *Transformation processes in Eastern Europe-perspectives from the modelling laboratory,* (Empirische und methodologische Beiträge zur Sozialwissenschaft 10), Frankfurt/M. a.o.: Lang.

EBRD – European Bank for Reconstruction and Development (1993) *Waterborne Transport Survey,* CIS. London: EBRD.

Fairplay – International Shipping Weekly (1993) 30th September, p. 10.

Fairplay – International Shipping Weekly (1993a) 7th October, p. 6.

Fairplay – International Shipping Weekly (1995) 1st June 1995, p. 10.

Foster, C.D. (1992) *Privatization, public ownership, and the regulation of natural monopoly,* T.J. Press Ltd., Padstow Cornwall.

Frydman, R. et.al. (1993) Needed mechanism of corporate governance and finance in Eastern Europe, *Economics of Transition* 1, No. 2, p. 171-207.

Gbl – GDR-Law Gazette (Gesetzblatt der Deutschen Demokratischen Republik), part 1 (several issues).

Ghaussy, G. and Schäfer, W. (ed.) (1993) *Economics of German Unification,* London: Routledge.

GKI – State Committee of the Russian Federation for the trusteeship of the state assets (1992) Ordinance No. 444-P: Concerning the particularities of transforming enterprises into joint stock companies and the privatisation of companies in air, inland waterway, sea and land based transport from 16.9.1992.

H. Böckler Stiftung (1994) In: *Wirtschaftsbulletin Ostdeutschland*, No. 1, p. 26.

H. Böckler Stiftung (1994a) In: *Wirtschaftsbulletin Ostdeutschland*, No. 2, p. 24.

HANSA – Schiffahrt-Schiffbau-Hafen (1992) 129, No. 9, p. 836.

Hanusch, S. (1993) Mittelständlern grünes Licht. *DAG-Schiffahrt: Zeitschrift für Seeleute*, No. 4, p. 60f.

Hinz, C. (1993) Improving conditions. *Seatrade Review*, September. p. 95.

Hinz, C. (1996) Transportalternative Küstenschiffahrt, *Dt. Verkehrs-Ztg*, 50, No. 132, v. 2.11.1996.

Holt, J.E.M. (ed.) (1993) Transport strategies for the Russian Federation. *Studies of Economies in Transition,* vol 9, Washington D.C.: The World Bank.

Holt, J.E.M. (1993a) *The World Bank's perspectives on investment priorities for waterborne transport.* Paper presented at 'Modernising Russia's transport system', Conference on the Transition to a Market Economy: 15.-16.6.1993, London: PTRC.

Huth, W. (1997) Das Aussterben des deutschen Seemannes – Auswirkungen auf die Seeverkehrswirtschaft, (*6. Seminar zu aktuellen Fragen der See- und Küstenschiffahrt,* 30.-31.10.1997), Kiel.

Interfax News Agency (1992a) *Russian Ministry of Transportation to receive controlling stock in Sovcomflot,* Moscow, 20.1.1992.

Interfax News Agency (1992b) Moscow, 6.3.1992.

Interfax News Agency (1992c) *Cargo volumes of Russian shipping declining,* Moscow, 8.5.1992.

Interfax News Agency (1994) *Russia puts heavier demand on shipping,* Moscow, 9.2.1994.

Interfax News Agency (1995a) *BMP sadolschalo innostrannuim kreditoram $60 mln,* IF0391 4 FON 382 [T3], Moscow, 18.8.1995.

Interview by the author (1994a) SNIMF (Ivanov, J.) - Director. St. Petersburg, 9.12.1994.

Interview by the author (1994b) Polish Ocean Lines, POL-Seal-Office (Socha, R.). Gdynia, 10.10.1994.

Interview by the author (1994c) Sojusmornijprojekt (Levikov, G.A.). Moscow, 14.12.1994.

Interview by the author (1994d) Baltic Shipping Company (source wanted to remain secret), St. Petersburg, 8.12.1994.

Interview by the author (1994e) Severnaja Verf (Tschernatskov, W.) - Marketing Department, St. Petersburg, 8.12.1994.

Interview by the author (1994f) Baltic Shipping Company (Filiminov, G.) - Vice President, St. Petersburg, 8.12.1994.

Interview by the author (1994g) Sojusmornijprojekt (Levikov, G.A.). Moscow, 13.12.1994.

Interview by the author (1995a) SNIMF (Ivanov, Y.M.) - Director, St. Petersburg, 27.6.1995.

Interview by the author (1997) Sojusmornijprojekt (Lerner, W.K.). Moscow, 8.5.1997.

ISL – Institute of Shipping Economics and Logistics (1992) *Shipping Statistics Yearbook 1992*, Bremen: University.

ISL – Institute of Shipping Economics and Logistics (1997) *Shipping Statistics*, April 1997. Bremen: ISL.

IWH – Institut für Wirtschaftsforschung Halle (1994) *Die wirtschaftliche Lage Rußlands*, (Forschungsreihe 8), Halle: IWH.

Jeffries, I. (1993) *Socialist economies and the transition to the market*, London: Routledge.

Karciewicz, P. (1995) Mass privatization programme for Poland, *The Coastal Times*, No. 11(29)/November, p. 14f.

Kikeri, P. et al. (1992) *Privatization – the lessons of experience*, Washington, D.C.: The World Bank.

Levikov, G.A. (1993) *The Russian port policies and future plans in the Baltic Area*. Internal paper, Moscow: Sojusmornijprojekt.

Littlechild, S.C. (1989) *Ten steps to denationalization*, in: Veljanowski, C., *Privatisation and competition*, Worchester: Billing & Sons. pp. 15-26.

Lloyd's Confidential Index (several issues), zugl: Southern, A.W. (ed.) *Index of Steam and Motor Vessels*, Colchester: Lloyds of London Press.

Lloyd's List (1996) v. 10th August, p. 2.

Lloyd's Ship Manager (1994) CIS Shipping Supplement, 15, August, p. 8.

Lloyd's Ship Manager (1995) 16th June. p. 5.

Lloyd's Shipping Economist (1994) An unconstrained German success? 16 , July. p. 25.

Maritime Conglomerate of the GDR (Kombinat Seeverkehr und Hafenwirtschaft) (several issues):DDR-Seeverkehr, Kombinatsinformation, Rostock: Komb., Seeverk.

Matzner, E. et.al. (1992) *Der Markt-Schock – eine Agenda für den wirtschaftlichen und gesellschaftlichen Wiederaufbau in Zentral und Osteuropa*, Berlin: Edition Sigma.

Nikpay, A.-R. (1993) *Privatization in Eastern Europe: A survey of the main issues*, (UNCTAD Discussion Papers 59), Geneva: United Nations.

OECD (1993) *Maritime Transport 1992*, Paris: OECD.

Ott, A. and Hartley, K. (1991) *Privatization and economic efficiency*, Edward Elgar, Aldershot, p. 12.

Preis, H. and Skurewicz, E. (1992) *Problemy reformy systemu transportowego kraju ze szczegolnym uwzglednieniem transportu morskiego w latach osiemdziesiatych*, Gdańsk: Instytut Morski.

President of the Russian Federation (1992) *Decree No. 1513 Concerning measures for the revival of the Russian fleet,* 3rd December.

President of the Russian Federation (1993) *Decree No. 2284 Concerning the state programme for privatising Russian state and communal companies in 1994,* 24th December.

President of the Russian Federation (1993a) *Decree No. 996 Concerning the implementation of priority measures for the revival of the Russian fleet,* 3rd October.

President of the Russian Federation (1994) *Decree No. 1535 Concerning the basic regulations within the state programme for privatising Russian state and communal companies after July 1st 1994,* 22nd July.

Propp, P.D. (1964) *Zur Transformation einer Zentralverwaltungswirtschaft sowjetischen Typs in eine Marktwirtschaft,* (Osteuropa-Institut Berlin Bd. 20), Repr. Köln: Edition Deutschland Archiv, 1990. S. 278-289.

Rau, S. (1994) Jüngste Entwicklungen des russischen Privatisierungsrechts und erste Ergebnisse seiner Anwendung, *WiRO,* No. 1, p. 11-13.

Reissig, R (1993) *Transformationsprozeß Ostdeutschland – empirische Wahrnehmungen und theoretische Erklärungen* (WZB-Diskussion Papers FS 93-001), Berlin: Wissenschaftszentrum Berlin.

Rodnikov Z., (1994) Logistics in command and mixed economies: the Russian experience, *International Journal of Physical Distribution and Logistics Management* 24, No. 2, pp. 4-14.

Russian Federation: Department für Seeverkehr im Transportministerium (1995) Document DMT-2633, MOR CAX.

Sadowski Z.L. (1991) Privatization in Eastern Europe: goals, problems and implications, *Oxford Economic Review of Economic Policy* 7, No. 4, pp. 46-56.

Schües, N. (1994) *Kerngeschäft soll europäisches Profil erhalten, Handelsblatt* v. 7./9th October, p. 18.

Seatrade - Soviet Maritime Guide (1990) Special Supplement, Colchester: Seatrade Publications.

Seatrade Review (1993), March. p. 31.

Seatrade Review (1993a) August. p. 67.

Seewirtschaft (1985) 17, No. 12, p. 586.

Sereghyová, J. (1993) *Entrepreneurship in Central East Europe: conditions, opportunities, strategies,* Heidelberg: Physica-Verlag.

Smith, G. et al. (1993) *Commonwealth of Independent States - a strategy for transport,* (EBRD Discussion Papers), London: EBRD.

The Economist (1995) 336, July 8th. p. 93.

The World Bank (1996) *World Development Report 1996: From plan to market. (Executive Summary).* Washington D.C.: The World Bank.

Treuhandanstalt (1993) Press Release, Berlin, 21st May.

Treuhandanstalt (1994) *Daten und Fakten zur Aufgabenerfüllung der Treuhandanstalt.* GVS. S/Dokumentation, Berlin.

VDR – Verband Deutscher Reeder (1995) *Deutsche Seeschiffahrt* 39/93, No. 7, p. 3.

VDR – Verband Deutscher Reeder (1996) *Seeschiffahrt 1996: Bericht des Präsidiums,* Hamburg: VDR.

Vernon-Wortzel, H. and Wortzel, L.H. (1989) Privatization: not the only answer. *World Development,* Vol.17, No.5, p. 633ff.

Vickers, J. and Yarrow, G. (1988) *Privatization: an economic analysis,* Cambridge/Mass.: MIT Press.

Von Seck, F. (1996) *Marktwirtschaftliche Transformation und Privatisierung der Seeschiffahrt Rußlands,* in: Breitzmann, K.-H. (ed.) *Marktwirtschaftliche Transformation und Strukturveränderungen im Seeverkehr der Ostseeländer.* (Rostocker Beiträge zur Verkehrswissenschaft und Logistik 5), Rostock: Universitat. pp. 7-44.

Von Seck, F. (1997) *Strategic reorientation and restructuring – the East German liner shipping industry,* in: Misztal, K. (ed.) *Economic reforms – the maritime sector in Poland and Germany,* Gdańsk University, pp. 43-62.

Willgerodt, H. (1990) Probleme der deutsch-deutschen Wirtschafts- und Währungsunion, *Zeitschrift für Wirtschaftspolitik,* 39 (1990), No. 3, pp. 311-323.

Williamson, O.E. (1992) *Private ownership and the capital market,* in: Siebert, H. (ed.) *Privatization – Symposium in honor of Herbert Giersch,* Tübingen, pp. 27-54.

Wiltshire, K. (1987) *Privatisation, the British experience: an Australian perspective,* Melbourne: Longman Cheshire.

Winiecki, J. (1993) *Post-Soviet type economies in transition,* Aldershot: Avebury.

Wirtschaftswoche (1993) v. 28th May, p. 10.

Wolkow, A. et al. (1995) Kak prowoschajut parochodstwa, *Kommersant* No. 5(116), v. 14th February.

Wright, V. (ed.) (1994) *Privatization in Western Europe,* Pinter Publishers. London, p. 109; 202.

Zurek, J. (1991) *Shipping and seaborne foreign trade economic correlations and relations, (Shipping and ports in the national economy – economic relations and models),* Gdańsk/Antwerpen University Press, pp. 87-106.

Zurek, J. (1994) *Shipping industry and economic transformation in Poland*, in: Vainio, J. (ed.) *Publications from the Center for Maritime Studies, University of Turku*, (Series A17), Turku, pp. 1-17.

For Product Safety Concerns and Information please contact our EU
representative GPSR@taylorandfrancis.com Taylor & Francis Verlag GmbH,
Kaufingerstraße 24, 80331 München, Germany


Printed and bound by CPI Group (UK) Ltd, Croydon, CR0 4YY
08/05/2025
01864369-0001